Nov. 28 - 17

*To Amy,
Congratulations on your
new Position, Best wishes —
Merry Christmas*

A Long Hard Ride

by

[signature: Richard R. Simmons]

Richard R. Simmons

authorHOUSE™

1663 LIBERTY DRIVE, SUITE 200
BLOOMINGTON, INDIANA 47403
(800) 839-8640
WWW.AUTHORHOUSE.COM

First published by AuthorHouse 03/11/05

ISBN: 1-4208-3248-4 (e)
ISBN: 1-4208-3247-6 (sc)

Library of Congress Control Number: 2005901637

Printed in the United States of America
Bloomington, Indiana

This book is printed on acid-free paper.

Dedicated To

My dear wife Joyce; for a lifetime of support and seeing me through my drinking years, my military career, my postal career and for giving me four wonderful children whom I am so proud of and thankful for. For her patience during the writing of this book, her ability to control our budget, permitting us to enjoy a lifestyle far beyond my wildest dreams

Alcoholic Anonymous and my many friends there who helped me through my first years of sobriety. To whom I am thankful for thirty one years of sobriety to date.

Acknowledgements

To:

Ross, my brother and best friend, for my racing career, (his intentions were good, the results were my own fault)

Dick Van Dyke, Movie, T.V. star, one night in London his public announcement on T.V inspired me to stop drinking, 31 years later; I still thank and admire him.

Sheila Black, My daughter, for her support and her help with my editing.

Mandy Black, Sheila's daughter, my first granddaughter. Because she told me I had to include her!

Bill McDonald Jr. my Postal friend, for his support, guidance and help in writing this book.

Joe Hartman, my colleague and mentor during my training in the best job I had during my Postal career.

Arleen Bowman, A good friend in Postal Management and fellow Toastmaster who also assisted me in my upward mobility.

Stella Studebaker, My sister-in-law, for the care and love she has given to her sister, my wife, Joyce over the years and her companionship during our trips

Table of Contents

Foreword

I thought I already knew and understood Richard Simmons—after all, I had an association with him for about 20 years. We had both been a part of the management team of the USPS in northern California, but after reading his autobiography, I was left feeling like I had never really known him at all. The life he presented to the public was just a shadow of the real man inside. This is the life story of a young jockey's journey through alcoholism, three careers, finding sobriety, and beyond.

Richard had his personal demons that plagued his life and followed him throughout his adult life. But if there was ever an actor who could hide his troubles and personal fears inside and out of sight—it was Richard. He never let people get that inside view of who he really was. Having read his life stories I am still not totally sure that I have all of the pieces of the puzzle that was his life.

His life story is one of true inspiration and redemption told in a way that makes you feel like the author is sitting in the same room talking to you. He gets right to the point in his told from the heart stories of his experiences. He doesn't dwell much on the emotional hurts he must have had from his earliest childhood days when his father died and he later dropped out of school. One can only image what he felt as a young boy thrust so quickly into manhood and responsibility. Later on, his love of horse racing and of booze formed the foundation of his young adult life. His service in the U.S. Air Force was a continuation of his downward spiral of drinking and hurting.

I found his autobiography to be so out of the ordinary that it is like reading a novel. I also learned something about the world of horse racing and jockeys—something that I would never have discovered without having read his story. It is hard not to feel for the author in his youth and how he tried to make a go of his young life. I could feel the spiritual and emotional frustrations even though Richard tries to under play any hurts and writes without revealing the full depth of what he must have felt. It is evident by his long drinking career that things inside him were not at peace as he was at war with who he was and what he was feeling.

This story is not about how someone lived his life but how someone rediscovered his life path and found true meaning to his purpose. I believe this is a book about a spiritual journey—one taken by a man in search of love and acceptance for who he is. The underlying message in all of his life experiences are about just wanting to be loved and accepted. There is emptiness in his life and you can feel it as he unrolls his life story. He finds as he grows older something more important than booze and getting drunk——it is called love. A love for his wife and family but more importantly he wakes up and finds that love within him for life. He finally realizes that life is too short to sacrifice any more "lost weekends" and he begins his rebirth as a sober man in search of meaning for his life.

I am sure that many men (and some women as well) will be able to identify with what he went through. His struggles with alcohol are a familiar tale for many people who served in our armed forces. The military has done so little to encourage sobriety and has actually been an enabler for as long as the history of war. Richard threw away many good years that he will never be able to get back again but it also brought him to the emotional and spiritual place he is now in. He learned from his life experiences and has grown and evolved in ways that even he doesn't fully understand.

Richard is my friend and a fellow traveler on this spiritual journey of life. I have found his life story to be both fascinating and moving. I think I am just getting to know who he is now. However, he keeps changing and moving forward with his life and his dreams so who I know today is already becoming history. I caution you to not judge this man unless you have fully walked in his shoes or ridden in his saddle. His story will grip you and hold you hostage until you finally finish the last page. Then you will be left sitting there on your sofa or easy chair wondering how the rest of this man's life story will end. He will get inside your heart and mind and emotionally you will become a part of his story.

W. H. McDonald Jr.
Author of "A Spiritual Warrior's Journey", "Purple Hearts" & "Sacred Eye".
President of the American Author's Association
Web sites: The Vietnam Experience www.vietnamexp.com
    LZ Angel www.lzangel.com
P.O. Box 2441, Elk Grove, CA 95759-2441
E-mail : Angelnet@citlink.net

Chapter One

It Begins

It is difficult to know where to begin in my life, for some reason I have very little memory of my early years. The most of what I can remember is from stories my mother repeated as I was growing up. I was the youngest of four boys; I had one older sister and one sister five years younger than me. My parents came from rural West Virginia; they were very religious people, as were their parents. My father's ancestors came from Scotland and my mothers were from southern Ireland, her grandmother and grandfather emigrated from a place called Killarney in the county Cork.

My father died of cancer on his fortieth birthday, leaving my mother, thirty nine years old to raise six children aged from four to thirteen years old. My father's death had a very deep impact on me; perhaps this is why I have little memory of my early years.

Times were hard for my mother. At the time of my father's death we lived on a farm in Maryland, where they had moved when my oldest brother Samuel was about four years old and my oldest sister Marie would have been about two. Dad worked as a share farmer for a wonderful man named Johnny Grafton, who owned two adjoining farms. As Johnny became ill and unable to manage operations of them, he trusted my father to run both farms.

1

Although there are many things about my early life that I cannot remember, there are some I do recall with stark clarity. One such memory is when Ross and I were very young. I do not know our ages but I can remember the event. Ross had a beautiful head of curly hair that mom was very fond of. However, Ross did not share her fondness of the curls. As we sat on our big back porch he was tugging at the curls saying he hated them, because when mom combed his hair it pulled. I asked if he wanted me to cut them off. He asked, "would you?". I told him if he would get the scissors, I would cut them off for him. He sneaked in the house for the scissors, the only ones he could find were mom's pinking shears. I carefully took each curl, cutting it as close to his head as I could one by one. Mom was very upset, she told me I had ruined his beautiful head of hair. I of course blamed Ross, saying he made me do it. Ross denied it, mom just picked up the curls from the porch and took them into the house.

I can also remember dad bringing a big tractor tire home from the main farm up on the hill where Johnny had most of the heavy machinery. The tire was taller than any of us kids. Dad took us boys to the top of our back yard where there was a large hill down across the yard, going off into a large meadow. He showed us how one of us could get inside the tire and ride it down the hill. I got in first because I was the smallest, I pulled my feet inside the tire, getting a grip on the rim, pulled my head inside, waiting while the others held the tire up for balance, then they let it go. As the tire started to roll down the hill I could feel myself getting dizzy but even though I had no control of the tire I felt like I was flying. As it picked up speed my fear turned to more and more excitement the faster it went. I could not see where I was going as I crossed the dirt driveway at the bottom of the yard, continuing into the meadow until the tire came to a stop and I climbed out with my head spinning. I stumbled around the meadow until I fell over shrieking with excitement. Dad could not stay to help get the tire back up the hill, it took all four of us to roll it back to the top and give the next one his ride. We spent many hours taking turns riding inside the big old tire.

3

I also recall my oldest sister Marie preventing me from choking, I was eating an orange while playing tag, wrestling with one of my brothers, running around the porch swing and acting the fool, when I sucked a piece of the orange down my wind pipe and started choking, Marie had to stick her hand down my throat to get the piece of orange. She probably saved my life, just another reason I love you Marie.

There was an apple orchard across from our house. There were about five or six various types of apples growing there. Each fall dad would have us kids climb the trees and shake the apples down then load them on a wagon. With a team of horses and as many kids that could pile on top of the load of apples, dad would head out to the cider mill about ten miles away up a winding dirt road. Depending how large of a load we took, we would get back two to three barrels of sweet cider and then head back home, getting home by nightfall. Dad would leave the barrels on the wagon until morning when he would roll them down into a root cellar under the house he had dug by hand, creating a large cool storage room. In addition to keeping the cider there, all the fruits, berries, and sausage mom had preserved in glass jars, were also kept there, stacked neatly on wooden shelves dad had built there. The cellar was probably about fourteen by sixteen feet, with a ceiling over six feet, the walls and floor were dirt, there was a set of double doors over the stairs leading down to the cellar. We kids were afraid to go down into the cellar until dad installed a light in it, then it was a great place to play in the hot summer as it was always cool. Before dad put the light in we were afraid of ghosts, goblins and other things that kid's dream up in their imaginations.

As dad was not a drinking man he kept a very close watch on the cider. As soon as it started to turn from sweet to hard cider he would turn it into vinegar by placing some strips of cheese cloth in it. Don't ask how this works, I have no idea, but one could probably find the recipe in an old "Farmers Almanac" the farmers bible, in those day's. Mom's brothers, who were drinkers, used to try to get to the cider before dad put his vinegar making magic on it, but dad was too clever for them. After all, he was the sober one. We kids would sneak down and get into the sweet cider until we found out it was a very effective laxative. Dad never punished us for getting in the cider; he didn't have to, he just let us learn the hard way.

In addition to the cellar dad dug by hand, probably shortly after they arrived from West Virginia, long before I was born, he also dug a well by hand. This was quite impressive. I can now appreciate how hard he must have worked to do it. The well was about thirty or more feet deep, about four feet across, after he finished digging down to the stream that fed it, hauling the dirt out in a bucket with a rope on a hoist, he then lined the entire wall with large river rocks from the water up to the top of the well, it must have taken him months, as this had to be done as well as working the two farms. Mom told us for the first few years water was drawn up by a bucket on a rope attached to a winch with a handle to wind the bucket of water up. Dad later installed a hand pump, making it much easier for himself, mom or one of the older kids to draw water from the well. I can remember how clean, cool and fresh the water was. When my wife Joyce and I with my oldest sister Marie, went to visit the home on our visit back east in 2001 I went to look for the old well, I asked the gentleman who now owns the farm, where the well was, he said he never knew there was one. I found where it should have been at the end of the porch, he had built a child's play area with a sand box over it. After explaining how dad had dug the well and describing how deep and wide it was he became concerned, saying he would remove the child's play area and check to make sure the well had been filled in. I will check again with him when we go to visit them, perhaps next year.

Another thing my father built was an "ice-house". This again was quite inventive. He needed a place to store the milk from the daily milking, especially in the summer, until the milk truck came by each day to pick up his daily quota. After the milking he would put the milk in cans that were five, seven and ten gallon sizes . There was a small stream that started near Johnny's farm up on the hill, it ran down across a field and two meadows between our house and Johnny's, behind the orchard on our place and down another pasture before emptying into a larger stream. Dad built a small stone shed construction across the stream, inside he made a cement trough about two feet wide, three feet deep and six feet long, he then had the stream split into two other troughs, each the same width and depth as the first, each of these were about ten feet long, this is where he would store the milk cans to keep them cool until the milk truck came by. The stream would continue out the back to resume its path toward the larger stream. He then used large slabs of slate to form the floor to the ice-house; it was usually too cold in there for us kids to play, but a great refuge from the summer heat. Each morning after milking the herd of about sixteen or eighteen head, around seven o'clock, or just before breakfast, he would load the cans on a wagon with a team of horses and take them over to the ice-house for storage until the milk truck came around eleven o'clock in the morning. He then would load them again on the wagon and deliver them to the pick up point at the end of the long lane between our house and the main road. The water going through the ice-house was very cold, as it was near the source.

Mom also used this place to store her freshly picked berries before preserving them in mason jars. She would also take two or three or her milk crocks that she had filled from the milk cans, to float in the cold water with the milk cans, this was to let the cream rise, then extract the cream from the milk to make butter, whipped cream and other delicious creations. One day in the summer mom went over to the ice-house to get a crock of cream, when she bent down to pick up a crock she saw three black spots floating in the cream, as she had some crocks of black berries us kids had picked for her along side the cream crocks, she naturally thought it was three black berries floating in her cream, as she started to pick one up a large frog leapt out causing her to tip over her crock, spilling her cream. Although it startled her, she often told the story and always laughed about it.

The fall was harvest time and also butchering time, these were events that brought together uncles, cousins, aunts as well as a few neighbors. They would slaughter about four hogs and share various parts. I suppose the closeness of the relationship determined how much and what part of the hog you got. It was exciting for us younger kids. The procedure was they would run one of the big hogs into a pen, one of the men would shoot him between the eyes, another would quickly jump in and stab him through the throat, piercing his heart so he would bleed out. Large barrels of boiling water were prepared under a block and tackle, the dead hog would then be hoisted up and dipped in the boiling water. This loosened the bristles so they could scrape him clean. It was then hoisted back up on the block and tackle again where they would clean and remove the various parts. The fat was stripped from the intestines and sides, put to one side to be rendered later into lard. The intestines were cleaned and used to stuff the ground sausage into. The livers, hearts, and prime parts of the meat were shared with relatives who had helped. We had some neighbors who came each year for the "sweetmeat" or sometimes called "mountain oysters" (the testicles). The kids always got the bladder that lasted about a week as a soccer-ball. When the fat was rendered into lard we would get the "cracklings" (pork rinds). Mom used to say they used every piece of the hog except the squealer, and if they could, they would sell that to a policeman for a whistle. Besides cooking the meals for all the workers, the women would assist in making the sausage, curing the ham, making the lard and putting it into jars. The men cut up the remainder of the hogs into hams, pork chops, and larger pieces. The hams were hung in a small building where a fire was to burn for three or four days to smoke and cure the meat. We had some great breakfasts from those hams.

Now I know people say the older you get, the farther it was to school and the deeper the snow. Well, Joyce and I went back east in 2001 to visit my sister Marie. We went to visit all the places we lived as kids, including our first homestead. I purposely measured the distance from our old home to the little two room wooden school we attended. It was 5 ½ miles!

One day in late fall, I was in the first grade, Ross was in the third and Simon (Bud) was in the fourth. The three of us were devising a plan to play hooky, our older sister Marie was walking ahead of us not wanting to be involved, she was a dedicated student, preparing to go into high school. At the first recess at 9:30, we met in the playground and decided to make our break. We had decided we would play in the big woods between our house and the school; the plan was to hide out and play until it was time to go home at the regular time after school, and then walk home as usual. We got to the woods around 9:45 and started playing various games, hide and seek lost it's thrill soon, as there were only three of us and it was difficult to hide with the noise the dead leaves made. We tried some imaginary bear hunting but found our stick rifles were not powerful enough and our attempts at making bows and arrows failed miserably. It was pretty cold and I was complaining about my feet being cold, Simon and Ross buried me in the leaves, covering me up making a game of it to keep me warm, but I was too cold and started crying. After about an hour of trying to keep me happy and warm they decided we would have to go home. Dad saw us coming across the meadow out of the woods. He waited by the gate at the end of the meadow sitting on the end of a wagon. As we slowly walked towards him we started with our previously made up alibis, Simon was holding his jaw and crying crocodile tears, he had a "tooth ache", Ross was doing the same, holding his stomach," belly ache", I just cried. Dad called for Simon to come over to him, saying, "As you are the oldest I will deal with you first". He reached in his back pocket and pulled out a pair of old rusty pliers and asked which tooth hurt. Suddenly Simon's tooth quit hurting. He then took Ross by the ear and asked if his stomach still hurt; Ross confessed we were playing hooky.

Dad loaded us onto the wagon, clucking to the team of horses and drove us back to school, where he hand delivered us to the teacher who stood us each in different corners of the classroom, much to the amusement of our class mates and to our shame.

There are not many things I can remember about my father before my school years, just sketchy memories, except for one incident I do remember very vividly, probably because I have a picture to remind me. I was about five years old, it was midsummer and my father was working in a field near our house. He was driving a tractor pulling some kind of hay rake, loading hay onto a wagon he was pulling behind the tractor. I was running behind the hay rake and, being in the middle of summer, I had very little clothes on. Dad ran over a large bumblebee's nest in the field. There seemed to be hundreds of bees all over me stinging every inch of my body. Daddy heard me screaming, grabbed me up and ran to the nearest creek that must have been over a hundred yards or more away and jumped in the creek with me, I can remember my mother running, as best as she could with her crippled leg. They carried me to the house and rubbed all kind of stuff over me, I don't know how long it took me to heal. I do know I still have a picture someone took of me all swollen up over my entire body.

As much as I hate the cold weather and Maryland winters (that's why I live in California) I have some fond memories of the winters. I remember dad hand making a wooden sled for us one winter. It was what was known as a bob sled, made of wood with metal runners made from old barrel hoops. We spent hours sliding down that same old hill in our back yard, now knee deep with pure white snow, where in the summer it was plush with green grass and we had so much fun with the old tractor tire dad had brought us. Our cousins Tom and Olbert Jr. lived a short way from us. There was a very long hill across the road from our farm where the hill went from very steep down a long, meadow like field, then it would gradually start to level off until it became almost flat about fifty yards from a barb wire fence at the end of the field, then there was about another twenty some feet to a creek. After a heavy snow my brothers, Tom, Jr. and I would get together after school and prepare a "sled run". We would some times spend two or three days preparing this run, starting at the top of the field, packing the snow down with our feet, going back and forth across the run until it was maybe ten or fifteen feet wide and then continue down the hill for maybe forty or fifty feet. The result would be a very fast head start down the long hill, where we would hit the unpacked snow and go rapidly down the rest of the hill until we could steer the sled around to avoid the barbwire fence at the bottom of the hill. Sometimes our neighbor's kids from near by farms would join in on the fun, helping pack the "run". One winter a few days after Christmas a couple of the neighbor kids came over with their new sleds. We could not afford store bought sleds so our contribution was to prepare the hill in return for a ride on their new sleds. There was a particularly heavy snow that week and we had spent all day preparing the run. With our cousins and the neighbor's kids, we were able to make the beginning of the run fairly long, about half way down the hill. We had made several runs down the hill and the more we used it the faster it got. Then it turned very cold towards dusk, as it was getting darker we decided to make one last run. We were not aware that the snow below the end of the run had frozen over making it even faster. One of the new kids had also got a brand new leather jacket for Christmas. We were all envious of him, even his younger brothers, who only got sleds, poor kids. We usually doubled up on the sleds as not every body had one, but on this last run the kid with the new jacket wanted to go alone so he took off on his new sled. When he left the packed run and hit the frozen snow, he could no longer steer the sled and headed straight for the barbwire fence at the end of the field. It was fortunate he did go by himself; he went under the fence, tearing his new jacket almost off his back, getting badly cut, shot straight onto the creek that had frozen solid, saving his life. I felt sorry for him about his jacket, but I'm sure glad he didn't let me double up with him for that run. After that we kids found another "run" to share the sleds of the more fortunate kids who had them.

About a year or so before our father died, Ross would have been about eight, I was seven, we were up at Johnny's farmhouse where we often went to play. Johnny was ill at the time so he was not around to supervise us and Dad was out working in the fields. Ross and I went into the house and started looking around; Johnny never objected to us being around and gave us free run of anything we wanted to get into. We came across a bunch of guns in a large closet. There were several rifles, pistols and shotguns. We were familiar with guns around and knew better than to play with them, however, our curiosity got the best of us. We were more intrigued with the shotguns than the others. We found a couple of twelve gauge shotguns that we were familiar with and had even fired at least once with an uncle or other adult around (although not our father). We knew how hard they would kick and they had earned out respect. The ones we were most intrigued with were an old ten gauge, an eight gauge and even an old "blunderbuss". It had a longer barrel than the others did and the end resembled a funnel. There was plenty of ammunition for the twelve gauge and a few rounds for the old ten gauge. I believe it was Ross who suggested we attempt to fire the old ten gauge. We both knew not to hold it to our shoulder, although we could not have if we had wanted to because of the size and weight. Ross suggested we prop it up on an old table we found, with the butt of the gun resting against a tree. We stood behind the tree, reaching around to pull the trigger. The thing went off with a deafening sound and the barrel just split in half, destroying the gun. Fortunately, neither of us was hurt, other than ringing eardrums for quite a while. Not satisfied, we decided to see how much noise the old eight gauge would make. We could not find any shells for the gun so we took one of the ten gauge shells that, when placed in the gun, just fell straight through the barrel. Not to be deterred, Ross took one of the ten gauge shells, wrapped some tape around it until it would not slide through the barrel. Using the same method of steadying the gun as with the old ten gauge we had just destroyed, we attempted to fire the eight gauge. The gun had a pull-back hammer that was hard for us to pull and hurt our thumbs so it took both of us to pull the hammer back. After the third attempt, and the gun not firing, we gave up. Of course, it was fortunate for us that it did not fire, as we would both probably have been seriously injured or killed. As our curiosity gave way to boredom, we could see our father coming across the field on a wagon with a team of horses. He had heard the explosion from the gun we had fired. Knowing that no one should have been there he came to investigate. As soon as he saw Ross and me he knew we had been up to something. Climbing down from the wagon, he demanded an explanation. We could not lie to him so we confessed to what we had done, showing him the gun we had destroyed. Dad never struck or even paddled any of us kids; however, he could give a stern lecture that left us feeling as though we almost wished he had whipped us. After the lecture he forbid us to ever come back to Johnny's house without a grown-up being with us and told us to never again touch any kind of gun.

I was eight years old when my father died April 15 1940; Johnny allowed us to remain on the farm as long as possible, but finally we had to leave as we kids could not run the farm and my father's brother and his family took our place. This began a long journey of rental homes for us, moving more times than I care to remember. We were living in our first rental home when WWII broke out. We had only what we could manage to grow in our small garden to eat and what our relatives could give us, which was very little. I can't remember for sure and my sisters cannot either, but it seems we received some kind of support from the county, perhaps $25.00 per month. I'm sure it would not have been anymore, there was no such thing as "welfare" as we know it today. We did receive a large basket of food every Christmas from our church. I shall never forget one year we received a can of "Del Monte" mixed fruit cocktail with the basket, we had never seen anything like it before; Mom rationed it out carefully for each of us, of course taking the least amount for herself, we thought we had died and gone to heaven, I can still almost taste that stuff and still enjoy it today.

During this period there was a government program, I believe it was called the Civilian Conservation Corps. (CCC) I think it was part of President Roosevelt's "New Deal". I can remember convoys of military trucks coming by our house each morning and returning in the afternoon. The men working with this unit were living in a camp near our aunt's home about ten miles away. Each day they would leave their "tent city" where they lived, traveling in old military trucks, to work on highways and other types of projects. I really don't know much about their work or missions, only that we received food from them. At first all of us kids would run to the side of the road in front of our house just to watch the truck convey go by;

then one day on their return trip, the trucks slowed down and some of the men in the back of the trucks tossed out brown paper bags, when we looked in them we found sandwiches and cookies. We were thrilled with our discovery of new found wealth. At first our mother was skeptical of them and talked to our aunt, who was familiar with the program. She assured mom the men were earnest in their gesture of good will, and we should be grateful for their generosity. As long as we lived there, which was probably only about a year, we waited anxiously each afternoon for the trucks to return. Some of the men saved their entire lunch for us, and many times this was the only food we had for that day. It also often served as our school lunches. The luxury of going to school with a crisp brown paper lunch bag, instead of sandwiches wrapped in a wax bread paper, was something only someone who has experienced such poverty could understand and appreciate.

We were looked down upon by our landlords, as we were not contributing much to their income, they were reluctant to even rent to us, and they treated us as a burden and offered us little if any assistance. I remember one year as winter was approaching, mom knew it was going to be cold in the house and we had no fuel for the old wood stove we used for cooking and heating the house. She went to the landlord to ask if there was any way we could get some wood from his property. He told her he did not feel it was his responsibility to cater to our needs. He later came to the house, I believe after his wife had talked to him, saying us kids could go out into the woods on his property and pick up old dead fallen limbs, but not to take any growing trees. Simon, Ross and me went out and spent the next few days gathering up what scrap wood we could, which did not amount to much.

Later in the month, when it had turned much colder, the landlord's wife came to the house and asked how we were doing. Mom said we were managing, when the lady asked if we had enough wood to last us through the winter, mom showed her the measly pile of wood left that we kids had gathered. She said she would see if she could help. She must have confronted her husband telling him he must do more for us, because he came to the house the next day and told mom there was a dead tree about 500 feet from the house that us kids could cut it down, he even loaned us an old cross cut saw that was dull and rusty, but it was better than the old dull axe we had been using. So, imitating lumber jacks, the three of us headed out for the task ahead. The tree was large, about forty or fifty inches in diameter. We had cut trees down many times when we were on the farm, so we were not new at it. However, what the landlord had failed to tell us was that it had been hit by a lightning strike. We did not find this out until we started sawing. The problem with sawing down a tree that has been hit by lightning is you cannot tell by the bark, as it is seldom broken, but inside the bark the tree is shredded and is like tooth picks. A dull cross cut saw operated by three young kids made it a very difficult task. We could not do much with the saw but with the help of an uncle we managed to finally cut it down with axes he had brought, we spent the next few weeks chopping it up. The wood we had chopped and gathered up helped some, but did not burn very well.

Just before Christmas that year, two of dad's brothers got together and brought us a ton of coal. We had never had a coal fire before, even on the farm, it was so much different than a wood fire, especially the smell. Instead of the smell of burning wood, it reminded me of the old coal burning locomotives that used to run daily behind our farm, where we would put pennies on the track for the train to run over. That Christmas was one of the happiest I can remember.

When I was in third grade we moved to a place near the village of Norristown. It was close to the Mason Dixon line in Maryland near Pennsylvania. Ross and I were going to a little two room school, the first three grades were in one room and the forth and fifth were in the other room. Ross was in the fourth grade but we managed to get together at recess and lunch.

I had a good friend called Earl in my class. We were very close and played together every day. He had a bicycle and took me everywhere with him. I would ride on the cross bar while he peddled. He even let me ride it by myself sometimes and being a new bike, I thought this was a great sacrifice for him. Apparently his mother thought so too. Although the family was well off, and I suppose very prominent in the village, Earl was not at all stuck up or pretentious. One day while we were out riding on his bike he stopped by his house to pick up a sweater. I stayed outside with his bike while he went in. As he was coming out of the house I heard his mother call to him saying, "I don't want you going over to that Simmons place to play with that kid; they are just poor trash, you have better friends to play with". I was out of her sight, but Earl knew I had heard her and was embarrassed by it. He tried to apologize for her but I pretended I never heard her. Although it hurt my feelings I didn't want him to feel bad for me. I do not know if things like that contributed to my low self esteem and played a part in my alcoholism or not. I have always thought it did. I do know it hurt me deeply. To think that someone could speak like that about a ten year old kid, and still hold their head up in the village was beyond me. I suppose it just hardened me toward the things I would later face in life.

After our second or third move my oldest brother, Samuel, quit school to enlist in the Army Air Corps. This was a great relief for us, as he could claim us as his dependents and we received a monthly allotment check from the Government. Small as it was, it was more than we were used to and we were very grateful. My mother was very wise in the handling of the money, although she had no experience at it; she was a very intelligent person. She too had to leave school to help her family.

We moved again in the spring to a larger house where the landlord told us we could have all the fuel we needed from a nearby woods. This gave us the summer to gather wood for the winter. Mom liked this place more than the others we had lived in. It was in a valley with beautiful surroundings and a stream where we kids could fish.

My oldest brother Samuel was now overseas in England with the Army Air Corps. Simon was working on a farm near our grandparents not far away. Due to the war, farm hands were short and able body hands were needed on farms, even willing children.

One day in early summer, 1942, Ross and I were playing in a cornfield near the house, as it was hot we were only wearing shorts. Ross found an old tube of lipstick at the edge of the field. We could see our older sister Marie sitting on a tree swing in the front yard. Ross decided to scare her. He took the lipstick and smeared it all over me as though I had been cut and was bleeding badly. When we got to the edge of the cornfield Ross picked me up carrying me in his arms. He started yelling, "I'm sorry Dick, I didn't mean it!" over and over. Marie looked up and saw us coming out of the corn field, took one look at me in Ross's arms and fainted, falling out of the swing. We laughed, and mom didn't.

In 1943 we moved back to Forest Hill Maryland, where I had first started school. It was the same school district but they had built a new school to replace the old three room school. I had never had bicycle of my own. One of our neighbors kids had an old bike he wasn't using and said he would sell it to me for $1.50. I ran across the meadow to our house as fast as I could to plead with my mother to buy it for me. Mom tried to explain to me that the money for the bike would buy bread, oatmeal, flour and other things we needed to survive. I whined and pleaded with her, as I always did to get my way. Being the gentle person she was, she finally gave in to me and gave me the money. That was the biggest rip-off I ever experienced. I was so excited about getting a bike of my own that I had not noticed how rusty it was or that it had no fenders and the spokes were bent and missing. I had to push it home as both tires were flat; the kid said he did not have a pump. When I got it home I found out it was one of the old type of bikes that did not have inner tubes. I went again to mom to beg her to get me new tires. They would cost about seventy cents each. No way was she going to put any more money out for that bike. One of my cousins came by with his father, who had a tire pump in his car and left my cousin with the pump while he went into town. We pumped the tires up, but they kept going flat as soon as we took the pump off. The only way to get the tire to hold air was to wrap tape around it; this was not very effective either. My cousin suggested we fill the tires with sand. We cut the valves off to make holes. Mom let us use one of her kitchen funnels to get the sand in the tire then wrap it with tape to hold it in. It worked. My cousin had experience riding a bike, so I let him peddle while I rode on the cross bar. As long as we were on a straight and flat road we could manage to control the wobble the sand caused. It also worked fine going downhill but we would have to push it back up to the top. After about an hour of riding he taught me how to handle it on my own. I started to go down hill, by myself this time. I was in my glory, pretending I was on my Harley

Davidson, when the handlebars broke, throwing me off. Crying and broken hearted, again I approached mom for assistance. She told me we could not afford repairs on the bike. She came out in the yard to look at the bike. When she how dilapidated it was, and what I had done with the tires, the broken handle bars and rust; although she tried to hide it from me, she could not help but laugh. She told me to remove the broken handle bar while she went back in the house, when she came back out she had a broom stick she had broken the brush off and stuck it through the holes where the handle bars had been. Mom had come through again. Soon I was wobbling off down that old dirt road on my very own $1.50 bicycle (Harley Davidson). I knew in my heart it was a piece of junk, but refused to admit it, even to myself.

The many moves we made and changes of schools had a very negative effect on me. As I remember, the reasons for us moving so many times were that either the landlord needed the house for farm tenants, or we did not have the money to pay rent. I never seemed to fit in with the other kids. I was usually the runt in school. Mom didn't start me in school until I was seven years old, most of the children started at five or six years old; she started Ross at five because he would be six in November. He had such a hard time she decided not start me until after I was seven, in August. Although I was older than the other kids I was much smaller, and I always seem to be the class clown, to the point of being nicknamed "monkey", even by the teachers. This, I'm sure, was due to my lack of self-confidence and low self-esteem, trying to be accepted by my peers. I was also held back in the third grade, making things even harder for me. The only person I could associate with comfortably was my brother Ross, who was just a little more than a year older than me but now two grades ahead of me. Simon and Marie were in high school and Anita was still too young to start school.

After yet another move and another school, we arrived at our first big school. It went from the first grade through the seventh, then four years of high school, all in one big two-story brick building. Being used to the little one or two room wooden schools I had been attending, it was very intimidating. This of course was still during the war and times were very hard for us. My mother had a difficult time providing for us, as provisions were short. My oldest sister, Marie, was in high school, and would handle our lunches. We would meet in some out of the way place where Marie would hand out our "rations" of lunches wrapped in a bread wrapper, as we could not afford lunch bags or lunch boxes like the other kids. The lunches consisted of bread and butter with sugar on it. We had butter because we still had the cow Johnny gave us when we left the farm. We got milk from her, which we then made into butter. As poor as we were, mom had her pride, and would not give us margarine, even when she could afford it.

While we were living at this house my brother Simon (Bud) had gotten mad at one of his teachers about six months before he was to graduate and left school, much to mom's displeasure. But it had its good side too; he went to work at a garage near where we used to live and attended grade school. He was able to help mom with expenses as he gave her part of his wages, and went on later in life to become a very good mechanic, rebuilding cars long after he had retired from the Air Force. One day when he was working at the garage, I had been playing hooky from school again and had gone into town. This is where I would usually go when I played hooky. I would hang around the bowling alley and pool room. Sometimes I would work as a pin-boy sitting up pins in the bowling alley to get pocket money, or play pool. Other times my friend Jack and I would roam about town looking for lawns to mow. On this day I hitch-hiked back to where Bud was working in the garage. I was going to get a ride home with him after he finished work. One of my buddies in town had given me a box of Feen-a-Mint laxatives. It was the type we used to get that looked like the chewing gum, called Chiclets only these were a little bit longer, and anyone looking at them could not tell the difference unless they knew what they were. Bud was using a welding torch and had his goggles on. I asked him if he wanted some chewing gum, he said, "Sure". I gave him three or four of them. He put them in his mouth and proceeded to chew them. It was about an hour or more before we left the shop for home. Bud was driving the car that mom had kept belonging to our father. He was the only one who could drive now as mom never did. It was an old 1934 Plymouth four door sedan, with all four of the doors that opened from the front (suicide doors). The driver's side had a bad lock and would sometimes fly open while driving, shortly after we left the garage to drive the 12 miles home Bud found he had to go to the toilet, urgently. He sped up and as we were going into a sharp turn to the right Bud's side door flew open, he almost fell out; I grabbed him and the wheel until he could get control. He barely made it in the drive- way when he jumped out, leaving the motor running, yelling for me to turn it off. He ran to our old out-side toilet, taking his pants off as he ran. I was laughing as hard as I could when mom came out to see what was going on. When Bud came out of the toilet, mom asked him what was wrong with him. He told her he just suddenly "had to go". She looked at me and said, "Did your brother give you anything?" Bud said, "Yeah, some chewing gum". Mom replied, "I think he may have given you something else". Bud took one look at me laughing, before mom could stop him, he caught me and beat the living daylights out of me. I don't think he ever forgave me. Mom didn't approve of us fighting, but she told me I deserved what I got.

I was in the fourth grade, my brother Ross wasn't doing much better in school than I was. A landlady of one of our aunts owned a large horse farm where she trained race horses. She approached my mother about getting permission for Ross to leave school and work on the farm. Ross pleaded with mom to allow him to go, telling her his wages could help with the family income. He was fourteen at the time. Mom finally agreed, and the powers that be permitted it. Ross began working on the horse farm and occasionally at the racetrack nearby. With my other brother Simon now working and my oldest sister Marie in high school, there was only mom, my youngest sister Anita, who had not yet started school, and me. I had no one now to associate with at school, and felt totally alone in the world.

While I was in the fourth grade we moved again; another move, another home, and yet another school. We were living near a place called Dublin, which had beautiful scenery, especially in the spring and summer. The autumns were picturesque; however, with the falling of the leaves, we knew the bitter winters were near. The old cook stove did not heat the entire house so we spent a lot of time in the kitchen. The snow made it difficult for us to get to the nearest store, which was nearly ten miles away, and wood for fuel was always difficult to obtain. I was by myself in school; in an attempt to be accepted by the other kids in my new school, I continued to act the fool, and the name of "monkey" was again appropriate.

One January it was extremely cold, all the ponds and the mill run near our house were frozen over. As we could not afford to buy skates, mom taught me how to make my own. She showed me if I took empty Pet milk cans, and stamped on them in just the right way, they would fold up around the arches of my shoes and create a pair of home made skates. The neighbor's kids, who the most of them had proper skates, but some who did not, had mom teach them how to make "tin can skates". We would spend many hours skating up and down the old millrun, or one of the many ponds. This was one of the ways I could entertain myself that we could afford. Thank God for mom's inventiveness, making all kinds of things for us kids, such as my tin can skates and my broom stick handle bars for my old bike. I can recall many happy hours when we would build a bonfire beside the mill run and skate long after dark. Mom was not able to join us due to her difficulty in walking, and inability to endure the cold caused by a childhood illness.

One day I took my "skates" to school. There was no millrun near the school. However, there was a pond at the end of the playground that was frozen over. We had been instructed several times not to go near it, but I was "monkey" and had to show off. I took my "Pet milk can skates" and ventured out on the pond, with all the kids telling me that I would get into trouble. Undaunted, I skated further out. Sure enough, I went through the ice and into the cesspool. I managed to get back to the playground, (without any help from my classmates). Due to the smell I was emitting, the teacher refused to allow me into the classroom. Although I had ridden a bus to school, it was just after the first recess, there was no bus available. I had to walk home. It was nearly ten miles to our house. I was wet and freezing when I finally arrived home. My ever-tolerant mother took me in, cleaned me up and sent a stern letter to the school; but nothing was ever done about it.

The rest of the school year was difficult to say the least; the other children were very harsh on me and the teacher was not much help.

Maybe someone did reprimand her for sending me home in answer to mom's letter to the school. Perhaps she was punishing me for it, but I do know I was a very unhappy child and became even more withdrawn.

These events soon took its toll on me; my attendance rapidly decreased. In August I turned 13 and began school in the fifth grade in September. I soon began to skip classes and play hooky. Eventually the truant officers came to see mom threatening to take action. This, of course, had no effect on me. One day when I was playing hooky, my older brother, Simon, and I went out looking for lawns to cut for pocket money. We found this lovely big lawn that Simon said we cold get $1.50 each for mowing, which was big money, so off I went with him. Around noon the gentleman who lived there approached and starting asking us questions. He asked our name and then asked Simon his age; Simon told him he was 17. Then he asked me how old I was, I told him I was 16. He left then returned after about an hour, just as we were finishing up. He walked straight up to me and said, "Richard, you are not 16. You are 13 and are supposed to be in school." It turns out he was the superintendent of schools.

Soon my mother and I had to appear in court where I was given the option to either attend school regularly or be placed in a juvenile home. I promised the judge and mom I would go to school, but I just could not handle it. I could not concentrate and was always acting up and being the "monkey". With Bud working on the farm the most of the time and Ross now working at the racetrack I felt so isolated. To draw attention to myself, I would act the fool, always living up to my nickname, "the monkey", thinking the other kid's would accept me. When they didn't, I guess I rebelled by playing hooky. Soon I started missing more and more.

One night I met Ross in the poolroom, he asked me if I had seen mom that day. I replied, "No, why?" He said the sheriff had been to the house looking for me and would be back tomorrow to pick me up. Well now I was concerned. Ross asked me what I was going to do. I said I had no idea. Ross said, "Look, we have a load of horses going to Hialeah Fla. tomorrow morning. I'll talk to my trainer and ask him to take you on as a groom. Do you want to go with us, or wait to see what they are going to do?" For the first time in my life

I felt much older than I ever had before. I did not feel like being the "monkey" anymore. I felt cornered, and it frightened me, although I would never let on. All of the sudden, as much as I loved Ross, I needed someone more. I wanted my father's love and guidance. It was in the fall of 1944, I was just thirteen years old, and had a serious decision to make. Without much time for me to debate the issue, I was on that box car with six horses headed for Florida at 6:00 o'clock the next morning. So ended my childhood, as most children know it, and the beginning of a new life and a career that lasted until the next officials came looking for me: the military.

Chapter Two

My first career

I soon learned that life on the racetrack was far different than any I had known. I always thought I was street smart from association with the gang in the bowling alley, pool room and bar, better known locally as the "Rat-Hole", but I soon learned that would not be enough to get me by and my brother Ross would not always be there to take up for me. I would have to fend for myself. I learned through some hard knocks and heartaches, but I was soon a full fledged race tracker, much to my mothers' dismay.

One of the first things I learned on the track was to drink, although I had some experience in the "Rat Hole". This was just an accepted way of life. I soon fell into the pattern, perhaps at first just to be accepted as one of the guys. After my experience in school, I felt the need to belong to any kind of group, no matter what the cost. Unfortunately, this was also in later years to become one of my biggest burdens.

Before I was fifteen years old I had experienced my first black out. This was probably due to one of my uncles introducing me to moonshine. He brewed the stuff himself on a farm where he and his family moved to from West Virginia. He met me one night in the pool room in Bel-Air, and took me out to his car and gave me some of his home brew. I remember it tasted like kerosene, but I had already had a few beers and this stuff seemed to get quicker results. He warned me not to tell my mother, (his sister) as he knew she disapproved of drinking in any form. After we finished off his pint he got me some more beer, I don't remember what happened next until I woke up on another one of my uncle's couches. This was an uncle who lived near us and the father of our cousins, Tom and Jr. that we used to play with as we were growing up. I made up some story about someone slipping something in my coke being the last thing I could remember. My aunt, who often looked after us kids from time to time after dad died, believed me. She never was comfortable with Ross and me associating with that racetrack crowd anyway. I know now that by the time I was sixteen I was a full-blown alcoholic. I did not stop drinking until twenty-six years later.

There was no moral discipline on the track, just instructions on how to take care of your horses. Another thing that assisted us was that we were required to have photo I.D. cards, similar to the type later issued to me in the military, in order to get into the stable areas. These were issued by each track we visited or worked at. As soon as we would go in the gate there was a trailer that we reported to in order to get ID's, have a blood test and blood type. Ross had instructed me prior to going in on what to say and how to act. I remembered Ross telling me the first time he went into the trailer for the blood type. He had never had one and didn't hesitate when the lady asked for his finger. He watched as she stabbed his finger with the little knife they used. He said he jumped up asking her what the hell she was doing. He said he nearly slapped her before someone more experienced stopped him. There was usually a lady typist behind a desk who issued the passes. She never looked up to see who was there, just asked for your information. If you told her you had green hair, red eyes, four feet tall or eight feet, that's what she put down, so naturaly the opportunity was there to get a fake I.D. card for the bars. Although I was born in 1931, according to some of my track I.D. cards I have been born as early as 1922 in order to facilitate my being twenty one years old in the states that required it. Some states only required you to be eighteen. I believe New York and Delaware were two that only required you to be eighteen at the time I never pressed my luck by going to bars that might question my I.D. instead I would usually frequent dives and places that only cared about getting your money. I was once challenged by a policeman in Atlantic City New Jersey who didn't believe my age, so he took me to jail until my trainer came to get me out the next morning. I don't know what transpired but I was on the next horse van going to Saratoga in New York.

This is where I first met "Whitie". He was working as a groom in our stables, and was an albino. I had never even heard of this term before and he scared the hell out of me when I saw him coming out of a stall about 6:30 one morning. He was very tall for a race tracker nearly six feet tall, but only weighed about a hundred forty pounds. He was as white as a ghost, but a strange kind of white, just plain scary. His eyes were a kind of pink and his hair white although he was only eighteen years old. I finally got to know him better and was not so afraid of him. He told me he was from Louisiana, that his parents were black, that he had six brothers and three sisters. He said he was the only albino in the family. He was shy but not ashamed of what he was. He turned out to be a nice guy, but stayed pretty much to himself. He never went into town with any of us. I guess to be honest, we never invited him.

Another character we had with our stables was Dicky Kline, he was also a groom who would exercise horses from time to time, his problem was he had a bad leg, he could not bend his knee properly, so he had a severe limp, when he exercised a horse he had to ride what was called "Acey Ducey", his left stirrup was pulled to put his leg in a sitting type of position, the same as any other rider, his right stirrup however, was lowered to where his right leg was almost straight; there were other riders who preferred this style of riding,

(One in particular, was Eddie Arcaro, who at the time was the leading rider in the states) I just could not get comfortable with it. Dicky was grooming our big stud "Yarle" who was notorious for biting and kicking grooms, or anyone else who was unfortunate enough to get in his way, one morning Dicky was walking Yarle around the shed row after a work out and a sponge bath, as he walked him, he became pre-occupied; he was walking along beside Yarle, tapping him under his chest and belly with the long end of the reins, Yarle had walked ahead of him until Dicky was near his hind quarters; when Dicky swung the end of the reins under Yarle, striking him in a tender, private part, Yarle leaped ahead of Dicky, kicking him square in the face. He was taken to the hospital where they found he had a broken nose, jaw and the bone under his eye was shattered; they told him he was lucky to be alive. I avoided Yarle as much as I could.

Chapter Three

Life gets serious

When I first started on the racetrack in 1944, I was mainly a "go-for". Although I was paid as a groom, I found my self walking hots, running errands, washing saddle towels, cleaning saddles, etc. I was also soon to be given my initiation to the race track, this was a trick played on all new comers. One of the trainers would come up to me and asked me to go over to another stable to get "the key to the quarter pole". Of course, when I arrived at that stable and ask for the key, they would tell me they had just sent it over to another stable, directing me over there, and so on until someone eventually told me it was a prank, there is no key to a quarter pole. Still, I was glad to get out of the situation I was in when I left home.

Yet I wanted more. This was to become a trait that would be characteristic of me throughout my life. As I boosted the exercise boys or the jockeys up on their mounts that I was grooming while leading them to the track for a race or workout, I thought, hell I can do that. After all, I did ride all the horses on our farm and my grandfather's farm as well, including his old mule and a few cows and heifers. As the matter of fact, Ross and I got our skills for breaking yearlings on the farm. We would sneak up on a young heifer or large calf that was laying down in the meadow, jump on its back and go for one hell of a ride. One time we were coming back from church in our best clothes, Ross and I started across the meadow where some young heifers were sleeping. We each jumped on one. Mine threw me off very quickly, but Ross's mount had other plans and headed straight for a large pond. She ran right into the middle and stopped. No matter how hard Ross tried, she would not budge. She just stood there until he had to dismount and come home soaking wet in his best suit. Dad was not pleased, and as kind of a man as he was, Ross got punished. Still, my trainer showed no sign of recognizing my talents. After somewhere between six months and a year on the track, I decided to approach one of our trainers. We had two, Fred Case and Joe Cerio, Fred always seemed the most approachable so I made sure he saw what a great job I had done that morning. The four horses I was grooming were all shinning like show horses and I had clean clothes on. I waited for him to return with the horse he had been training in the starting gate and helped him dismount and undo his tackle. I think he knew what was coming; after all he had been around for a long time. I said, "Fred, what do you think about putting me up and giving me a chance to exercise some horses for you?" He looked at me and replied, "I think you would fall on your ass before you got out of the shed row". Of course my spirits were broken, but also my anger raged inside me, how dare he judge me without giving me a chance? Fortunately he picked up on my anger more than my hurt pride. "So you think you are ready to start riding do you?" I said, "Yes, and I think you will be surprised." He said, "I doubt that".

My brother was grooming a big horse named Our Dandy at the time; he had exercised him often and said he was pretty gentle, I asked if he would persuade Fred to let me take him out for a work out the next morning. Fred agreed and Ross put me up on my first horse. I was never so proud of anything I had ever done. I felt like my idol Eddy Arcaro, (leading rider at the time and the only rider to win the triple crown twice; the Kentucky Derby, the Preakness and the Belmont stakes 1941-1948) Fred told me to just take him to the track and let him have his head, not to try anything fancy, or try to impress anyone. Well, old Dandy seemed to understand me and gave me a great ride. I completed the course then slowly galloped him back to the barn. I gave him the best wash down and rub down he ever had, then I gladly walked him out to cool him down and put him in his stall and gave him a good dinner.

There were many more experiences after that as Fred decided I could make it from the shed row to the track without falling off. My first mount was a much more pleasant experience than my first attempt at the starting gate. Now that is another world. The first time in a gate has to be the most intimidating thing for any rider. I asked Ross for any advice he could give me. He said, "Dick, it's just a big metal box with pads on both sides and doors that close you in, don't sweat it." I said, "How do I know when the gate will open?" He said, "When it opens, just be ready." I asked how you do that. He said, "When you are in the gate and it is closed, take a long hold, a handful of mane, get a deep seat, keep a stiff upper lip and a tight asshole." Ross always had a way with words.

The morning I was to take a horse out of the gate the first time, after I had saddled up and headed towards the track, I realized the saddle I was using had been used before me by someone much shorter. The stirrups were much too short so I took my feet out of the stirrups to made adjustments as I was going down the track toward the gate instead of doing it before I left the shed row. Fred was standing in his usual place at the quarter pole with his stop watch to time the horses. I got in the gate with four other horses, before I had a chance to get scared or do any of the things Ross told me to do, Fred opened the gate and all hell broke loose. It must have been the most comical sight my stable mates ever saw as I snatched the horses head both left and right; bumping horses on both sides of me and very nearly fell off. Finally I got control and finished the course, when I got back to the barn Fred was already in the shed row. I pulled my saddle off and turned to Fred asking how I had done. Without even looking at me he said, "Well, when I saw you going to the gate adjusting your stirrups, I thought to myself, that can't be the smartest thing he has ever done. Then as I watched you come out of the gate I thought, yeah, that it probably was the smartest thing you've ever done". Fred had hurt my feelings again with his sarcasm, I told Ross about it, he said don't pay any attention to him, hell; he talks that way to everybody, even other trainers.

Fred did allow me to try my hand at trying to win a few races, first at the fairgrounds at our own track then finally at the bigger tracks, but only in small claiming races. I had a few 3rd places at Atlantic City and two 2nd places at Monmouth Park in New Jersey, I also had several mounts at Delaware Park, where I rode my first race on a muddy track, I had exercised in the mud before but never rode a race in the mud, I did not fare well, as I broke about sixth in an eight horse field, it was pouring the rain down, not being experienced as much as the other riders in the use of riding with goggles in the mud, where they would wear at least three pair of goggles. When one pair got too muddy to see they would pull that pair down giving them clear vision again and so on, I had three pair of goggles on ok, but as soon as I left the gate they were muddied up, I reached to pull down the first pair down as I was trying to get a better hold on the wet reins and trying to avoid running up on the heels of one of the horses in front of me, instead I pulled down all three pair, there is no way to get a pair back up and control a horse at the same time, I could not see a thing, just mud and the backs of horses, to prevent an accident I just eased my horse back and finished last, I don't think anyone other than me thought I would do much better anyway.

Most of my mounts for a while were just small races and got nothing. Until the spring meeting 1947 at Pimlico in Maryland; Fred came to the stable one morning as I was getting ready to exercise one of the horses Bob Flowers was grooming. A mare called Abbey Gail, she was a twin of Abby Mae, another mare in our stable, they were sired by one of our studs "Yarle" out of Abby Peire, I knew she was fast, her mother had been one of our fastest horses in short races, and Yarle had never lost a race, I had worked Abby Gail out of the gate before and was well aware of her speed. Fred asked if I thought I could handle her the following day in a race. I had hoped I would get the opportunity to ride her in race where I would be given the chance to possibly win. I tried to appear as confident as I could with my guts churning with nerves. I realized this was the opportunity to win my first race. I said, "Sure, I've waited a long time for this. How should I handle her?" He said, "You know she is the fastest thing we have out of the gate, so I'm putting her in a five furlong race tomorrow. Just make sure you get her out of the gate in front, she will do the rest."

I got little sleep that night. I must have ridden that race in my mind all night, and the next morning I had three horses to exercise. I just pretended each one was Abbey Gail and got very comfortable in the gate. Fred walked with me to the jockeys' room that afternoon and talked to me as he never had before. He said, "Dick, you know you can win this race and break your maiden. (A term used for a jockey's or a horse's first win) Have confidence in yourself and do not do anything stupid, just get her out of the gate in front and she will take you home". I thanked him for the mount and opportunity to win my first race. I got into my silks and walked to the saddling enclosure without saying a word to anyone. I only wish Ross could have been there, but he was preparing one of his horses for a race himself at Bowie about 30 miles away. When the bugler played "call to post" I was surprisingly calm. Bob Flowers brought Abby over from the stables and held her while Fred lifted me up on her. I could feel the power this mare had. I felt a bit tense on the way to the starting gate, but I kept telling myself, "Ok it's up to you now". When they closed the gate I remembered how fast this horse could come out of a gate, I had seen her leave an exercise boy on his butt in the gate. I remembered what Ross had told me on gate protocol. I was next to the last of seven in the gate; I took a long hold on the rains and grabbed a hand full of mane. I didn't have time to stiffen my upper lip or tighten anything. When the starter, Eddy Blind, swung that gate, Abbey shot out like bolt of lightening. There was no doubt I was in front but I dared not look back to see how far or anywhere except straight ahead. I could hear the horses behind me, but nothing on either side of me. I wondered how far in front I was, Abbey was still pulling me out of the saddle and I remembered what Fred told me, "Just let her go, she will do the rest". She did just as Fred had promised. I could hear the crowd as I approached the wire, it seemed to be over a lot sooner than I expected. I never moved my whip from where it was in my right hand when I left the gate; I knew I would not need it. As I crossed the finish line I realized I had just won my first race. Finally I looked back as I was pulling her up. I found out later I had won by five lengths and I never felt so proud.

Bob Flowers was waiting for me in the winner's circle with Fred, they both congratulated me on a fine race and breaking my maiden; I realized I had arrived.

I rode a few more races at that meeting before going back to our stable at Bel-Air where we were getting our horses ready for the winter trip to Florida. It was colder than usual that fall and I was grooming five horses at the time. One morning after washing down one of my horses, I dried him and threw a blanket over him and was walking him around the shed row. It was normal to have buckets of water around the shed row to give the horses a drink while walking them out. We had a bucket warmer for cold mornings such as this was. The water was warmed by placing an electric heating ring in the bucket to warm the water, and then of course, remove it when the water was warm before a horse drank from it. On this morning I was not completely awake, or more likely hung over. As I walked my horse he started to walk to the water bucket. Not thinking anything about it, I could see there was no ice in the bucket so I just let him stick his nose in the bucket. Suddenly all hell broke loose. The horse jumped almost straight up, knocking me over and took off down the shed row, with me picking myself up yelling, "Loose horse!" as loud as I could and wondering what had happened. Then I saw the bucket rolling around the shed row with the heating ring still in it, I realized what had happened, someone, maybe even me, had left the electric heating ring in the bucket still plugged into the electric socket. That horse got one hell of a shock and I got sober fast. Fortunately only my brother Ross, Bob Flowers and me were at the barn, as the trainer had not shown up yet. Ross caught the horse before he hurt himself. He put him in the stall and gave me hell for not checking the bucket before I let the horse drink from it.

One year at the fall meeting at Pimlico, our trainer, Fred entered a horse in a race at Laurel Park. He was sending Ross and Bob Flowers down as grooms in the horse van with the gelding he had entered, along with three other horses, he asked me to also take a mare along that he wanted to get familiar with the track, and work her out for the three days we would be there. Although I had asked Fred to let me ride the gelding in the race, he said he had already given the ride to Jimmy Stout. As I had no offerings of other rides,

I decided it was better than cleaning out stalls, so I gladly went along. I worked out each of horses for the first two days. On the third day Jimmy worked out the gelding while I exercised the mare. Jimmy won the fifth race on the gelding and my mare had become familiar with the track and was prepared for a race the following week. We loaded the horses back on the van for the ride back to Pimlico. Usually all three of us would ride in the back of the van with the horses; we had each bought bottles of whiskey to drink on the ride back. Bob was a friend of the van driver and offered to share his bottle with him if he could ride in the front. The driver of course agreed. Although there was a seat for the passenger, there was also room for someone to stand on the driver's side between the driver and the door. Bob got bored just riding, and he had hit the bottle pretty heavy on the way back. As the driver was going through Baltimore, Bob was checking out the school girls. At one of the school crossings there was a large metal sign in the middle of the road warning of the crossing; normally the signs are portable and are rolled out of the street when not being used. Bob poked his foot out of the window of the van to kick the sign, thinking it would just topple over but it was permanently cemented into the road. Bob broke his foot and was in a cast for the rest of the meeting. When we got back to the track, Fred asked where Bob was, we told him he would be along shortly, after he got his cast on. Fred was pissed but he let me ride the mare at Laurel Park the next week, she went off at twenty to one and I won by three lengths.

The trainer was usually the one to lift the jockey onto the horse. One day Ross and I were each taking a horse that we were grooming at the time to the saddling enclosure. Both of the trainers were there at the time, Fred was lifting Johnny Longden up on the horse I was running and Joe Cerio was lifting Jimmy Stout up on Ross's horse. Jimmy had been drinking a lot of beer and eating pizza the night before and he had no inhibitions about relieving himself of gas when he felt like it. As Joe lifted him up, Jimmy cut loose with a very loud report, right in Joe's face. Instead of Joe just boosting him up enough to make the saddle, he gave him an extra shove, lifting him clear over the horse where he fell over the other side onto the ground. Fortunately Ross had a good grip on the horse and managed to control him, Jimmy however was laying on the ground in the saddling enclosure laughing his head off while everyone watched him. Joe told him if he ever did that again he would throw him clear off the track.

One race I enjoyed very much was a stake race where I rode with a guy I had a great deal of respect for. Bobby Strange was riding our best horse Yarle, who had won every race he had ran so far. Our trainer Fred knew he had a great chance of winning if he could get him to the front early. Fred put me in the same race on Abby Gail, the horse I had won my first race on. He wanted me to pace Yarle who was a distance runner. This was a mile and a quarter race. Abby was more of a sprinter, but she could beat any horse out of the gate. The plan was for me to take Abby to the front an hold the pace for Yarle to follow, then as Abby would hold her position on the inside rail I would make room for Bobby on Yarle to come on the inside and go to the lead. Yarle was in the # 4 stall in the gate, I was in #2 on Abby Gail. When the gate opened Abby Gail did her thing. I was three lengths in front at the quarter pole. I could see Bobby on the big gray stallion was in about third place moving toward the rail, about four and a half lengths behind me. I started to move out from the rail to give Yarle room. He moved in beside me on the rail, we held our positions as we went into the first turn. As we came out of the turn Abby Gail started to tire. Bobby looked back and said, "I'll see you in the winner's circle". Yarle took off and as I started to ease up on Abby she seemed to sense she had done her job. Yarle went on to win by five lengths. I finished fifth, I felt good about that and Bobby and Fred treated all of us that night.

I had a very good buddy in my home town, a guy named Jack Haggy. We were very close in age and would get together every time I went into Bel-Air. He also played hooky from school but he was more discrete than I had been and did not get in trouble over it. He was very good at playing pool and bowling. I could hold my own in both games but Jack was very good, we used to challenge the local school boys to get their allowances by betting with them. Jack also had a friend, Red, that he used to work for to get his pocket money to play pool and gamble with whenever he would take off from school. Red used to hire Jack to help him with his deliveries on his beer truck a few times a week. He was driving for the National Bohemian beer company. I went with him and Jack a few times but it was crowded in the cab with the three of us. Red had a friend who drove for the Gunther's beer company. He said he would talk to the guy and get me the same type of work Jack was doing for him when I had spare time from the track. I would work with Red's friend a couple days a week while Jack worked with Red. Jack left school when he was sixteen and wanted to move into town. His parents lived about 12 miles from town and he had to hitch hike into town. He asked if I would rent a small house with him he found in town that was very cheap and just a short walk to the race track. I agreed and this worked out great for both of us, we felt we had more freedom and Jack could afford it with my help. When I was on the road I would send him the rent money. Jack started working pretty regular with Red and through him we found out Red had to take a big tractor and trailer into Baltimore once a week for a large load of beer to supply his warehouse. The beauty of this was his company allowed three cases of breakage each trip. I talked to Red's friend that I had worked for and found Gunther's had the same deal. The drivers were very careful not to break any bottles and they agreed to take two cases for themselves and let us helpers take one each. This meant Jack and I had two cases of free beer each week. We also had a lot of visitors.

In the spring of 1945 we went to Delaware Park in Stanton, near Wilmington, we went up in a horse van with four horses. There was me, Ross and Bob Flowers on the van. I screwed up before we left; I was supposed to prepare the water barrels. We used big wooden kegs for the water in the vans and on trains. The kegs held about fifty gallons of water. We would put a round flat wooden float on top of the water to keep it from splashing around during transportation. The horses could drink by just pushing the float down and the water never splashed out. I had filled the barrels but I did not put the floats in. Fortunately the road from the barns to the highway was rather rough and we soon found out what I had done, or rather, not done. Ross ran back to the barn and got the floats and placed them in the kegs, not without telling me how stupid I was. It was a very nice ride and some beautiful country side both in Maryland and Delaware.

Delaware Park was a beautiful racetrack and one of my favorites, although I always liked going back to Delaware there was always the sad memory of my first trip there, that year we lost one of our best jockeys, Joe DeFacco, he was one of the nicest guy's I ever met, he had just turned 21 while we were at Pimlico a few months earlier. I had exercised a horse with him earlier that morning and he was excited about the stake race he was riding in that afternoon. I can't remember the horse's name, but every one in the stable had a bet on it. It was the third race on the card and although the track was a bit wet that morning it was fairly warm and with the sun shining, the track dried out and was fast by race time. Ross and I were in the grandstand near the finish line, we did not have binoculars so we could not see much of what happened. It was a mile and a quarter race, they broke in front of the stands. We watched Joe laying in third place on the back stretch, he had a good hold and in the position he wanted to be in, as he was coming out of the last turn. Another horse tried to pass him on the outside; it looked as if he cut in a bit close. We saw Joe's horse's head first seem to rise up then suddenly drop. He couldn't pull his head up and he went down like a sack of flour. He fell about three feet from the inside rail, the worst possible place, in the path of the rest of the horses. We could see other horses trying to avoid trampling him. Joe's horse had to be destroyed on the track. They took Joe to the hospital where he was pronounced dead. One of the horse's hooves had hit the side of his head tearing off his scull cap and another in the back of the neck, he never had a chance. Joe's parents came down from Brooklyn to take him back and pick up his things. Joe was always a flashy dresser and loved to buy new clothes, he was the envy of all of us for the wardrobe he kept. He even had a small trailer he pulled behind his big yellow convertible Buick to carry his wardrobe in. We all helped gather his things and even our owner Mr. Bryson came down from New Jersey to see them and presented them with a set of the stable's riding silks, he thought a lot of Joe as well.

On a lighter side of that year's trip to Delaware, our stable had run two big races one day and won both of them. The owner and trainers had invited all the stable hands to the club house, which was a big deal for us as we were usually in the grand stands or in the center field. Both of our trainers were there for the races and were feeling rather generous treating us to several drinks. After the races Ross had a date with a girl he met at the track earlier and was taking her to the movies in town. He asked if I wanted to go and see if I could get lucky at the movies. I jumped at the idea of going to town and of courses I felt I could get lucky. We were both pretty drunk before we left the track but still felt we needed to stop in a local bar before going to his girl's house. By the time we left the bar he was about an hour late for his date. As we were approaching her house Ross said he should take her some flowers to make up for being late. Of course, there were no flower shops around, and its unlikely Ross would waste good money buying them anyway when there were all theses lovely gardens along the way. It had turned dark when he spotted a nice garden full of flowers under the street lights. He stepped into the garden that had recently been watered and pulled up several flowers, roots and all. When we came to her house, he rang the bell. Her father answered the door and there stood Ross and I both laughing our heads off. Ross held the flowers out with the dirt and roots still attached to them and said, "These are for Gloria, you want to tell her I'm here?" Needless to say, Gloria and her father were not impressed and let us know. He told us to get out before he called the cops. We decided to skip the movies and went back to the bar where we found a couple of the bar's regular gals and tried our luck at wooing and dancing with them. We were not so lucky at this either, so we stayed until the bar closed then headed back to the track.

We went from Delaware back to our home stables which were at the Bel-Air race track. Bel-Air was a one mile track that belonged to the owner of our stables, it was a part of the big farm where the horses were raised, and it was used mostly for training our horses and breaking yearlings. The county fair was also held there each year. During the fair races were held, mostly for small purses that were more for entertainment, this is where I got a lot of my early riding experience.

There was not as much discipline and protocol here and this where I learned about unethical practices, such as using a "buzzer". This was a device similar to a cattle prod only much smaller. Exercise boys and jocks would use this devise early in the morning work-outs to get the horse used to it. It was small enough to hold in your hand while riding, it held a dry cell battery and two sharp prongs. When you hit the horse in the back of the neck it would give the horse a shock and make a buzzing sound. It was used early in the morning when there were no officials around. It took some getting used to using because the first few times the horse is hit he may dump you. The whole idea was to get the horse to know when he was going to get shocked and he would run faster. Of course you could not use this at bigger tracks but there were advantages to knowing how to use it. After the horse had been hit a few times he would respond to any similar action. The reins on the bridle have a buckle at the end to join them together. If some unscrupulous rider wanted to, (of course I never did; "ahem") he could file the point on the buckle of the rein to make it sharp. Then, when working out a horse or riding him in a race he could lean down near the horse's ear, jab the horse in the neck near the base of the mane with the sharpened buckle and make a buzzing sound. Usually the horse would respond, but the jockey had better not get caught. Of course other jockeys knew of this practice so he may get reported to the Stewards, or get hell beat out of him if it cost some other guy a race. As I said, this was usually only used on small tracks like fair grounds.

One of the times I got into trouble with the track officials was at Bowie in Maryland. It was a spring meet and I was riding one of the three French horses our owner had bought. No one liked them because they were nervous, very hard to discipline, and difficult to ride. They would give a rider a hard time, especially in the starting gate. This particular time I was the first in the gate and the horse started acting up right away. He reared up in the gate then tried to go under the gate. I held him the best I could, finally taking my whip and hitting the horse over the head with the blunt end. The starter cautioned me, but the horse was still acting up. I hit him again when I thought the starter was not looking, but he was. He said, "Simmons that will cost you $100.00." The horse would just not settle down and I snatched his head with the reins. The starter said, "That will be $200.00 Simmons." Well I had a temper too, and yelled back at the starter, "Hell why don't you make it $300.00?" (You don't argue or smart off to a starting official.) The starter said, "No, $500.00!" and swung the gates open. The horse finished out of the money, and so did I. Ross told me later that I should have known better. These officials had a lot of power and used it when they thought a horse was being abused or a jockey was doing something illegal. The first time I was fined was shortly after I had won my first race, for something I thought was stupid. It was procedure after the race, when you were coming back to the unsaddling area and approached the scales where you had to be weighed in before and after a race, that you wave your whip to the judges upstairs in a salute. I failed to do it one time at Pimlico and was fined $50.00 for it. I should have learned to respect the officials then.

One of our exercise boys was an Italian guy named Ralph Sansaverino, Ross and I used to take him home once in a while for mom's Sunday dinner. He loved this and always brought mom a gift of some kind. He was from Yonkers in New York and had no experience with country home cooked meals. He always enjoyed talking to mom, who used to tell him his name, Sansaverino, sounded like an opera. Mom enjoyed listening to classical music and Ralph could play some on our old piano. They enjoyed each others company, especially after one year when Ralph, Ross and I bought all the fixings for a Thanksgiving dinner and mom cooked one of her famous meals. Ralph was in heaven. Before we went back to the track mom gave him a couple jars of her home made canned peaches. He asked Ross and me why we ever left home.

Ralph was twenty one years old and single when they started drafting for the Korean War. He was one of the first to be drafted; after he finished his basic training and was on leave he stopped by the stable to see us before going on to New York. The trainer was not at the stable that morning and Ralph wanted to take a horse out for the last time. Bob Flowers got a horse out he was grooming and put Ralph up. Before he got out of the shed row something spooked the horse and he reared up, throwing Ralph into the railing then fell on him pinning him against the rail. We called the ambulance and they took him to the local hospital. When Fred, our trainer and the rest of us visited him the doctor told us he had broken his neck and back and was paralyzed from the neck down. The military would not take responsibly for his accident as it was not service related; the race track insurance said he was not authorized to be in the stable area. Ross and I visited him one time in Yonkers while we were in Atlantic City. He was never the same and very depressed. Mom was very upset over it and regularly sent him cards, he of course could not respond.

One year when we were usually scheduled to go to Florida around late October or early November, we took six horses to Bowie Park in early November; it is not far from D.C. and close to Laurel in Maryland. It was extremely cold and there were no sleeping quarters for us. The trainer told us we were only going to be there for 10 days and we could bed down in an empty stall. The first two nights we nearly froze even though the three of us, Ross, Bob Flowers and me huddled together with all our cloths on, covered up with loose straw and hay to try to keep warm. The next night we decided the horses had had two good nights so we were due one. We pulled blankets from the horses for ourselves, we only took two and all three of us slept under them. Unfortunately, the trainer came in before we got up and really gave us hell. Though we showed him the conditions we were sleeping in, you could actually throw a cat through the cracks in the walls and the wind was blowing so hard the noise kept us awake, he said that was no reason to take the blankets from the horses. He promised to find some old blankets for us and he did. I think they were ones the grooms had been using to haul the stall cleanings out on, but at least they were warm.

One year we were coming back from Florida early for some reason. It was around mid February and still very cold in Maryland. I was in a box car with five horses, my brother Ross and Bob Flowers. When we reached Savanna Georgia we always stopped for water. We usually only stopped for about a half hour and it was still warm in Georgia so we had the box car door open for air when this old black guy came up and asked if we were going to Baltimore. We said yes and he asked if he could bum a ride in the car. This was of course against all rules and would surely get us fired, but Bob Flowers being the opportunist he was, looked across the station platform and saw a stack of crates of oranges awaiting shipment, along with some bags of coconuts. He told the guy, "If you get us a crate of those oranges and a sack of coconuts when I tell you to I'll let you in." The station was deserted so the man agreed. Bob waited until the conductor blew his whistle and the train started moving slowly out of the station. Bob yelled to the guy, "Now! The man came running with a crate of oranges and threw them into the boxcar then went back and grabbed a bag of coconuts and threw them in. Bob yelled, "One more bag!" As the man ran back for the second bag of coconuts Bob slammed the boxcar door leaving the poor guy not only without a ride but probably having to explain to the station master what happened to the oranges and coconuts. I know that was a dirty trick Bob played on the old guy in Savanna but it may have saved us from starvation. When we got to Baltimore it was snowing hard. We loaded the horses into a van and headed for Bel-Air track 25 miles away. By the time we got there it was a full blizzard, we got the horses in the barn, bedded down and fed. By then it was after five in the afternoon and we were too tired to go to town in the snow so we went to bed early. We woke up the next morning and it had been snowing heavily all night, with about 3 foot of snow on the ground and no sign of it letting up. We just fed the horses, cleaned out the stalls and went back upstairs in the barn where our sleeping quarters were and started playing cards and eating oranges and coconuts and of course we each had brought at least one bottle of whiskey with us when we got off the train in Baltimore and proceeded to drink that as well. We played cards all day and after bedding the horses down for the night settled in our selves, as it was snowing too hard to go into town, and it was a good half mile walk. We decided to have some more coconut and oranges for supper. When we got up the next morning we could see we were completely snowed in, the snow was up to the rail around the track. It was over 4 feet deep and still falling; we had to dig our way to the stables to see to the horses. We had no phone available we were isolated and after three days and nights of this we were getting desperate. Finally the city or county cleared the highway in front of the track but that was not much use to us as we were at least 200 yards from the road. On the fourth day the trainer came with a crew from the main farm and dug a road from the highway to the barns so we could get out and go into town to eat. I never have cared much for oranges or coconuts since then.

Chapter Four

The storm

We went to Florida early in 1945. Instead of our usual route of Delaware, Maryland, New Jersey and New York, we went to Hiealia in late August. This was unusual as normally the meet didn't start until November. I'm sure Mr. Bryson, our owner had his reasons. We were out working the horses very early each morning, around 4:00 am, and we had more horses than normal that year. We needed to work the horses early because by 10:00 am the temperature and humidity was too much for the horses and us. This was my second trip to "The big white city", Miami, and I loved it. The evenings were free as long as the horses were bedded down and fed for the night. Someone was always at the stable to watch out for things and of course there were always the night guards. It was off to downtown town Hiealia or Miami for as long as our money held out. My brother Ross his best friend Bob Flowers, I and some other guy decided to go to Miami on the 13th of September. We had heard weather warnings throughout the day but never paid any attention to them. The wind was picking up as we got into town and some people in the shops were acting nervous, but we were there to party. By 9:00 pm the storm was starting to get nasty and we decided we had better head back to the track. The buses were full so we took a cab back splitting the fee. We checked on our horses who were all acting more nervous than normal and we tried to calm them down. About that time our trainer showed up and told us to stand by the stalls throughout the night as he expected some real serious weather, there was a hurricane warning out for the entire area and we were in the direct path of it. Our shed row faced the back of the track which was enclosed with what must have been a fourteen foot fence, completely covered with ivy, making it about sixteen feet high and at least two feet thick. We were later grateful for that fence. We of course got no sleep that night and around 3:00am it must have hit full force. I thought all the roofs were coming off the barns and any thing that was not tied down was in the next county by then. Fortunately, our trainer made sure all our tack, buckets, tools and anything loose was secured. We found out later Miami was hit full force, and Florida City near Miami had winds from one hundred thirty five mph with gusts up to one hundred seventy one mph. We were really lucky we had no more damage then we did, and not one horse was hurt or got loose. However just outside of Hiealia they were not so lucky. Between the track and Hiealia was a zoo with a large assortment of animals, and an enormous amount of monkeys. The zoo was spared in most part, except for the monkey cage, it seems there were some very large palm trees near the cages, and palm trees do not fare well in high winds. Several of these large trees fell on the cages breaking them open. When the storm subsided enough for us to evaluate the damages, we heard lot of noises coming from the large ivy covered fence just in front of the shed row that probably saved us from more serious damage. There were hundreds of loose monkeys as far as you could see. Over the next few weeks the race track was inundated with monkeys. Some became quite bold and ventured toward the barns looking for food. Some guys tried to catch them for pets but I don't think anyone was successful. It was nearly a week before we could get to the track to workout any horses so we did a lot of walking them around the shed rows.

Another event I shall never forget happened later that meeting; we had a groom named Seagraves in our stables. He was either the luckiest guy I ever met, or he knew things the rest of us didn't. I do know if you wanted to win money betting on a race, it was a good thing to keep your eye on Seagraves. I've seen him come back to the stables after running a horse in a race with money stuffed in every pocket he had, I did not witness this event first hand, but was told about it by Bob Flowers, Ross's friend. Our latrines were set up the same as the ones I later encountered in the service, except these were ones like I have only see before in the last school I attended, the stool was designed where the seats were elevated about four inches, and on a spring. When you sat down, the seat would go down, when you stood up it would automatically pop up and flush by itself. Bob told us that once, as he walked into the latrine, he saw Seagraves franticly grabbing the contents out of the toilet bowl. He was slinging money, paper and everything else from the bowl around the room. Bob yelled and asked what the hell he was doing. Seagraves said, "I dropped a wad of money in this damn toilet and it flushed on me. Help me get it!" Bob said, "You on your own pal."

Later that meeting in December just a few days before Christmas one of our jockeys and I went to Miami for a night on the town. We had made a few of the back street bars as neither of us was anywhere near 21 and avoided the big bars that might question our I.D.s. After about the third bar we met this gentleman and his wife. She was a beautiful woman, very shapely, we got talking to the man and he ended up inviting us to their house for some more drinks. After we had been in his house about two hours we were all getting pretty drunk, the man asked me if I would like to go outside and help him get some more wood for the fireplace. He and I went outside and were out there about a half hour. As we were talking he was showing me some of his trophies he had in the outside room. When we went back in the house, I went to the living room with a load of firewood and he went into the kitchen where he found my buddy and his wife in a compromising position. He started yelling at both of them. I went in to see what was going on, he grabbed me in one arm and my buddy in the other and started shoving us towards the door, telling us to get the hell out of his house. We made it to my friend's car and took off. I gave the guy hell for messing up a great evening and risking getting our heads blown off, I never went to town with him again.

After the winter in Florida we went back to our stables at Bel Air, Maryland. It was a mild spring for a change and the weather exceptionally nice. Our trainer Fred Case came to the stables one morning calling about six of us who had experience exercising horses together; he said they had several yearlings on the farm that required breaking. This was an opportunity I had been waiting for. I was as excited about this as I was getting up on my first horse for Fred. Some of the guys were not too comfortable about breaking yearlings, you could get hurt and it was hard work. I was the first to jump forward and say, "Fred, let me have a go." Fred, being the critic he always had been said, "What makes you think you could break a yearling? I have heard about you and your Brother Ross's great achievements of breaking heifers, calves and steers, but these are horses, not cows." I was determined and had learned to ignore his criticism. I said, "Hell, they have four legs and have never been ridden, right?" He just shook his head and replied, "I guess it's about time you got dumped on your ass and taught a lesson; I hope your brother can teach you something." Ross slapped me on the back and said, "Let's go break some horses, cowboy."

There were four of us that went to the farm where the yearlings were; Ross, me, Ralph Sansaverino, and a real comic, Stanley Nelson. Stan was the tallest guy in the stable; he was around 5ft 8 inches tall, skinny as a rail, weighing about 125 lbs. It wasn't that Stan had nerves of steel; he was just crazy, and usually drunk. He would take on the wildest, meanest horse in the stable. He enjoyed exercising the three crazy French horses that no one liked to work out and Yarle, our big stud that everyone else avoided. Yarle was a groom's nightmare; he had injured more grooms, putting two in hospital, by kicking or biting than all of our other horses combined. I was scared to death of him and avoided him, not that Fred would let me go near him. But to Stan, this was entertainment. As Yarle was such a big horse, Stan's size and weight was no problem. It was really comical though to see him get on one of these yearlings, his feet almost touched the ground on some of the small ones, but Stan was good at it and really enjoyed it.

When we got to the farm Ross taught me the procedures. First, a groom would herd one of the yearlings into one of the several small enclosures where we would very slowly and gently walk around the pen with the yearling to gain his confidence, feeding them oats or perhaps an apple out of our hand, finally rubbing his neck and eventually getting him to allow you to put a halter on him. Once we had the halter on we could walk around the pen with him for an hour or so depending how he responded. Then, gently laying our hand on his back would get him used to some pressure on his back. Later, laying a saddle towel over his back we very slowly added the girth, slightly tightening it as we walked with him. Once we got him calm enough to trust us, the groom would hold him by the reins and halter while I would lay across his back, until he would object and try to run away for the first half a dozen times. This all took patience and after a period of several hours I could put a saddle on him and just lead him around the pen several times.

Then the test came. At first we rode them bare back, before we had saddle broke them. Fortunately, the first two I got on were fillies and gave me little trouble, only a few bucks and attempts to run away. Then they just settled down and seemed to enjoy galloping with someone on their back. Then Ross asked me to try out a certain fairly large black colt. He was much more spirited, it took me most of the day before I could get him settled down enough to put a saddle on him, he did not like that at all and let me know it. He charged the groom holding him several times and nearly jumped the fence once. I walked him around for about a half hour before I attempted to mount him. As soon as I threw my leg over him, before I could get my other foot in the stirrup, to Fred's amusement he threw me ass over heels and took off across the pen. It took me another fifteen minutes before I could catch him and grab control of the reins again. As he was fairly tall, Ross helped the groom hold him and give me a leg up; I got my feet in both stirrups and grabbed a hand full of mane. When they turned him loose he gave me one of the best rides I had for a long time, I felt like Roy Rogers. He ran, bucked and pitched turning in every way he could to unseat me, but I held on and had him in a controlled gallop after about fifteen or twenty minutes. Even Stan told me I gave him a great ride. Fred, he just rolled his eyes, but I knew he thought I had potential, and I became one of the regulars for breaking yearlings each spring. In just over two weeks we had added ten more horses to our stable, most of which would be destined for claiming races or traded for more favorable prospects by the trainers.

Chapter Five

Mardi gras

The majority of my racetrack work was done on the east coast; Maryland, Delaware, New Jersey, New York and Florida. One spring in 1947, our owner decided to take the three French horses he had bought and everyone had so much trouble with, to New Orleans to race at the fair grounds. Bob Flowers did not want to go so they sent my brother Ross and I. Ross had been the year before and from what he told me I was glad to go. It sounded like fun the way he described it. The weather was fair, better than Maryland and more humid than Florida, but it promised to be a fun trip if we could control these crazy horses. It was a short meet of about three weeks, but it was during Mardi gras and I was anxious to find out if all the excitement Ross had told me about was true. We arrived on Wednesday and the Mardi Gras was already going on. We had taken care of our stable duties early in the day. We were both grooming horses for the meet and neither one of us were exercising any of the three horses so we were free to go in town around 2:00pm that first Saturday. When we got to town the festivities were well under way and drinks were plentiful. Ross introduced me to what he said was a traditional drinking tradition. I was given a large schooner of beer that looked to me like a big dish used for a banana split. After downing that, we chased it with some kind of wine. By six or seven that evening I was legless, Ross was not much better. We caught a cab back to the track taking with us a few bottles of the wine; we finished those off during the evening and passed out on our bunks. Someone came and drug us out of bed around 10:00am to take care of our horses, which was no pleasant task. We were both hung over, but I was worse. I was never so sick in my life, I was terribly thirsty but anything I tried to drink I threw up immediately, and the smell of food from the café was nauseating. The worst thing though was this old wino working at the stables. Word was he was some relative of our owner and was just kept around. He never did any kind of work, other than walk a few horses and run some errands. He was sitting in the shed row where I was washing a horse, drinking what I guess was his last bottle of cheap wine. He motioned for me to come over to where he was sitting; he said something I could not make out so I leaned over nearer to him to hear. He looked at me and asked me what time it was; well he kind of blew the word "what" right into my face. The smell of that stale wine filled my head. I just let go of the horse I was holding and proceeded to heave my guts out, and as much as I drank in my life, from that day on I could not stomach the smell or taste of any kind of wine. Even though both of my daughters are wine drinkers and connoisseurs of good wines, visiting the wineries in Napa and other popular tasting places, this does not bother me, nor does it bother me if I go to their homes and they drink, I was very fortunate that when I stopped drinking, the craving for any kind of drink left me entirely, but the smell of that wino's breath still haunts me today.

There were quite few of these old guys around, it was known they would take a can of the fuel, Sterno, used to heat up wash buckets. They would take these cans of fuel, strain it through two or three slices of bread then drink it. They also used a fluid we called "leg paint" that was used on a horse with bruised tendons to deaden the leg so he would not limp. I suppose it was like morphine, anyway the winos would use the same procedure to get a drink from this medication; I do not know how many of them went blind from this habit. I finished up the meet without going back to New Orleans, and have no desire to go back.

When we got back to our stables in Bel Air, Ross got together with Bob Flowers and went into town to pick up some girls. They didn't come back to the track that night. I went into town the next morning after I finished my work to get something to eat and shoot some pool. I met my buddy Jack and had a hamburger or something then started shooting pool. Ross came in the pool room around noon. I asked him if he and Bob got lucky that night. He said, "Why don't you and Jack come up to the hotel room and see?" The hotel was a flop house over the pool room. I asked Ross where Bob was and he said he had gone back to the track. Jack and I went with Ross up to the hotel room. When we got there we could see someone in the bed covered up. Ross nudged me and asked, "You want some?" I looked at Jack who was grinning from ear to ear. He said, "Yeah, I would!" I said, "Go ahead". He walked over to the bed and patted the person in the bed and they giggled and wiggled about. Jack took his pants off and started to get in the bed when Bob Flowers threw the covers back laughing, He jumped out of bed roaring and yelled at Jack saying, "You're sick." I thought Jack was going to kill them both as he chased them out of the room. Jack wouldn't speak to any of us for nearly a week; he thought I was in on it too. I finally convinced him that I did not know it was Bob under the covers, that I could have been the one who got into bed with Bob, had he not jumped in first.

One day in the spring of forty seven or forty eight while we were at Pimlico, I was resting on my bunk with the door open when I heard something in the room. I looked up and there was the prettiest golden cocker spaniel dog I had ever seen. He was just standing at the foot of my bed wagging his tail and seemingly smiling at me. I called to him and he jumped up on my bunk licking my face and acting like we were life long friends. I had not had a dog since the one I had while living at home with my mother. He had been killed by a motorcycle and I thought I would never get over it, but this one seemed to really like me. Although I had not seen him around the track, he was very comfortable with the horses and followed me around, obeying me when I told him to stay while I took a horse out for a workout and was there when I got back. He would follow me back to the barn. I asked all around but nobody knew where he came from, although he was fully grown probably around two years old and very well groomed, no one claimed him; actually, I never looked too hard for an owner as I wanted him for myself. I named him "Boots" as he seemed to enjoy playing with mine and the name seemed to fit him.

After we had been at Pimlico for about two weeks I got a call from my mother telling me my grandmother on my father's side had passed away. She thought me and my brothers and sisters should attend the service. I talked to my trainer, asking for some time off; he said things were slow for the next two weeks so I could have the time off. My mother was staying with my brother Bud (Simon) who was in the Air Force stationed at Aberdeen Proving grounds in Maryland and living at Edgewood, about ten miles from the base; about the same distance from our home town of Bel-Air. My brother Ross was married and living near the track in Bel-Air, he and Bob Flowers would drive each day from Bel-Air racetrack to Pimlico, about fifteen miles away.

Later that week Ross, Boots and I loaded up in Bob Flowers' car and headed out for Bud's place in Edgewood. As soon as my mother saw Boots she fell in love with him and the dog responded with the same greeting he had given me. I told mom she could keep him as he would be better off with her than at the track, and I could see how much the dog meant to her. She was very happy about it and kept the dog for years, until someone stole him one night; Bud said it nearly broke mom's heart.

Ross and Bob Flowers went back to Bel-Air after making arrangements to meet up at grandmother's funeral the next day. After the funeral Bud asked me if I would like to stay with him and his wife for the rest of the time I had off, I agreed. Bud's wife Louise was a wonderful woman and put up with much more than most women would. Bud and I were both drinking more than she liked, but she never complained, at least that I knew of. Bud and I both made asses of ourselves with our drinking. He had a tab running at the local grocery store, where they also sold beer. I remember us going to the store and Bud getting a case of beer on credit. Louise was upset with him about it, but him and me, being the fools we were, proceeded to drink it anyway. I got pretty drunk and Bud suggested we go into Bel-Air. He said he needed to shave first, so I decided to join him and have a shave myself. We were laughing and fooling around while attempting to shave, I must have cut myself in a half dozen places and proceeded to patch the cuts with toilet paper, this of course amused Bud even more. He had taken a week of leave himself so he and I continued to drink and fool around the house. One day he showed me an old 38 pistol he had gotten from one of his drinking buddies. It was a very old gun; it was rusty and the cylinder was loose on it. We decided to go out into the woods in back of his house to practice some target shooting. We were both half drunk and neither one of us very experienced with guns. After he fired a few rounds he gave it to me. I said I would practice my quick draw. I pulled the gun from my pants and proceeded to do some rapid fire. After the third shot, I realized the thing was spitting lead as I fired due to the loose cylinder. It is a wonder we did not kill each other or at least lose and eye from the flying lead. Fortunately for us the gun fell apart and Bud decided it was not worth fixing, so he threw it away. After making my peace with Louise and my mother, I went back to Pimlico where my drinking did not affect anyone other than myself

Chapter Six

Giant of a mare

We had a little mare named "Videl" in our stable that was a favorite of everyone, she was as gentle as a lamb, and not much bigger, she was barley 14 hands high, she was the smallest horse in our stable or anyone else's as far as I know, she was very easy to work out and loved to run. She also had something few horses have, the ability to wear another horse down and break their spirit. When I read the book "Sea biscuit" and saw the movie, I was reminded of Videl. Whether in a work out or in a race, she just loved to pull up beside another horse and pause when she got even with them. Then she would pull a nose in front of the other horse; then allow it to catch her again, and then she would pull away again. Doing this again and again she would tire the other horse out; she seemed to enjoy this and got very good at it. One day at Gulf Stream Park in Florida I believe it was 1948 or 1949, Ross and I were both working as grooms at the time and he had Videl. She was running a race that afternoon and I went with him to take her to the saddling enclosure. We then went into the grandstand to watch her race. We were both knew she had more than a fair chance of winning, even at twelve to one so we placed our bets and went to our regular place near the finish line, only this time we crossed the track to watch from the center field, we knew Fred had told the rider to keep her on the rail. There was another horse that was the favorite in the race; he was a big gelding from Brandywine Stables called Our Dollar. He was a year older than Videl and was at least seventeen and a half hands high; he just dwarfed her. When they opened the gate she broke from stall five and Our Dollar was in stall six. They left the gate in fourth and fifth place, with Videl in fourth in a fourteen horse field, they were all closely packed with the big horse appearing to be in front, they kept this field most of the way until they hit the last turn into the long stretch, the big horse had pulled well in front of the rest of the field, about six or seven lengths in front, the announcer calling the race was giving Our Dollar most of the attention and never mentioned Videl. We could see from the infield with binoculars that Videl was doing her thing; she was between the big horse and the rail "dogging" him. They were just over a hundred yards from the wire when Videl made her move. The announcer almost fell out of the stands when he saw her head pulling in front. He yelled as loud as he could, "No it's not Our Dollar, here comes Videl, and she is taking the lead!" She won by a half length. When jockey Bobby Strange brought her to the winners circle he was grinning from ear to ear and I swear Videl had a smirk on her face. Just about everyone in the stable managed to get in the winner's circle for the picture, (another picture I lost when Ross's house caught fire and burned to the ground), we headed for the cashiers cage to cash in our tickets. All was well in Gulf Stream that night.

Gulf Stream Park had a beautiful center field with a large pond, there were the traditional flamingo's a few swans and a lot of mallard ducks. One of our trainers made a comment one day how his wife could make a great roast duck dinner. Without him actually telling us to do it, when we ask him if we got some ducks would his wife cook them for us, he said yes, it would make for a great party, half joking and half serious. A few days later after the last race and all the horses were bedded down and about an hour before dusk Ross, Bob Flowers and me each took a feed sack and started across to the center field. There was a guard at the entrance and as we approached Ross just casually said were going to get some fresh grass for the horses. The guard just nodded and we walked across the track onto the center field. Ross and I had experience in wringing chickens' necks on the farm so this would be no different. We were well out of sight of the guard or anyone else. The ducks were sitting on eggs so it was fairly easy to sneak up on them, we each managed to get two or three ducks each. We pulled some grass to fill the sacks, as we approached the guard he just asked, "Did you get your grass?" We said, "Yeah, thanks a lot." We had a great duck feast that Sunday, but the funniest part of the story was a few days later an announcement came over the PA system at the track saying the guards would be monitoring the center field more closely as it appeared some one had been stealing the ducks eggs that were normally collected for the local park; they didn't realize they were missing the ducks to lay the eggs.

When we finished the meet at Gulf Stream we took our horses to Atlantic City for an early spring meet. I was exercising and grooming there. We had a mare called Abby Mae I was very fond of. She was the twin sister of Abby Gail, the horse that I had won my first race on. I had exercised Abby Mae several times and even rode her once when we were giving her a race for experience. I was grooming her at that time and she wasn't acting right, not eating much and sleeping a lot. I called the trainer over, after checking her out he called our veterinary, the vet checked her out and said he thought she had pneumonia. This was serious for a horse and Abby Mae was not all that strong and I was concerned. The vet left late in the afternoon leaving Fred some medicine for her. I sat up with her most of the night, sleeping with her in the stall until around 2:00am when I went to bed. I went down the next morning and she was lying down in the stall and could not get up, she was panting heavily and having cold sweats. I covered her with blankets and called the trainer. Fred took one look at her and said, "I'm afraid we have lost her." I asked him to at least call the vet. He said, "Ok, but I don't think it will do any good." When the vet came I saw him talking to Fred and could tell by they were acting what was coming. I could not stand it any more, so I went back up to my room and lay on the bed, hoping they were wrong. Bob Flowers came up to the room after about an hour and said they had to put her down. I felt like crying, but I don't think I did. I went back to the stable and worked around some other horses trying to avoid her stall. Around 1:00 that afternoon Fred came back to where I was working and said, "Dick, they are coming for Abby this afternoon. I want you to go in the stall and take those new shoes off her we put on last week." I said, "You are kidding." He said, "Do you know how much a new pair of shoes cost?" I said, "No and I don't give a damn. If you want those shoes, you take them off yourself." and stormed out. Bob Flowers told me later that was normal that the trainer asked the groom to do that, I said I just couldn't do it, Bob Said he would do it for me, I guess Fred understood too, he never mentioned it again, I lost a good friend with Abby Mae, but I still had her sister to comfort me.

That evening I decided to go into Atlantic City, as I needed something to cheer me up. It was that night I met a girl named Pat. There was a show going on at the steel pier with Gene Kroupa playing drums and Gene Kelly tap dancing around the entire ballroom floor. I met this beautiful girl at the refreshment stand and struck up a conversation with her. I thought I was making pretty good time when this tough looking guy in a three piece black suit came up giving me an evil look. Before I could make an ass out of myself by some smart remark, Pat introduced him as her father. He gave me the look a father gives any guy wondering what they are doing with his fifteen year old daughter. When he asked who I was and what I did, I told him I was with Elray Farms, riding out at Atlantic City track. He suddenly took a different attitude towards me and invited me to join him and his party where he plied me with drinks; we spent the rest of the evening talking about racing. After the show he invited me back to his place, which turned out to be one of the biggest night clubs in the city. After being quite generous with his drinks, around one o'clock in the morning he called a cab to take me back to the track and gave me a pass he told me to show anytime I wanted to come to the club, he said he would see me around the track so I could introduce him to my trainers, I thought, fair enough.

That year I dated Pat several times and we seemed to get along very well, except she did not care much for my drinking. When I returned the next year I called her and asked her out again. I didn't have a car so I asked her if she could get a date for my friend, Johnny Savagio. Johnny was a jockey riding for Calumet Farms at the time and had won several big stake races. He had just bought a new Buick convertible, so he was anxious to show it off to some girls. Pat said she had a friend she would ask to join us. She said there was a show she wanted to see at the Steele Pier, but the first shows were sold out so we could go to the late show that started at nine that night. I said it would be fine, that we would pick her and her friend up around six thirty and we could spend a few hours at the beach. She asked me to wear something nice as she had a new sweater she wanted to show off. I only had one suit, it was the blue suede I had wore for my grandmother's funeral, but she would never know. Johnny and I were dressed to kill when we showed up. We picked Pat up first it was nearly dark and being male, I did not notice what she was wearing, by the time we picked up her friend and got to the beach it was dark, we sat in the car at the beach and watched the moon come up over the shore, it was a beautiful sight, but I was otherwise distracted in the back seat. Around eight thirty we headed for the theater. After Johnny parked, we got out of the car. As we waked under a street light, Johnny and his girl were behind Pat and me. They started laughing uncontrollably. When we stopped to ask what was so funny Johnny said look at you, I looked down at the same time as Pat did, she just howled with laughter, I was covered with white hair. Pat was wearing a white angora sweater, I was wearing a blue suede suit, they do not fair well with two teenagers in the back seat of a Buick.

Johnny and I had both been riding that day and neither of us had been drinking so Pat was pleased; however I had no mounts for the next few days so I proceeded to drink pretty heavily. On the second day I ran out of booze, I had no way to a bar about ten miles from the track, Johnny was riding all that afternoon and had left his key's to his new Buick on his bunk, I did not have much experience in driving, especially a new car with automatic transmission, what little driving I had done was in a stick shift, but I needed a drink, and there was a car, so I took off. I got a fifth of whiskey and headed back, I had no idea how fast this car could go and how soon it would get to a high speed, when I came to a hill top on a narrow road I damn near lost control of it. Fortunately there was no one else on the road. I made it back without any more problems. I made sure I parked in the same spot Johnny had left it and I never told him about it.

One weekend just before the beginning of the meeting at Atlantic City Johnny asked me if I would like to go home with him for a good home cooked Italian meal. I had always liked Italian food in restaurants so I gladly accepted. I had been to New York a few times with Ross and some of the other guys, but we either went up town, to Manhattan, Staten Island and once to Yonkers with Ralph Sansaverino but I had never been to Brooklyn, where Johnny was from. We left early Sunday morning and arrived at his house around ten in the morning. There was his mother, a very large Italian woman, hugging every one she met. His father was a quiet gentleman with kind of beady shifty eyes. We had a few drinks and around noon Johnny's uncles and cousins started arriving. I wondered just how many were coming, as the relatives started gathering in little bunches and talking among themselves in Italian. Soon there were about a dozen of them in the small apartment. I began to feel uncomfortable; these guys would make the people in the godfathers group look like choir boys. Johnny saw I was nervous and asked me what was wrong. I told him they made me uncomfortable. He kind of whispered, "You'll be ok, just don't make any quick moves." Then he laughed and told one of his uncles, in Italian, what we had been talking about. They all laughed and I felt more at ease. Johnny had told me on the way up what to expect at an Italian family dinner, he said they are going to keep bringing you food, you must keep eating, it is an insult to refuse any of the food offered, when we started eating around one o'clock I found out what he was talking about. My God, I have never seen so much food, let alone try to eat that much. There must have been at least six different courses. I thought I was going to burst. Johnny just kept telling me I had to keep eating and not to say I didn't want any of it. We did not finish dinner until after three. We went into a small living room where these uncles and cousins started talking to Johnny in Italian. I could not understand a word but soon got the drift of the conversation when one of the uncles brought out a large box of very expensive looking binoculars, they gave us each a pair and took us out on a landing to show us how powerful they were, they were the best binoculars I had ever seen, much better than any I had seen the trainers using. It soon became evident to me what was going down, these men obviously had a large supply of these glasses (I wasn't going to ask where from) they were making a deal for Johnny to sell them at the track. Before we left they loaded about four large boxes in the back of Johnny's car, he told me what the deal was on the way back to Atlantic City. These things sold for around $350.00 wholesale, they told Johnny anything we got over $200.00 for each pair we could keep. We made a lot of money from them as trainers, owners, and bookies were coming to our stable almost daily. Johnny kept most of them over at Calumet Stables and I sold some from the stable I worked for, my trainers both took a pair each and were very pleased.

Chapter Seven

A legend in the making

In the spring of 1950 I was stabled at Laurel Park in Maryland. There were some pretty big stake races scheduled for the meet and there was a lot of hustle and bustle going on. I was getting pretty good at handling a horse and Fred had more faith in my abilities, enough to trust me to be loaned out to other stables to exercise horses for them. I felt rather important the morning he asked me to go over to Calumet Farms stable to work out a few horses for a friend of his there. Calumet was one of the top stables at the time, this was a stable that used jockeys like Johnny Longden, Bill Shoemaker, Eddy Arcaro, Joe Culmone and other famous riders and I felt quite honored by the opportunity. At that time I knew of Bill Shoemaker's fame around the track and had seen him on several occasions around the jock's room and on the track working out. I had seen him ride and was in awe at his ability to control a horse, especially in the gate, I had only spoke to him in passing by saying "Hi" or mention to him in the jock's room, "Nice race". He always acknowledged anyone's comment graciously, he was a true gentleman. As I approached the barn where the horses was stabled that I was to work out, there he stood with a cup of coffee. Although I knew we were very close in age, (I was ten days older) I was still intimated by him. I said, "Good morning Mr. Shoemaker." He looked at me with that toothy grin hesitating a moment and said, "Mr. Shoemaker? My father hasn't been around for years. I'm Bill, and you are?" I introduced myself, he said he recognized me from being around and seeing me in the jock's room, and asked what stable I was with, I told him Elray. We struck up a conversation and I asked how his mounts were going and what races he was in that day. He said, "Things are great and I'm riding the 1st, 3rd, 5th and 7th today. Slow day." He flashed the famous smile. I said, "Don't you get tired riding a full card as I have seen you do?" "Yeah," he said, "but I get rich.", again with the wry grin.

I knew from the talk around the track the reason the "Shoe" was in town, at the time he was leading rider in the states, and a gentleman from England, Gordon Richards was there that week. He was leading rider of Europe; they were there for a match race for leading rider of the world. This was Wednesday and the race was scheduled for the following Saturday. I asked Bill how he felt about the race. He said, "Mr. Richards is a great rider, so I guess I have my work cut out for me." I wished him good luck and said, "I know where my money will be." He said, "Thanks." Our grooms bought out our mounts that we were going to work out, we shook hands. As the groom lifted him up he said, "Have a good work-out." I said, "Thanks Bill." I felt as high as a kite as my groom lifted me unto my mount. I had just shook hands with a legend. I galloped out onto the track and worked my horse behind him. The match race was run that Saturday, it was the three o'clock race with only the two horses, I can't remember the names of the horses, but it was one heck of a race with Bill winning. He was very gracious to Mr. Richards in the winning circle, as was Mr. Richards to Bill. He of course later became Sir Gordon Richards, having being knighted by Her Majesty Queen Elizabeth. He went on to enjoy a long and successful career. I was only privileged to see Bill ride in live races about three more times, he rode mostly on the west coast, I was usually on the east coast, but I did see him a two races in Florida, and again at Atlantic City. I followed his career with admiration all the time I was in the service. I was stationed in England in 1953 when he set the record for most winners in one year, (485), a record he held for twenty years. I sent him a card of congratulations. I sent him another one when he retired after forty one years of riding races. Out of 40,350 mounts, he had 8,833 winners, 21.9%. He was the only jockey to have over 50 percent of his mounts finish in 1st, 2nd, 3rd, or 4th place. (There is usually purse money for fourth place) He was a magnificent rider, a great lover of horses and a gentleman. I am honored to have know him and to have had the privilege to shake his hand.

After this meet we went over to Pimlico, then up to Delaware, then onto Monmouth Park in New Jersey. We ended up the fall meeting at Atlantic City where we ran several races.

This had been a pretty successful meeting for me and I had enjoyed myself. I had seven winners plus a few seconds and thirds, I had been kept busy but I liked that. The last week of the meeting I asked my trainer Fred to let me ride Videl in a stake race. I was a bit surprised when he agreed. I asked if he minded if I invited my girl friend and her father down for the race on Saturday. I had introduced him to Pat's father. He remembered, and liked him; he knew he was a big gambler. Fred had been to his club in Atlantic City, and said he would arrange to get passes for him and Pat to sit in our owner's box in the club house. I called Pat, asking her to join her father for the race. She was excited about it and handed the phone over to her dad. Her father was pleased about the invitation and said he would see me on Saturday. I worked Videl out all week and by Friday I was sure she was ready, I talked to Fred about his instructions for the race, he told me I knew her pretty well and to give her plenty of room to do her thing. I was well aware of her ability to wear a horse down by pulling up along side, then dropping back just a head or less, then pull in front again, she was a champion at it, and enjoyed it. I was not able to meet Pat and her father when they arrived, as I was also riding in the first and third races, but they came to the paddock with Fred to see me off in my first two races. Videl was in the fifth. I knew I had some tough competition, in both horses and riders. Bill Shoemaker was riding the favorite, Joe Culmone was riding also, as well as Bobby Strange, and I knew I had my work cut out for me. I had no luck in my first two races, sixth and fifth place. By the time for the fifth race I was eager to win a race, especially this one, after all my girl friend and her gambling father was there. They met me in the saddling enclosure, Pat said Videl was "so cute", I told her that was not the image I wanted to present to my competition. Fred gave me my final instructions and lifted me up when the bugler played "call to post". As I entered the track I looked at the tote board, Videl was five to one, not a bad price I thought, and I knew Pat's father would be pleased. On the way to the starting gate I noticed the two horses I would break in-between; they were both very big geldings. I was in gate five for the break. All the horses loaded well and we were sent off shortly. When the starter swung the gates, the two big geldings leapt out of the gate with Videl leaping right in-between them; they bumped us on both sides, knocking Videl to her knees. That is the closest I ever came to a serious fall, it was all I could do to pick her head up from the track, she stumbled a bit, and then regained her balance, and she instinctively took off after the field, which was now about seven lengths ahead of us. Videl seemed to sense she was in trouble; she gave me every thing she could, by the turn she had gained considerable ground, as she came out of the turn she passed the two big geldings and a few more. By the 3/4 pole we had gotten to fourth place, but she just could not catch the others, we finished fourth. Bill Shoemaker won the race by a head. As soon as I returned to the unsaddling area, I claimed a foul for the two horses that had damn near took me down. An objection notice was posted on the tote board, but after the judges' inquiry, it was taken down and I lost the decision. I was mad as hell, and made no secret of in at the scales, until Fred told me to settle down before I got fined again. I stomped off to the jockeys' room. When I got there Shoemaker was changing silks, he said he thought I got a rotten deal, but said "These things happen, don't let them get to you." I said, "Yeah, I suppose, but it ticks me off, and by the way, congratulations on beating me, but a good race." He gave his famous toothy grin. He was one of a kind.

I took a shower, got dressed and headed out for the club house to join Pat and her father. Pat was upset; I gave her a hug and said it was alright, it happens. As I turned to her father to apologize, he interrupted me, saying, "It's ok Dick, its only money. I've done alright by you, so you don't owe me anything." and slapped me on the back. He said he was glad I did not have a spill and came out ok.

That year we were at Monmouth Park in New Jersey, where we were going to run Yarle, our best horse. He had not lost a race; the owner was going to retire him after this race although he had not let it be known yet, this was to be his last race before being put out to stud. I had never run him in a race as a groom, nor had I ridden him. Bob Flowers was grooming him at the time. I asked if he would let me lead him to the saddling enclosure and to the winners circle if he won. There was no doubt in anyone's mind that he would win, and I wanted my picture with him.

Bob said sure, now I am so glad he did, as he won by half a length and I got to have my picture taken with him in the winners circle. This is the only picture I have from my racetrack days, although we had many pictures taken in the winners circle both as riders and grooms, when I went into the service I gave Ross all of my memorabilia for him to hold for me. This included all my pictures, a pair of riding boots, my favorite riding whip (made of whale bone) that had been given to me by a great rider and good friend of mine, Bobby Strange, and a set of our stables silks I had managed to somehow get mixed up in with my clothes. Silks were the owner's property and he was very possessive of them. You can't blame him for they were very expensive. After Ross left the track he was living upstate in Connecticut with his wife and family, in the dead of winter his big three story house caught fire and burned to the ground, he got out without being able to save anything, even his clothes. He said he stood in the front yard in his underwear in four feet of snow and watched every thing he owned go up in flames, of course my things as well. Years later after I had retired from the Air Force and was living here in Folsom California, where we still live, Ross came to visit me and said he had something for me. He handed me the picture of me with Yarle. I asked how he got it and he said he had left it at mom's house one day when he visited her and forgot all about it, some how it survived and he managed to get it and said he wanted to be sure I got it as he knew it meant a lot to me. I had some recovery work done on it and it hangs on the wall in my office at home now, proudly displayed.

Unfortunately I lost Ross a few years later to cancer, it runs in my family, as I had lost my father and mother to cancer, and a few years ago I lost my oldest brother Sam to cancer, and just recently, my other brother Simon. I'm the only boy left along with my oldest sister Marie in Pennsylvania and my younger sister Anita in Texas. I am also a survivor of prostate cancer I was diagnosed in 1993 and received radiation treatment for five weeks; I still take shots three times a year and have been clear for over ten years, again God takes care of his weaker ones. Ross was the first of us children to die; he was in his early fifty's, when his wife called to tell me was getting worse and was in the hospital. I asked for his number in the hospital and called him. He seemed to be in good spirits as he talked, but he told me he knew it would not be long for him. I said I wanted to come to see him and he said, "Dick, I wish you wouldn't. I would rather you remembered me as I was when we were last together on the track." I agreed; then he said you won't believe my weight", he said. "I weigh 88 pounds." He gave his famous sinister laugh and said, "I guess if I had to make my riding weight, they would need to drop about 20 pounds of lead in my saddle." This was typical of Ross's sense of humor, I sure miss him.

Chapter Eight

Marines not interested

One of my more unpleasant memories happened during Christmas of 1950. One of my buddies and I went to Miami for some partying on Christmas Eve, and really got drunk. I don't know how we got back to the track, but somehow we did. My friend and I each had three horses to exercise that morning, Christmas day. We should have been on the track by five a.m. but we didn't wake up. Our trainer came and drug us out of bed. My friend got his horse out and went to the track, I stayed in bed. The trainer came in again at seven a.m. and I was still in bed. He yelled some obscenities at me and told me to get out of bed and clean out some stalls, as some one else had worked my horses. He left and I went back to sleep. Around nine thirty he came storming in the room and told me I was fired, to get my stuff and get out. On Christmas day? I gathered up my belongings, threw them in a small bag and headed downtown to Miami. (God I loved that city) As I was hung-over, feeling sorry for my self being 1,400 miles from home with no job and very little money, I got a cheap bottle of booze and headed for some flop hotel room and spent the night feeling sorry for myself. I guess I passed out some time later. I woke up the next morning with one heck of a hang over. I stumbled around town for a few hours trying to get my head together until I found a small coffee shop and spent about an hour and a half thinking before going back on to the street.

As I got to one of the main streets I started to walk past the Post office. The military recruiters from all the services were there. I had never paid much attention to their pitch; The Army's sign with a big Uncle Sam pointing his finger at you with the caption, "We Want You", the Navy's "See the world" and something lame for the Air Force. Well I had always wanted to be a Marine; I just pictured myself in their dress uniform. I suppose because of seeing my cousin Kenny come back from the war in his marine dress uniform had made a big impression on me. So when I walked by the Post office and saw their logo, I was impressed; as you may remember, they had a replica of an M-1 rifle under a sign saying "WE NEED A MAN BEHIND THIS". Well that did it. I must have weighed at best 98 lbs at the time soaking wet and stood almost 5 ft. tall. Looking like something the cat drug in, I headed through the big doors and lo and behold, the first one in the line seated at the tables was this big burley marine Sergeant. I walked straight up to him all cocky. He looked at me and said, "What do you want?" I said, "I understand you need a man behind that gun out there." He looked at me and said, "Does your mommy know where you are son?" My Irish temper was never more prevalent. I told him what he could do with the gun and anything else he could find to fit in the same place. He took off after me, both running full out. I beat him to the door and saw a bus standing at the station for Hiealia and jumped on. From the window I saw him shaking his finger at me and yelling something; I gave him a similar gesture (with another digit) and went back to the track. I found my trainer in the shed row cleaning a saddle. I approached him humbly, apologized for my actions and asked him to take me back on. I convinced him he would need me when we got back to Maryland to break yearlings, and he knew how good I was at that. I don't know if I convinced him or maybe it was because it was the Christmas season, but he took me back, with strong warnings. (Yeah, yeah, yeah!)

My racing career was not one of the kind that went down in any annals of history. After my trainer let me start exercising horses for him, I did not actually start in a race to try to win until some time early in 1946. My job was mostly to give a horse a race; I was to get on a horse that was not yet ready to compete in a race to win, but needed experience from the gate, running in a race with other horses, and to get them prepared to compete in actual races. I was what could be called an exercise boy with a riding license. This is common practice probably not known to a lot of the betting public. I would just take him out of the gate and keep him in the pack, but not get too near the lead horses and not get in the way of other serious runners. I enjoyed this type of work. As I rode these sham races, I couldn't help but remember a jockey that had been riding for our stables doing the same thing. He was an experienced rider, unfortunately too experienced. On one occasion he was to give a horse a race at Atlantic City, there was another horse from our stables that was the favorite to win and had been heavily bet on by the local mobsters from Atlantic City. On paper the horse our jockey was riding, and was supposed to just give a race, had a good chance to win and this jockey had convinced the mobsters he could win; So it seemed the mobsters had paid him off pretty well to pull the race, making sure the favorite would win. Well apparently he took there money and ran, because he won the race at a good price. Evidently, he had bet the money they paid him on the horse he was riding, going against their wishes, as well as his trainers, and then intended to ship out leaving them stuck with the money they had bet on the favorite plus what they had paid him. That is the last anyone heard of that jockey, word was he became a part of the New Jersey turnpike. I won a few more small races at Monmouth N.J, Atlantic City and Bowie MD. I won my first big race at the fall meeting 1949 at Hiealia Park in Florida, it was a $50,000 purse and the 10% sure came in handy. This was to be one of my toughest races as I was up against some pretty big boys, my biggest challenge would be Joe Culmone, there were other big time riders in the jockey's room at the time, there was Bill Shoemaker, Johnny Longdon, Bobby Strange, Jimmy Stout; and a few others; Culmone and Jimmy Stout were the only two riding in this race with me, but Culmone was the one I was concerned the most about. He was very possessive about his position in a race and would not hesitate to cut a rider off. He was leading rider of the states at the time; Shoemaker took the title from him later in 1950). Both Shoemaker and Longdon wished me luck; Culmone didn't acknowledge I was in the room. I was riding a mare named Mystery Lady, owned by the Brandywine stables and went off at four to one in the betting, she was a feisty little thing and tried to take control of things on the way to the gate and was sweating up, one of the out-riders saw what was going on and took hold of her and led us to the gate, she was fine once we got in the gate and broke in about 5th place among a twelve horse field. She soon moved in fourth and I held her there until we hit the top of the stretch. I moved her up into 2nd place on the outside, but she would not pass the lead horse, I had plenty room on my right so I went hard to the whip, she hung there until a few yards from the wire when I had to push her head forward right at the wire, I was lucky, my timing and motions was just right as we crossed the wire together in a photo finish. I was not sure I had got it, but Jimmy Stout, on the lead horse nodded to me as we were pulling up and said congratulations, good race. I still wasn't sure I had it until I got to the unsaddling enclosure. Another concern I had was the way I had to use my whip on the horse, I was afraid I may have cut the horse with the whip, which was a finable offence. If you draw blood while whipping the horse, the Stewarts would haul you up and you could be fined or even suspended depending on how severe the Stewarts saw it. I went on to win two more stake races before I finished my riding career, one at Laurel Maryland and one at Delaware Park. The rest of my winners were either smaller purses or claiming races but I enjoyed my time on the track very much.

In the spring of 1951 I returned from the winter track meets in Florida, after Fred had taken me back on. We arrived in my home town of Bel-Air Maryland. Work was slow and the next meet was at Pimlico, a few months away. The only thing to do was groom work; washing horses, cleaning out stalls and walking horses around the shed row. Not a very exciting life. The horses would not begin serious work-outs for a few months and there were not as many yearlings to be broke as anticipated. Although that was my favorite job, there were just not enough to go around so there was a lot of dead time. I went into town to my regular hangout, "the rat hole". It was a natural hang-out for such as us race trackers and other ne'er-do-wells.

I began to notice that none of my old town buddies were there. Asking around I was told most of them had been drafted or enlisted in the service. It suddenly dawned on me the Korean War was on, they were drafting guys eighteen years old and I was twenty. I thought uh-oh, I'm in it again. One of my old drinking buddies was at the bar in a navy uniform, he called me over, gave me a beer and we started shooting the bull. He was in town to re-enlist and asked me to join up with him. As he put it, they were on my tail anyway and it was just a matter of time before they caught up with me. I said no way in hell would I join the navy, and after my recent experience in Miami, the marines were out. He called me chicken and bet me $20.00 I would not join any service. Big mistake, betting against a race-tracker. By this time we were out on the street, still arguing about me joining up, when we walked past a store dummy that had been placed on the street in front of the drug store, across from the recruitment office. It was dressed up in an Army uniform. It seems we had a very ambitious recruiter in town that had obtained the dummy from one of the local men's stores, dressed it up in a very sharp Army uniform and had installed a two way P.A. system to it. We were both pretty drunk and struck up a conversation with this dummy. The outcome was us going over to the recruiting office. My buddy got with the navy recruiter and was going to re-up. It turned out they only had Army and Navy recruiters in town, the Air-Force and Marines were in Baltimore, 23 miles away. I had two brothers who both were in the service. My oldest brother Sam was a tail gunner in WW-2 on B-29's in the Army Air Corps during WW-2 and another brother, Simon, who was serving in Korea with the Air Force. I decided they were going to get me anyway so what the hell, I'm going to get my $20.00, so I signed up for the Army. The little recruiter said we had to go to Baltimore for my physical and be sworn in so he drove me to Baltimore. When I went into the main recruiting office I was handed a batch of papers to fill out, after completing the forms I took them into a line of officers sitting at a long table, I handed them to the first officer I came to; he was with the Air Force. I noticed he quickly held them below the table. He looked up and kind of whispered to me, "You know you qualify for the Air-Force, wouldn't you rather join us?" I said I really didn't care; I got my $20.00 out of this anyway. He handed me another batch of forms, slyly disposing of the original ones, and asked me to go back to the table and complete the new forms he had given me. I filled out his forms and returned them to him. I was very quickly processed through the physical and sworn into the United States Air Force.

The officer who swore us in told us we were to go to a hotel across the street that we would be taken by bus to the train station at five a.m. the next morning for transportation to San Antonio, Texas. I quickly raised my hand and said in a loud voice, "Whoa! Just a minute!" He said, "What?" I said, "I'm standing here in front of you in what I came in, shorts, dirty T-Shirt, no socks and sneakers, I didn't even bring a tooth brush or a razor." He replied, "So what, we will furnish you with everything you will need when you get to Texas." I said, "I haven't even said goodbye to my family, as the matter of fact, my mother does not even know where I am." He looked at me with utter surprise and said, "I don't believe this, you've been in the service less than an hour and you are asking me for a pass??" I said, "Yes sir". He thought it over for a minute, then said, "I'm going to grant this against my better judgment, but I will tell you this, you had better be at that train station at five a.m. tomorrow or I will have two of the biggest, meanest AP's I can find to pick you up in Bel-Air, do you understand?" I said, "Yes Sir, Thank you sir!" As I left the swearing in area and started back to the entrance, I met the little Army recruiter who had brought me to Baltimore, he was beaming as he approached and asked did you pass? I said, "Of course, why wouldn't I?" He asked where I was being posted. I told him Lackland in Texas. He looked at me with pure puzzlement and said, "That's Air Force", and I said, "I thought they were all the same, what's the difference?" He turned on his heels and marched off. I called to him and asked if I could get a ride back to Bel-Air, well, I need not repeat what he told me to do. I hitch-hiked back to Bel-Air. I did make the train; I was there at four a.m. to be sure. So started another life, another career and many more memories. (I might add I received my draft notice the third week of my basic training, whew!)

Chapter Nine

My new career

When I arrived at Lackland AFB in Texas they must have been as disappointed as I was. There I stood 5'1", 98 pounds at best, with about three months of hair growth and as cocky as any street smart ass as you would ever want to meet. I don't know what they fed me during my basic training, but I left there weighing 126 pounds and stood 5'4". I felt as big as a house. The first order of the day was of course the hair cut, which I didn't mind as it was 7 June and over 100 degrees, next was the clothing issue. This was a joke; the fatigues they gave me must have been for someone over 6 feet tall. The crotch came between my knees. They had issued us a sewing kit from which we were to alter our own fatigues. There was a sight to behold. The rest of the issue was in proportion including the shoes. I was used to wearing size 5 ½ boots or shoes, the smallest they had were size 7. When I pointed this out to my training instructor he said, "Stuff some socks in the toes and be prepared to learn to march in them". The first night was rather restless, I guess partially because I was wondering just what the hell I had gotten myself into this time and the fact a lot of these kids were a bit younger and it was their first time away from home. I felt sorry for a few who were home sick and were crying through the night, but I finally fell asleep, mostly from fatigue from that long train ride from Baltimore to San Antonio. The next morning we were herded from the barracks to the chow hall, my first experience with S.O.S. (shit on a shingle). It was beef gravy poured over toast. I liked it but some of the guys who never saw it before didn't. The southern boys were longing for grits and this was as close as they were going to get to them.

Next was our first attempt at moving from one place to another in a group, they called it marching in formation. I was not impressed, nor was the instructor. At the end of the day when we got back to the barracks I knew I had blisters, (the socks in the toe did not work) but I did not realize how bad until I took off my brogans. My heels had blisters larger than a fifty cent piece, both had broken and were bleeding, I went to the training instructor to show him. He made some sarcastic remark about me being a candy ass and told me to report to sick call in the morning. I found my way to the sick bay and when the doctor saw my feet and the brogans I was wearing he asked what size shoe I wore. I told him 5 ½ but this was the smallest size they had. He said that would change. I guess he must have called the commander who in turn must have called my training instructor and told him to get shoes to fit me. The instructor was not pleased with me and let me know in no uncertain terms. I guess they had to order my shoes as it took three days to get them and the doctor had put me on quarters until my feet cleared up. I was put on various details around the barracks because I could not leave the barracks in my stocking feet. Some of the others resented my position and I was again shunned by my peers, but I was used to that; remembering my school days, I just shrugged it off. The T.I. did not forget easily, he felt I was responsible for him getting chewed out over my shoe experience and decided to get even one day on maneuvers. We were training for gas attacks. We were issued gas masks and taken to a building where we were lined up outside. We were ordered to enter the room, five or six at a time. Once inside we were told to put on our masks, then a canister of tear gas was set off. The plan was for us to take off our masks briefly, just enough to get the gas in our eyes then put our masks back on rapidly, clearing the mask, as previously instructed, then exiting the building. Things went fine until he got to me. He made me keep my mask off by holding my arm until I had to take a breath, then he blocked the exit so I could not get out, as I pushed pass him choking and gagging he laughed and asked, "How are your new shoes, Simmons?" I damn near choked, and my eyes burned the rest of the day. The rest of my basic training was pretty uneventful. Well, perhaps with the exception of one night I was put on guard duty. I was guarding the officers' swimming pool (a real strategic post) as it so happened it was a weekend and they had been having a pool party. Ok, officers + party = booze. Now this was the longest I had been without a beer or any kind of drink for several weeks. As any drinking man knows, one develops a nose for booze, and sure enough I found a few cans of beer around 2:00 am and helped myself. It sure tasted good. When my replacement showed up around six am, I was asleep (on guard duty) fortunately I woke up when I heard the jeep. I stayed clear of anyone to prevent them smelling my breath, lucked out again. Things did not go well for me in basic training at all. One of the worst things that happened to me, after my shoe incident, was with a dental procedure. About a week after we arrived we were scheduled for dental check ups and dental work as they deemed necessary. I've seen more humane treatment from a veterinarian castrating a horse. It all started around ten in the morning. We were herded into a large wooden barracks where the "dental chairs" were placed (they were wooden stools with arms). There were about thirty in my group. Four or five of us would sit at the stool while the dentists examined us; the ones that needed work were given a shot of Novocain and told to wait until we were called back for the required work. The doctor found a cavity in one of my bottom molars. He gave me the shots and told me to wait. As each of us were seen, the paperwork was being stacked in a pile on a table near an open window. Evidently, a gust of wind blew some of the papers on the floor and they got mixed up. When I was called back in after the Novocain had taken effect, the dentist sat me down and proceeded to pull out a tooth; only it was perfectly good top tooth. I started screaming with pain. He yelled at me, "Be quiet Simpson!" and yanked the tooth out. I damn near passed out. He kept calling me Simpson; I grabbed his shirt and pulled him towards my chest pointing to my name tag. I managed to yell out, "My name is Simmons!" He never apologized, just pulled the bottom tooth as well and gave me some aspirin, then called for Airman Simpson. I had similar events happen to me twice after that, while I was stationed at Chanute Field in Illinois. As a doctor was trying to pull a tooth he broke it off and attempted to chisel it out; somehow the instrument slipped and he cut a three inch gash in my gum that required eight stitches. When he told me to return the next week to have the stitches taken out I told him to go to hell, I would take them out myself, and I did. The next time I was stationed at Mildenhall in England. Some quack, who I believe was nearly as drunk as I was, attempted to drill a tooth on the opposite side of my head that he had deadened. I thought no way in hell was I going to go through this again, and jumped out of the chair. He told me he thought I had been drinking and was going to report me. I told him if he said a word to anyone about it I would report him to the Inspector General. I'm not sure if he had been drinking or other people had complained about him, in any case, I walked out, and he never said anything. I went to a nearby base and had the work finished. I refused to go to a dentist after I retired for a long time, until Joyce took me to her dentist. I was very uneasy with him until he worked with me a few times, he turned out to be very good and we have used him since.

When we graduated from basic we were all promoted to PFC, except a few who were going to be washed out and sent home as unsuitable for service. We were each assigned to an AFSC (air force specialty career), that was to become our permanent job. I had hoped to get into gunnery school so I could follow in my oldest brother's foot steps as he was a tail gunner on B-19's & B-29's in WW-2. No such luck. Some were going to sheet metal school, auto mechanics, aircraft mechanics, food service, motor pool etc. I went with a guy named Jullio another named Brown and checked the bulletin board for our assignments. We were going to be "Rubber Products Repairmen". We looked at each other and said, "What the hell is that?" We caught a lot of flack from the rest of our graduating group; they of course put the word out that we were going to be repairing condoms. As it turned out we became assigned to the fabric, leather, rubber products and parachute training school at Chanute Field in Illinois, where we first ran sewing machines. This got us the title of "tit-less WAFs". Then we went through parachute school and finally survival equipment repair school. Shortly after arriving at Chanute I found the only beer they served in the canteens was this 3.2 stuff that was like water and just did not get the job done. I had only one stripe I could not go to any of the clubs where they served the proper stuff, so I made my way into the town of Rantoul just outside of the base. As I was still only twenty years old, I would normally wear civilian clothes into town and I still had my race track ID cards. This became pretty much a nightly thing. One night I decided to bring a pint of whisky back to the barracks with me. We were not permitted to bring alcohol back on the base so I hid it in my shirt. That night I was wearing a loose dress shirt with slacks. I was pretty high at the time, without much imagination or common sense. When I reached the gate the Air Police asked for my pass and he had me stand under the light. When he asked if I was bringing anything illegal in I of course said no. He could tell I was feeling no pain, and then the idiot took his night stick and smacked me in the stomach right where I had the bottle, smashing it and soaking my shirt. Before I could ask him what the hell he thought he was doing, he said, "Don't ever try that again." I kept my mouth shut and went on to bed, probably the best move I had made all night. While awaiting school assignment to classes we were given casual status and we were assigned various details. I wound up on KP a lot for some reason. It couldn't have worked out better for me, the mess Sgt. found out I was an ex race tracker and he was a fan of betting on horse races. We got to talking and he found out I knew people at a track near Chicago and with my track IDs, could get passes. I was in; he would sign us out for some reason he made up and headed to the track in his car for the day. We made this trip several times while I was stationed there and KP was not too bad as I got prime assignments from him. I got out of technical school in November; this is when we were given our next assignments. It was 1951 and just about everyone was being sent to Korea. When I got my assignment, it was for England. I had just assumed I would be going to the Far East and didn't mind, as my brother Simon was there. One of the guys I graduated with wanted to go to Europe, as his brother was stationed in Germany. We went to the First Sergeant to try to get our orders switched but he had no heart, he told us to take our assignments and shove off. Years later, when I was sent to Korea and Japan for a temporary assignment, I was glad I didn't get the assignment in 1951. This was for many reasons, the most obvious being I would have never met Joyce. Before leaving for England I went into Chicago for the first time. My oldest brother Sam was living there with his wife. He worked in construction. I thought I had seen cold weather in Maryland, but I had never seen anything like it was in Chicago. I spent three days with Sam and told him I couldn't take it any more. I wanted to go home to Bel-Air to spend the rest of my leave with Mom before I had to report to Camp Kilmer in New Jersey to await shipment over seas.

Chapter Ten

Overseas bound

As soon as I arrived in Bel-Air I headed for my old stomping grounds, the rat hole. I didn't even stop by to see mom. All the guys from the track were in Florida for the winter, so I just belled up to the bar. I continued to drink heavily while I was home for the next two weeks; embarrassing my mother, other relatives and generally making a fool of myself. At the time, my youngest sister Anita was living with our mother. She was fourteen and had gotten quite a bit out of hand. In finding her independence, she was dating a guy mom did not like or trust. When mom found out the guy was 23 years old and married she got in an argument with Anita. I told mom I would take care of the matter. Mom cautioned me to be careful as she didn't know what this guy was capable of. I replied he had no idea what I was capable of either. I headed for the "rat-hole" where I knew he would more than likely be. I asked around and someone pointed him out to me, he was sitting alone at the end of the bar. When I approached him I asked him if he was dating a young dark haired girl in town named Anita. He made some smart remark about her and I asked him to step outside in the alley by the bar. He made another remark about my size and said, "Let's go boy". He made the mistake of going out the door in front of me; as soon as the door closed behind me I cold-cocked him from behind, knocking him to the ground. As he attempted to get up he appeared to be reaching in his pocket. I assumed he was pulling a knife so I kneed him in the face and as he went back down. I jumped on him and proceeded to pound hell out of him. I wrestled him all the way down this narrow alley that had walls on both sides with a roof. It was dark as there were no lights in the alley; we just rolled towards the parking lot at the end of it. Three of my buddies coming out of the parking lot recognized me and came over to pull us apart. One of them was my best friend Jack. I yelled to him that this was the guy that had been seeing Anita. Jack jumped in and took over beating on him; finally the guy broke loose, ran to his car, jumped in and took off. After I was overseas mom wrote to me and said the man never showed his face in town again. She said it may have been because Jack had put the word out if he ever showed up in town there were a few of my friends he would have to deal with. I knew Jack would have the pool room gang on him plus any race tracker he could get together including my brother Ross. Although I still had nearly a week left on my leave I felt I had better get out of town before I got the crap beat out of me by some of the other local boys, ones who still remembered me from the racetrack, or I got in trouble with the law. To be quite honest, I was ashamed of how I had acted around my mother and felt I had better leave.

I arrived at Camp Kilmer around eleven p.m., dead tired, hung over and feeling sorry for myself. When I went to sign in, the orderly took my orders and asked me to put my name on a roster. I asked what the roster was for. He said, "You're on K.P at three a.m.." I said, "Like hell I am. I still have four days left on this leave, just tell me where my bunk is and I'll go to bed." He said, "Oh no, you won't. If you don't sign that roster, you don't have a bunk." We exchanged a few words, mostly mine. I grabbed my bag and orders and stormed out. I caught a cab at the gate and went back into town. Not knowing anyone in the town I decided to go to the bus station and take a bus to Atlantic City. I got a room in some cheap hotel so I could try to drink my self sober with the fifth of whiskey I had picked up. I woke up the next morning feeling even worse, which should be no surprise. I took a shower, shaved and got dressed. I called Pat, the girl I used to date when I was in town with the track. She sounded glad to hear from me and asked me to come over to her place. She was a senior in high school, still living at home with her father. He was the big gambler I knew from the track and I knew he was not one to mess with; he owned a big hotel and night club on the board-walk where they lived. He greeted me with a whiskey sour, which did not please Pat. She never did approve of my drinking and had told me on several occasions when we were dating. Later we went to a local high school football game. She had been dating the quarterback. She called him over and introduced us. I made some smart ass remark about him being a jock and told him I was a real jock. It's a wonder he didn't slap the stuffing out of me, but I guess he had more respect for Pat than I showed; perhaps that is why she went home with him and left me and my bottle at the game. Again, with my tail between my legs and my head hung in shame, I headed back for Camp Kilmer, but before I left town I just had to go back one more time to the board walk. I had so many fond memories of the board walk and the Steel pier. It was the end of November and freezing cold on the pier, which was completely deserted. I stood there looking out to sea, feeling sorry for myself, wondering what the hell I had gotten my self into. I wanted to be back in Miami with my mates and horses who were now at the winter meeting enjoying the sun. I stood there for a long time on the edge of the steel pier, with the cold salty water splashing on my face; wondering what fate had in store for me across the cold dark waters of the Atlantic Ocean. I debated whether to go to Pat's fathers club. I knew Pat was pissed off at me for the way I had acted and would probably be in bed anyway. Her father would be hanging out with his cronies. I was in uniform and GI's were not particularly welcome in the club anyway. Reluctantly, I headed back to Camp Kilmer. The same clerk was on duty when I reported in, it was thanksgiving eve around nine p.m.; I asked him if he was going to put me on K.P. again. He grinned and said, "I'll give you a break, you don't have to start until four a.m., and I will personally make sure you make it." I was too tired to argue and said, "Just tell me where my barracks is located."

We were only supposed to be at Kilmer for a week and then ship out. Well, it was 1951 and any ship worth putting to sea was on the west coast to take troops to Korea and Japan. While we were at Kilmer awaiting shipment we of course were put on all kinds of details to keep us occupied. Each morning we would fall in and be marched to breakfast, then fall into formation again to be marched to some area where some were pulled out for various details. During the march from one point to another, as we would round a corner or near some buildings, some of the troops at the end of the formation would disappear down an alley or into a vacant building. By the time we arrived at our destination there were very few men left of the original group. Once about six of us were assigned to paint the floor of an old theater that had not been used for a long time and probably had no future plans for it being used, it was just something to keep us busy. We were given about four five-gallon cans of gray paint and told to paint the floor and aisles. The young Lt. in charge showed us where the equipment was and took off saying he would be back in a few hours. He left a SSgt in charge of us. After the Lt. left, we had a long smoke break, and then the Sgt. told us to paint the floor up to the top of the aisles. He then took a five gallon can of the paint to the top of each of the slanted aisles and tipped them over, allowing the paint to flow freely down the aisle all the way to the front seats. The lighting was very dim in the theater and when the Lt. came back, the Sgt just opened the door enough for him to look inside the dark theater. He stopped him at the door telling him the floor would take the rest of the day to dry. The Lt was satisfied and we all got the rest of the day off. I wonder if that paint ever dried.

The longer it took to get us a ship, the more troops were coming into Kilmer waiting for transportation to England, Germany, France and other European posts. Finally we heard they had gotten the USS General Patch, the USS General Rose, and some other ship, I didn't find out the difference between ships until we got to ours, the USS General Heresy, which meant nothing to me, yet. It was mid December when we finally boarded and it was freezing cold. I found out later this ship was from the 1920's, had wooden decks, one stack and was meant to carry 1200 troops, there were 2500 of us on board. It wasn't even a naval ship; it was run by the Merchant Marines. This was going to be the trip from hell.

I was fortunate enough to meet an old Master Sergeant who took me under his wing for some reason. He told me before we left dock, "Do not drink any water at all the first day at sea, and try to make it at least two days, and eat everything they throw at you, otherwise you will get sea sick." I stayed by his side for the most of the trip, which turned out to take twelve days. He was right, I never got sea sick, but I was among the few. To say this ship was crowded is an understatement. There were no provisions to sit down to eat, at our first meal that night I found out why. After we went through the long chow line we were led to these long narrow tables that resembled a bench more than a table. They were just over waist high, the width of the mess tray, with and lip on each side to keep the tray from sliding off. There were hand holds to balance you with one hand while eating with the other, standing up all the time. It was very important to hold your tray with your thumb while you balanced yourself. Otherwise, as the ship pitched, which it was very much, the tray would take off up or down the tray holder, (table) depending on which way the ship pitched. If the tray took off you never knew what was coming back in it; usually your meal, and most likely someone else's as well. That turned a few stomachs also. Sleeping quarters was just as bad. The bunks were stacked nine high; with the bottom one being about four inches from the floor and the top one being about as close to the large steam pipes that ran the length of the ship. In order to get in, the first guy had to lower his bunk and get in, then the next guy, and so on until the last guy was in. The men on the top and bottom bunks had disadvantages. The man in the top bunk would burn up from the steam pipes and the bottom man would freeze. The man on the bottom also had to deal with the men in beds above him throwing up so he didn't get much sleep. If you could call it luck, I was on the fourth bed. One day they attempted to pull a regulation fire drill, until they realized the ship would capsize if too many troops went to one side so the drill was canceled. The weather in the Atlantic in December is freezing cold. To get away from all the men that were throwing up, I would go upon deck. I would have to climb four or five flights of open metal stairs to get on the deck. The wind was horrendous and near gale force all the time. As I stood between the aft portion and mid ship, holding onto the railing covered with ice, I could see the entire front of the ship go under water almost to mid ship, then raise up again crashing over and into the waves. It was all I could do to hang on as the wooden deck was oily and slick and it was difficult to keep my balance. It was too cold to spend more than fifteen or twenty minutes at a time on deck, even with our warmest clothing (Don't let this discourage you from taking a cruise ship). I didn't find out until after I arrived in England and was my shop with the survival unit that the ship had sunk in New York harbor. I did not think I would ever be glad to see a ship sink, but this thing was long overdue. We also learned the ship was used to ferry the displaced persons from WW-2 and the Berlin Air Lift to the states. It also had been in a collision with another ship in Germany before the trip back to the states to pick us up from Kilmer, and had a temporary bow put on it to get it back to the states for repairs. They still loaded it with D.P.s to transport them to the states. When it got to New York and unloaded the D.P.s, it was scheduled to be put into dry dock for repairs but there were all of us troops at Camp Kilmer awaiting transportation to Europe. The decision was made to make another trip before the repairs were made. That was our trip; it was rumored that when we were half way across the ship was leaking so bad they were debating whether to turn back, but decided hell; we were half way and decided to go for it. We were told our baggage in the hole was in six foot of water. Fortunately, most of us had to have our duffel bags with us, even though we had little use for them onboard the ship. It was too crowded to try to unpack anything or even get into it. Most of us arrived in England with the same clothes we boarded with. Shaving was next to impossible, between the lack of hot water, and the way the ship pitched and rolled. We were allowed to shower, if you were lucky enough to get in. One day we would have regular water, the next was salt water. That was an experience; there was a large lever to switch from fresh water to salt water. We soon found out in salt water, do not use soap, it turns to wax on your body. To amuse myself, I found if I caught someone in the fresh water shower, all lathered up, I could reach in and switch to salt water and get out of the area before someone beat the crap out of me. Another source of amusement was to take a knife and slit the bottom on the burp bags, there were stacks supplied on each bunk. Actually, they were only brown paper lunch bags, but a few of us got pleasure from others' misery, especially on those open metal stairs and there was no chance anyone was going to kick hell out of us for this, they were too sick. (Some of us are sicker that others) After 12 days we arrived in South Hampton, England and we were glad to see land. It was wet and it took the most of the day to disembark. I don't know how long it took us to get to Warrington on what seemed like a cattle car to us, it was not even as comfortable as the horse cars I was used to, but at least we were off that damn ship. Outside of basic training, those were twelve of the longest days I had gone without a drink of some kind. Damn, I was thirsty for anything. I was willing to even try English beer that my brother Sam had told me about, warm and bitter. Believe me; I soon developed a taste for it in a big way.

Chapter Eleven

First trip to England

When I first arrived at Burtonwood RAF Station I had no idea how large I would find it to be. It was the largest base in the world at that time in land mass, it covered fifty two square miles of country. This was deceptive really; the way the base was laid out, there was an area for living quarters containing about fifteen or eighteen quansent huts. I lived in one of the larger areas that had a mess hall, theater and base exchange. There was a large farm area adjacent to that, then some hangers for work shop areas, then another large farm area then some more living areas, farm, hangers, farm etc: the entire base was laid out like that. We used military trucks to get to our work area. It took us about forty five minutes to get to and from work. The base was situated between Liverpool, a main docking area, and Manchester, an industrial center. Both towns received very heavy bombing during WWII. The base was a large bomber base during the war, with B-17s and B-29s. Although there was heavy bombing as Manchester, fifteen miles away and Liverpool about the same distance during air raids, the base had only one bomb dropped on it. It was later learned this was from a damaged German plane that dropped it to lighten his load so he could make it back to his base in Germany. The Germans could not find the base, between the layout of the base and the English fog they just never located it. That bomb landed in a field was about one hundred yards from the NCO club, I wasn't there but I was sure glad he missed the club.

I was assigned to the survival shop when I first arrived at Burtonwood. I made my second stripe in just over six months. This was before they changed to ranks to Airman, so I was a corporal, which was then considered an NCO. I was put in charge of the survival shop over five other men. I enjoyed my status but took my duties seriously. Once there was a contest where NCOs could nominate outstanding employees for a special pass. There was one pass that gave a deserving person a weekend in Spain with a flight there and back. One of the men working for me was a very good worker, I thought. He wanted to go so I made up the formal report outlining his strengths and value to the unit. When the Major called me in to discuss his merits he started asking me questions. I had put down the airman was very punctual in reporting for work, completed his work with great satisfaction, completed all assigned duties without complaining, was always neat in appearance etc. The major asked me what time the airman was due to report to work, I said eight a.m.. he asked if there were any men in my shop who did not do their work, I said no. He asked if they came to work late or untidy, I again said no. The Major handed me the paper back saying, "It sounds to me like this airman is doing what I expect him and all others to do. When you find someone doing things other than their appointed duties come back to see me." I was too embarrassed to tell my friend what the major had said, I just told him someone else was selected.

One day there was a very bad accident on base. A navy aircraft was sitting on the runway with a load of eighteen sailors aboard awaiting clearance for take off. Another plane, an air force C-47 was landing. He came in short of the runway, hitting the ground bouncing over a small hill, landing on top of the navy plane, both planes went up in flames; there were many fatalities and many were badly injured, mostly burn victims. That night at the NCO club we talked with some of the medics involved with the victims. They told us the worst problem they were having with the injured was their treatment made it necessary to turn them in their beds every so many hours to prevent their internal organs from damage. The medics said due to their burnt skin it was difficult to turn them and very painful for them. This airman, who worked for me and had dreams of becoming an engineer, listened intently. He went back to the hut early that night and sat up the most of the night working on the plans for a temporary type bed device that would aid the injured. It involved several of the shops in our hanger; he designed a type of a bed made of steel pipes welded together with two sheets of heavy plywood covered with sheets of thick foam rubber and covered with nylon fabric. The end result was a sort of a cot that the burn patients would be placed in, clamped between the two foam rubber mattresses. The metal frames were designed so they could be turned every hour or so without having to touch the patients. He took his plans to the hospital commander who immediately accepted it and had it implemented.

While I was still single and living in the quansent hut there was a guy we called "Irish". He was from Belfast, Ireland and had enlisted in USAF. There was a program that foreigners could enlist in the military and obtain their citizenship while serving. This guy was rather sloppy and not many associated with him. I considered myself of Irish decent but this guy was from Belfast, in the north and my family was from southern Ireland. As I remember my mother saying to me, "Never the twain shall meet." She said you could not trust the northerners. Irish was a heavy drinker and would go to town by himself. One night he came back pretty drunk. I found out later that he had bought some itching powder from a novelty store in town. When he came in I was asleep. As he attempted to sprinkle some on my back he must have tripped or staggered and dumped the whole box on me. I don't know how long it took before the stuff worked, but I woke up with my back burning up and driving me crazy. I ran to the shower across the street from our hut. As soon as I got in the shower I got relief, but when I got back into bed it started all over again, I kept running to the showers all night and in the morning I went on sick call. The doctor took a look at my back and asked if there were any practical jokers in my hut. He told me someone had given me a heavy dose of itching powder and that I should have all my bed linens changed. I suffered from that stuff for years, every time I would get nervous, excited or upset it would react on me. This dumb Irishman told someone in the squadron about it and they told me. I decided to get revenge. My oldest brother had told me about a prank he had seen played on someone in his quarters while he was stationed in England during the war. He told me if you took an old shoe shine brush and cut the bristles off about a ¼ inch long or shorter, spread out one of our old GI blankets and rub the bristles in on both sides, no one could see them and it would drive anyone nuts, showers of course would not help, and he said it was impossible to detect. I spent one whole afternoon "fixing" this guy's blanket; after about the third trip to the showers that first night, he came back and accused me of doing the same to him as he had to me, I told him I didn't know what he was talking about and let on I never knew what he had done, he suffered for about a week when he asked to be transferred to another hut, I got rid of the blanket, I felt vindicated.

Shortly after being assigned to the 59th Services Equipment Squadron, I was living in the quansent hut. We had a SSgt assigned as chief of our hut; I was a corporal at the time as assigned as his assistant. He had just came from Korea where he had been serving for about a year. I never knew why he was sent to England from Korea, he never talked about it, but I believe it was because he had been wounded; I noticed when we were dressed for a parade or anytime he had to wear a dress uniform he wore a purple heart ribbon, I never asked him as he never volunteered any information about it. He was a very rough looking man, from Maine and obviously a heavy drinker, he had a big red nose that is typical of a heavy drinker (I should have had one like a watermelon, but didn't). The first thing he did when he came into the hut was to start unpacking his duffel bag. He pulled out a fifth of whiskey and offered me a drink, I knew from then on we were going to be great buddies, and we were. A short time after he was there we were sitting on our bunks talking and drinking, when he looked up and noticed the light over my bunk was burnt out. He said, "You're the assistant, run down to supply and get a new bulb to replace that one." I brought the bulb; I had never seen one like it. American light bulbs had screw type bases on them. This thing had two prongs, like the old bulbs in automobile head lights, what was called "bayonet" type of bulb. I just thought it was another English antiquated appliance. Our bunks were prepared for "open air", which meant the mattress was folded toward the top; the blankets and sheets folded and placed on top of it, leaving the metal springs exposed. I was in my bare feet when I stepped on the bed springs to reach the burnt out bulb. I found it needed to be twisted to get it out; apparently it had not been changed for a while and was stuck. I was too short to reach properly so I grabbed the brass fitting and the base of the bulb at the same time. In the states we have 110 volt electricity, I had been shocked with that before and it was not a pleasant feeling. This was English electricity, 220 volts; it knocked me ass over tea cups, off the bunk, into the pot belled coal burning stove, knocking it over. The stove pipe came down throwing soot all over the entire hut. Fortunately, the stove did not have a fire in it but I made one hell of a mess of our hut, and learned all I needed to know about English electricity. My hut chief picked me up and offered me another drink out of his bottle.

During this time I was drinking every night either in town or at the club. One night I was coming back from town loaded. A friend of mine who was in the air police was on the gate that night. He saw I was in pretty bad shape and said he was just being relieved of duty and would give me a ride to my hut. It was just a short distance but I thought it best to take him up on it. When he stopped outside of my hut I tripped and fell as I was getting out of his jeep. I just laughed, got up and staggered into my hut. What I didn't know was our new first sergeant was outside across from my hut and saw me fall out of the air police jeep. The next morning he called my shop, telling my NCOIC to have me to report to the orderly room. I knew this guy was what was known as a "ninety day wonder". This is someone in the air force reserves doing a three month tour of duty overseas. They were not liked or respected by the regulars. When I reported he proceeded to reprimand me for being drunk the night before. I had a hangover, and always the smart ass, I did not feel like listening to this bull and let him know. I called him a damn ninety day wonder and told him I had no intention of being chewed out by some part-time Tsgt. What I did not know was our commanding officer was listening from the next office; he had a small sliding wooden panel between the offices, he slid it open and said, "Send that airman in here". This commander was known for being very strict and took no mercy on the likes of me. He had the nick name of "iron jaw"; he had a very large head, with an exceptionally large jaw, I think of him every time I see Jay Leno on "The Tonight Show". When I reported to him he made me stand at attention for the entire time I was there. He had a large book on his desk; he told me it was the new "USAF Article 15" to take effect that day. It was the manual to replace the one for the old articles of war 104. The manual used to mete out discipline. Under the old one he could recommend a court martial, assign me extra duty or restrict me to the base and other minor penalties. Under this new manual he could reduce me in rank on the spot. He told me he was busting me to Private, taking both stripes. I have the unique distinction of being the first airman to be busted under the U.S A.F. article 15. As I was leaving his office he told me in addition, I was to move a coal pile of about three tons from one end of the squadron to the other in a wheelbarrow. It took me the rest of the day.

When I got back to the shop the next morning my boss asked me about what happened, when I told him he said he did not think the commander could do that, and made an appointment for me with the Inspector General. When I explained everything to the I.G. he became angry and called my commander demanding to know what he thought he was doing. He also told him he had better acquaint himself with the article 15 procedures; he could only take as many stripes as he could give, which in his case was one. He instructed "Iron Jaw" to give me back one of my stripes and told him he was wrong in punishing me twice by making me move the coal pile. He also told him he thought his first sergeant was a little too ambitious and should be returned to the states until he had more experience dealing with suburbanites. Even though I only got one of my stripes back, I felt much better, feeling I had gotten even with the "ninety day wonder". It has always been my personal policy not to carry a grudge, (once I get even). I didn't even get very drunk that night, just a little high.

It was only about three months until I got my second stripe back, however even that got me in trouble. In the time between me losing my Corporal stripe and getting it back, the air force had changed the ranks of Airman for the first four ranks; it was now airman basic, airman third class, airman second class, and airman first class, instead of the old way, which was private, private first class, corporal and buck sergeant. Payday was only once a month and was always quite an event; first an inspection, a parade, a commander's call and then we would line up alphabetically to report for pay. If you made a mistake you were sent to the back of the line. I kept saying over and over to myself, I must say airman second class, not corporal, I must say airman second class, not corporal. When I got to the pay officer with the first sergeant beside him I saluted very sharply and reported, "Corporal second class Simmons reporting for pay, sir." I didn't even wait for the first sergeant's order; I just went to the back of the line.

During this time I was also restricted to the base, which was no big problem at first, I still had the beer bars on base. There was a guy in my hut who had just purchased a little motor scooter from the BX; it was similar to the old Vespa only much smaller. He brought it into the squadron area and let us take turns riding up and down the street in front of our hut. I had taken several rides on it and felt quite confident in handling it. A few days later I talked my buddy into letting me ride his scooter some more, not telling him what I had in mind. On Wednesday my friend went to the movies around eight p.m. As soon as he was gone, I jumped on his scooter and took off to town; although I was restricted and needed a pass to get though the gate near our hut, there was another gate at the other end of the base where they never checked passes if you were in a vehicle or on a bike. I went the long way into town, right through the center of town. On the way back to the base I was following a Double Decker bus, in the rain. When the bus stopped I could not and slid right under the rear of the bus. I got quite a bit of "gravel rash" on my hands and arms. The bus conductor wanted to call a policeman but I refused (I did not have a license to operate the scooter) and took off again. I got home before my buddy got out of the movies and parked his scooter where he left it. The next morning my hands were torn up. The little finger on my right hand used to have a big wart on the knuckle. I had torn most of it off and it was turning blue. I signed up for sick call and they sent me over to the hospital, where they burned the rest of the wart off, damaging the knuckle. The medic bandaged it up and sent me back to the squadron.

A few days later my finger became badly infected and I was put in the hospital, they found I had osteomalacia in the bone of my little finger. I was admitted to the hospital and spent nearly three weeks there, some very funny things happened during the time I was in and some not so funny. The most unpleasant thing was I was to get as shot of penicillin every hour for ten days. This was in the early 1950's and penicillin was new and untested. It was thick stuff and felt as if they were shooting butter milk in my butt every hour. On the fifth night I started choking and could not breathe; it was a reaction to the penicillin, my throat was closing up and they nearly had to cut it open to get air into my wind pipe. Before I started getting the reaction, the first night around two a.m. the medic came to give me a shot, he asked me if I wanted it. I said, "Hell no but what choice do I have?" He said his buddy would take it for me; this shot was also used to treat VD, if you came to sick call for it, it was put on your record. This would be bad news at promotion time; so the medics would treat each other when necessary and if they found someone like me willing to give up a shot. I gladly gave up my shot, and a few more, as the treatment for VD required three shots in three days. It's probably as well that I did, I would have suffered more from the shots. I became quite well liked by the medics.

During the time I was in hospital, there were three men in my ward who had came in to be circumcised, this became a common thing. Part of their treatment was they had a wire hoop type of an apparatus over them to keep the weight of the covers off them while they healed. A nurse came by about every three or four hours, pulled down the cover and sprayed their "injury" with a penicillin powder spray. I had a similar apparatus on my bed, but it was a heating unit to keep my finger dry. I was sound asleep one afternoon, apparently having a "nice dream", when the nurse came by and started pulling my cover down. I fought back saying I had just had a shot but she insisted and kept pulling on the cover. I fought back but she won; when the cover came off, there I was in all my glory. She looked surprised and asked, "What are you in here for?" I held my hand up and said, "My finger". She dropped the cover and the men in the

96

beds next to me that she had just sprayed, roared with laughter as she made a hasty embarrassed retreat. One of the men that had been circumcised was a medic. He had busted his stitches twice already (he had dreams too). One afternoon a very attractive nurse, who had worked with him in another part of the hospital was a good friend of his, came by to visit him. After they talked for a while she sat down on the side of his bed, crossing a very shapely pair of legs. In a short time he said to her, "You had better leave now". She told him she had all afternoon to visit. He squirmed a bit in his bed and repeated, "You had better leave now." She said "Don't worry, I came to see you." Suddenly he yelled, "Get the hell out, I'm busting my stitches again." She jumped up, embarrassed, and ran out as we all shrieked with laughter. She never came to visit him again while he was in hospital.

The damage the medic did to my finger when he used the electric needle to remove the wart damaged to tendon and caused me trouble throughout my military career. The osteomalacia in my little finger on my right hand caused my finger to be bent down at a forty five degree angle permanently, this of course was my saluting hand, every time I would salute an officer I was questioned about the way I saluted and had to explain each time. It became a nuisance but I got used to it and later had fun with it; the only solution they had offered was to bring in a surgeon specialist from Germany, when I asked what he could do, I was told he would break it and make it permanently straight, I said "no thanks, at least now I can get in a fight without poking someone's eye out".

Chapter Twelve

My most fortunate encounter

When I arrived in England in early December 1951 I was not impressed with the weather or what appeared to be to be their antiquated ways, but I soon learned to enjoy their way of life, what I had difficulty with was their drinking habits. The pubs opened at ten a.m., closed at two p.m., opened again at five p.m. until ten thirty p.m. During the summer months, it was still daylight when the pubs closed, so we would go back to the base and go to the NCO club to finish up the night. We were living in quansent huts with usually six or eight men to a hut. One of the men in my hut was bringing his wife of a few months over from the states and needed a house. There was a lady named Alice,(Mom) a cook at the BX cafeteria that acted as an adopted mother to all the GIs. She got to know everybody's business. She talked to this friend of mine and told him her husband could help him find a house. She invited him to her house. He didn't want to go alone and asked me to go with him. We found the house and were greeted by Alice and invited in. Alice introduced us to her husband, Bill and three daughters. One girl, I thought, was the most beautiful girl I had ever seen. Sitting there in the middle of the floor cleaning a rifle was Joyce, their middle daughter. I later learned she was not only in the Territorial Army (similar to our national guard) but was also the north of England champion in competition shooting. I was awe struck by her; it was love at first sight. Her older sister

Rena was about 6 years and older very attractive; she ran a hair dressing salon in the front part of the house. The youngest sister, Stella, was about 12 years old. The father and my friend talked about the house while I pretended to be interested in the conversation, but my mind was doing its own thing, I could not take my eyes off Joyce. Finally, Bill offered to take my friend and me to the movies. We left the houses and a short distance from the house I asked if he minded if I asked Joyce to join us. He said, "You ask her, its ok with me if she wants to go." I ran like hell back to the house and knocked on the door. When I finally saw her again, and she accepted my invitation I thought, my god, I'm taking an English lady out for a date. I had never been with anyone like this before; she seemed so full of life, and actually interested in me. I only hoped I wouldn't make a fool of myself. I was cold sober for the first time since I don't know when and did not even think of having a drink all night. I wish I could say that feeling lasted for as long as I knew her; but that was not to be our fate. Early in our courtship Joyce was not comfortable with calling me Richard, a name I never cared for, and she had an uncle named Richard, all my family called me Dick, but that was what they called her uncle, she asked if I minded being called Rick, I of course said call me what ever you want as long as you call me often, so came the moniker Rick I still have today among my family, my work mates and supervisors always called me Richard, so I used that as a business name. I do not know if I went back the next night or not but it was not long before our second date, our first time out alone we went to the movies again. I can't remember for sure myself, but Joyce tells me I proposed the first time that night, she refused anyway. I proposed several times after that and she kept refusing saying it was too soon; but one night she finally did accept. I don't think my feet touched the ground all the way back to the base, and that began a long and wonderful friendship.

There were some differences in our language that we both found alarming. I was visiting after work on day, wearing my 1505 khaki uniform. We had arranged to go out that evening, but I wanted to change into nicer clothes. I announced that I first needed to go back to the base and change out of my khaki pants. Her family stood there, stunned. They pronounced "khaki" differently, more like "car key". The American pronunciation that I had used was a crude slang term meaning shit. Another time, Joyce was visiting me on base and her mother came with her. As they were leaving Joyce's mother turned and called to me and called, "Keep your pecker up!" I had never heard the term before, nor had any of the men in the room. Joyce told me later it was an English term used to mean "Keep your chin up" the men got quite a charge out of it.

One of my shop mates invited Joyce and me to their house for Sunday dinner. The problem was the difference between what Americans call dinner and what the people in the north of England take it to mean. Where Joyce was from, the meals are breakfast, dinner then tea; supper, if taken, is a light snack before bed time. For the American couple dinner was after six p.m., (past tea time for Joyce). Joyce and I had gone to Sunday mass and communion that morning, meaning we had no breakfast. Mass was eleven a.m., so we arrived at the couple's home around twelve thirty, expecting to have dinner. They were just getting up so we visited for the rest of the day, without eating. They did not start preparing dinner until around five p.m., and to make matters even worse, the hostess asked Joyce to help with the meal by peeling the potatoes. Joyce was insulted and thought the woman was very rude. An English guest would never be asked to prepare their own meal. It was not until later that Joyce realized the difference between the terms of the meals and somewhere in America today there must be a couple talking about the two nuts that showed up for dinner at lunchtime.

The scariest time for me was when the time came for me to ask her father for her hand in marriage. I had put it off as long as I could, mainly because Joyce and her sister Rena had connived between themselves to convince me it was the English custom that I had to get on my knees in front of her father while the two of us were alone in order for him to accept my request. This of course was a load of crap, and they told me it was not true just a short time before I was to ask him. On the night when this was supposed to happen, Joyce, her mother and both sisters made an excuse to leave the house, leaving only me and her father. All the time I knew him, I did not know how to address him; for some reason Mr. Mulholland did not seem right. I don't know if that was his decision or mine, but when ever

I addressed him, whether to ask him a question, offer a cigarette or comment on something all I could manage was, err, or ahem or, aah, or cough-cough. He seemed to understand my discomfort and played along. Well, this time even I knew this would not be appropriate, so we both just sat there staring at the open fire in the fire place. God it seemed like hours, and maybe it was, when finally I said "Mr. Mulholland", he damn near jumped out of his chair and said, "Yes Rick", as it turned out he was just as uncomfortable or as uneasy as I was, perhaps even more. He broke the tension with some calm remark and asked, "Was there something you wanted to say Rick?" I cleared my throat a few more times and finally said, Yes sir; I would like to ask for your daughter Joyce's hand in marriage." He said, "Do you think you are both ready for marriage?" I said, "Yes I do and I love her very much." We talked for quite a long time about the possible difficulties in getting married as what he considered our young ages, but he never discouraged me in any way. He said he would support Joyce in her decision. He shook my hand and made some comment about welcoming me to the family; I don't know how the rest of them knew when to come in, but eventually they returned and her father informed them of what had taken place. It turned out to be a wonderful evening, he was truly a gentleman and supported us the remainder of the time we were courting. He never once said anything to me about my drinking as long as I knew him, although after I sobered up I can image what he must have gone through, being a father myself and having two daughters. I always respected him; I only wish he could have lived to enjoy my sobriety. Unfortunately he died about 10 years before I got sober.

Soon after we got engaged we of course started planning for a wedding, Joyce and her family were devout Catholics, I had been brought in the protestant faith, my parents were Nazarenes. I had not attended any kind of church probably since I was ten years old, so I had no objections when I was asked to convert to Catholicism, and my mother had no problem, as long as we were happy. Our courtship was the happiest time of my life; I felt so overwhelmed by Joyce and was afraid if she knew of my past life, especially my life on the racetrack, she would not accept it, or me. I just never talked much about racetrack life. I wish I could say I continued to behave like a gentleman but even though I covered it very well, my drinking was getting worse. If Joyce noticed, she never let on; I know I disappointed her on several occasions when I found myself in the NCO club or in a pub in town, calling her at the last moment making up some lame excuse. She was always graceful and never questioned my actions or motives, I'm sure her mother and father must have suspected, but they knew Joyce loved me and allowed her to set her own boundaries without interfering.

We had a very nice courtship; I know I loved her very much and wanted to spend my life with her. We had a wonderful catholic wedding with papal blessings and all, her parents really put on a spread. I had no one from my family there and no one from the base, all my so called friends were drinkers and I did not want this spoiled.

Our Wedding

Joyce on the other hand had a very large family and many friends. After the ceremony Joyce and I were loaded into a Rolls Royce and her parents and sisters, who served as bride's maids, and the best man and other important guests followed in other Rolls Royce's. I do not know how many guests there were but the church was filled and they had hired two double Decker buses to take them to Walton Hall, a very large castle of a looking place for the reception. It was a wonderful place where Joyce and I had spent many happy hours walking around the beautiful lawns and gardens; it was the most serene place I had ever been. When Joyce and I first started courting she used to take me out there. We would get a bus from town; it was about a half hour ride to the hall. In addition to the beautiful grounds there were English bowling greens, tennis courts and a nine-hole golf course that we used to play. We had never played before, but we got pretty good as we went there often. One day I thought I was getting ahead of her in score so I was going to let her win the next hole. It was a short hole so I let her go first. She got a hole in one; I think I shot a four. So much for chivalry.

Joyce and I left the reception, changed and went to the train station for a train to Rhyl in Wales where we spent our honey moon. It was a wonderful time and I never thought of drinking, I guess I was just in love. One day while we were on our honeymoon, strolling along the sea side, we came upon a tennis court where we could rent equipment and play. I jokingly told her I had let her beat me at golf, but I would take her on the tennis court. Having never had a tennis racket in my hand, I had no idea how to play; I had watched Wimbledon on TV so I figured it can't be all that hard. They only gave us one ball and two rackets. Being the gentleman I was, I let her serve. She got the first one over the net, in my effort to "return service" I hit the ball as hard as I could and it not only cleared the net, it went clear out of the court and out into the North Sea. I had to pay two pence for the lost ball; we never played another match while we were there.

Unfortunately, soon after returning to duty I picked up where I left off with my drinking, at the NCO club, just up the street from my workplace every evening and some times stopping off at a pub on the way home. Joyce never nagged me about my drinking, I guess she just hoped it would get better, but it didn't.

As much as I was drinking, there were others that were as bad as or worse off than I was. One of my SSgt's for example, a guy called Cod Rogers, was the NCOIC of our shop and stayed drunk also. He used to take some of us other drinkers out almost daily to a nearby pub for darts and ale. He invited Joyce and me to his house for fish & chips; when we got there Cod was passed out in a chair. His wife, an English lady, was embarrassed. Cod sat near the window and there was a large fish tank by his side. He came to and poured himself another glass of whiskey from a bottle by his chair. Not even aware we were there, he called to his wife to get him a glass of water for a chaser. She told him to get it himself. Cod just picked up the water glass, dipped it into the fish tank, took a drink of whiskey, drank the water from the fish tank and went back to sleep.

I was riding a bike all the time and would have to ride through the town of Warrington to where we lived in the village of Stockton Heath. There were many pubs on the way home and I would usually make as many as I could. One afternoon when we had been married about six or seven months I took off from work early and started a pub crawl, I must have made most of them before I started home. I don't remember a lot about it, I apparently had a black out. When I came to I was riding hell bent for leather along the side of the canal that ran between Warrington and Stockton Heath. There was a narrow path along side the canal where the locals walked and rode bikes. This canal was very deep, as it was used for barges and fairly large ships going between Liverpool and Manchester. Had I fallen in, I would have never stood a chance of getting out, as the bank was over four feet high. I have never figured out why I was there in the first place, it was a long way from the route I should have been on; I suppose God looks after fools and drunks. There were many more of these events, more than I care to remember, but writing about them somehow gives me a strange sense of relief.

We had a small apartment for a while in a lovely village called Stockton Heath. One of the nights when I came home drunk, I fell into our landlady's hedge row, it was after dark and I passed out, Joyce had no idea where I was, the landlady found me the next morning still in the hedge, I think that was when she asked us to move. We went to live with one of Joyce's aunts, during her pregnancy with Ann, who was born about two weeks after the nine-month mark (Joyce's mother was doing the finger count). Joyce had complications and an infection after Ann was born. That is when we went to live in a very small house with her parents until it was time to be shipped back to the states. We got a rotten deal in that shipment. I of course, with two stripes, did not have the sense or courage to fight the fact that Joyce and the baby could not come back on the same ship with me. I went on the General Patch and she came later on the General Rose, about two weeks behind me. She had a hell of a bad crossing; traveling with a six month baby all by her self, the other dependent wives would not give her any kind of help. I spent some time with my mother in Maryland and awaited her arrival. She docked in New York and then had to catch a train to Baltimore. One of my cousins took me to meet her and bring her home to Bel-Air. We only had a few days there before I had to report to Gary AFB in San Marcos Texas.

Chapter Thirteen

San Marcos, Texas

Joyce stayed with my mother until I could find a place for us to live. I found a very nice house where the landlady rented a part of the house to us. Joyce made the long six day ride across country on a slow moving train to Texas, just her and Ann Marie, who was about eight months old. She must have wondered what ever was she thinking about, but she never complained and loved the place I had found; it was convenient to all the shops. We soon made it a very comfortable home and we were very happy there. We did not have a car at the time; I just never got around to getting a car all the time I was on the track. I didn't even had a driving license, as I really did not have a need for one; some one always had a car so there really was no reason to spend money on one. Finally we got our first car, a 1949 Hudson. I followed by getting about four or five more (I sure liked Hudson's). The first year we were doing very well, then I started drinking heavily again; I had kept it pretty much under control for the first year or so. When we moved to another house I got another Hudson, a 1953 Hornet, that was one of the fastest cars on the road at the time, but it got about eight miles to the gallon. Even with the price of gas in those days, it kept us broke, along with the car payments we could not afford, but that never stopped me. My damn ego just got us deeper in debt and finally I had to let the car go back for repossession. I was working part time at the NCO club and my drinking pattern soon returned. One night I was helping stock the bar at the club. As I came out of the walk-in refrigerator I tripped and fell, falling on the big iron knob used to push the door open, striking it with my chin and causing a bad gash. I knew I was too drunk to go to the emergency room so I went home, when I got up the next morning I had bled all over the bed and Joyce made me go to the hospital. I had to fill out an accident report, so I just put down what happened, except for the fact I worked there and was drunk.

About a year after we arrived at Gary AFB they changed the name of the base to Edward Gary AFB, the full name of the person the base had been named for. Shortly after that our first son was born. Joyce had to call a friend to look after Ann while she took a taxi to the base hospital; I was probably either at work or at the NCO club. When I did go to the hospital, the nurse asked me what I was going to name the child. I said, "Edward Gary". The nurse laughed and said, "No, what name do you want to give your son?" I said again, "Edward Gary". She blushed and said, "Oh, you were serious!" I said, "Of course." She apologized, and so that became my son's name.

San Marcos was my first experience with aircraft crash recovery. My first recovery was a X-H21, what at the time was the biggest helicopter in the air force. It was the first double bladed chopper and was called "the flying banana". I was working in a tire shop at the time and this thing was coming in for a landing when one of the engines froze, throwing it on the tarmac about fifty feet from my shop. After the rescue team removed the crew, the hanger chief sent me and my crew out for reclamation of the craft. San Marcos was a primary training base and this was the first experience the pilots had at flying. They were trained in an all fabric aircraft, the L-21 and an all metal one, the L-19. These were small liaison trainers with which pilots were given initial training before going on to small helicopters, the H-13s. These things were little more than a glass bubble with a rotor on top and a small tail rotor. With the inexperienced pilots, there were several crashes we had to deal with. Fortunately, there were only a few fatalities but a lot of bruised egos.

The biggest victim in this category was our base commander. He devised what turned out to be a very practical and inventive device for crash rescue; it consisted of a quick disconnect system that would hook up to a large CO2 fire extinguisher, connected with a cable to the undercarriage of an H-19. According to his design, in case of a crash, the rescue crew would hook this CO2 container to the belly of the helicopter and board the craft. The H-19 would fly to the crash site and set the CO2 bottle as close as possible to the crash. When the weight was taken from the line, the commander's hook-up system would release and set the CO2 bottle off. The chopper pilot would then use his prop wash to direct the CO2 into the fire. It was demonstrated several times at practice sessions and seemed to be a solution to a lot of our crash problems. The commander was not satisfied with the demonstrations so he put on an exhibit for some visiting dignitaries. Using his quick-disconnect system he took off with an automobile hooked under the H-19, he flew the length of the air strip at low altitude setting the auto down in front of the stand where the spectators were. All went well and he received applause. Still not satisfied, he returned to the hanger and had a maintenance crew hook up an L-19 training plane in the same fashion. Although the crew chief cautioned that he did not think this was a good idea, the commander told them to hook it up. The H-19 took off with the L-19 underneath hooked to the quick disconnect apparatus. Things seemed to be going just fine until about half way down the flight line. Fortunately, before he reached the stands where spectators were, the wind caught under the wings of the L-19 causing it to rise, releasing the tension that was keeping it hooked up. When the weight was released from the hook-up, it did just what it was designed to do, release. The L-19 crashed into the tarmac. The concept was later successfully used in crash rescue, it was later improved on and used with the H-43 helicopter which had a much more powerful prop wash, but I never heard of it being used to transport fixed wing aircraft again.

In 1956 I had purchased yet another Hudson car, it was a 1952. It was not as fast as the Hornet, but a nice family car, until one night while I was out with my buddies drinking. I crashed it into a bridge totaling it and was jailed for drunken driving, another heart break for Joyce. I managed to get out of it pretty light as the base was closing and my commanding officer came to court with me and explained to the judge that I was being sent to Laredo near the Mexican border. The judge suspended my license and I never even tried to get it back until I was stationed at MacDill in Florida in 1963.

Chapter Fourteen

Laredo, Texas

After they closed Edward Gary AFB in San Marcos Texas in 1956, I was sent to Laredo AFB about two hundred miles south. After getting out of trouble in San Marcos with my DWI, anyone would think I had learned my lesson and could control my drinking but it only got worse. When I arrived at Laredo I was assigned to a fuel cell repair shop where I worked alone for about six or eight months. When SSgt. Dave Hoffman was assigned to work with me, there was not much work for us and we were assigned additional duties with a crash rescue team. Our duties there were to be available to respond when the siren sounded to alert the crew of a crash or pending emergency. Our responsibilities were to secure the crash site for the inspection team, clear as much of the area we could, preparing for the pick up of debris. This base was a primary jet training base and the crews flying these air craft had no experience in jet aircraft. This led to numerous emergencies and crashes; many were on take off or landing. As long as there was no fire, they were usually not serious or fatal, except for the aircraft, which was normally salvaged and cannibalized for repairs on similar aircraft.

Unfortunately, there were several fatal crashes because when these things lost power they would drop like a sewer lid. At least two of these crashes involved people I knew personally. As a bartender at the officers club, I would get to know them. The first one happened around ten a.m.; when we were notified to respond we saw the smoke not far from the end of the runway and knew it was a bad one. When we arrived the plane was still on fire with the crew members, a 1st Lt. and a 2nd Lt., still inside. The pilot had come in too low and hit about a mile short of the runway. As the plane hit the ground it slid onto a small hill pitching it upward again. As it rolled on its back and came to rest upside down in a small ravine it caught fire. I learned later from the medics who pulled them from the cockpit after we had cut the side open to gain access that they were still alive during the fire as they had torn their finger nails completely off trying to escape. When we got inside the cockpit we could see where they had torn the side panels off with their hands tearing the wiring out from the cabin. The next crash I knew the test pilot, a Captain I had talked with many times at the club. He took a T-33 up for a test flight after major maintenance on the wings and tail sections. The aircraft barely cleared the runway when it went into a roll, turning upside down and crashing into the runway and immediately catching fire. With a full fuel load, he never stood a chance. When we went to pick up the crash after the inspection team made their initial check, they had us load it on a flat bed truck and take it to an empty hanger where they reassembled it. They spread it out on the hanger floor and removed the skin from the wings and tail pieces. They discovered the aileron cables in the wing section had been crossed. These crash inspectors were really professional and could pinpoint a problem or cause of an accident. Apparently, when the pilot attempted to raise the aircraft to go into a bank, the controls caused the craft to do the opposite and go straight into the runway. He had barely cleared the runway and had no chance to make any corrections before crashing. I also knew the crew chief, who was court marshaled for dereliction of duty for signing off on the aircraft logbook.

Dave and I had a lot of spare time on our hands; we got very inventive in our work schedule. We were never checked on because we always were ahead in our workload, put out very impressive production and our shop was in a remote area from the other hangers and shops. We found we could go to the hanger where an aircraft was being worked on and find out from the crew chief if there were any fuel cell changes being made; we knew it took three days from a cell being pulled to clear the work scheduling process and reach our shop. We would sometimes go three or four days with no work in the shop. We also used an old trick I had learned years before about sign out boards; we would sign out to two or three different places on base or even off base, then make arrangements for someone in the area we were supposed to be to say we had just left in case anyone did call. We were always covered. Dave had a couple of friends just outside the base who owned bars. One lady, called Lou, had a bar with a large deep fry pan in the rear. The guys from the base would bring their catches in and we would have a fish fry about every Friday.

When I look back at these times, it hurts to know how I deserted Joyce and the children by abandoning them. Even when Joyce was pregnant with our third child, Sheila, and had a severe ear infection, I would still leave her and continue drinking. This deprived them of my support, the money I was making at the clubs no where near covered what I was spending. They went without most of the time, yet Joyce stood by me. Whenever I did have a sober thought, it tore at my guts; to realize I could be so distant and hurtful to someone who had given me all the love she had, just did not seem to be me. As much as this tormented me, I just did not seem to be able to take any control, the thinking would just make me more remorseful, and I would drink even more, it was a vicious circle I could not control.

Dave had the only transportation as I lost my license in San Marcos for the DWI, although I still took Dave's truck at times when he would stay in the shop to finish some work. One afternoon I took his truck into Laredo and got pretty drunk. I forgot I had driven his truck in and caught a bus back to the base. When I found the shop closed I knew he would be at the club; I just walked on up to the club and had a beer with him, he said, "Give me the keys and I'll take you home". I said, "Whoops. Dave, I forgot I had your truck and caught a bus back." He just shook his head. Dave caught a bus into town and I walked home; we lived in a trailer park just out side the base.

After Dave and I had been stationed together about two years, he came in the shop one morning from the hanger where our orderly room was and said the First Sgt. wanted to see me. Our First Sgt was a good friend of mine so I had no concern. When I reached to orderly room he said, "Simmons, get your bags packed, you are going to the Bahamas." I said, "You can't be serious." He said he was and I asked, "Why me?" He said they needed a fuel cell man there and I was the senior. I asked if it was a concurrent tour. (so I could take my family) He said, "I'm afraid not, it's an eighteen month tour." I was madder than hell; when I got back to the shop where Dave was, I told him about it, he said it wasn't fair. A few days later the First Sgt. called me back to the orderly room. He said they had revoked my orders and were sending Dave in my place. Dave never said a word about it to me but he had gone to the Commander and asked to be sent in my place. He thought a lot of Joyce and knew what a hardship it would be on her, and being single, he felt it was the right thing to do. Dave had to sell his beloved truck as it was classified commercial and you could not take a commercial vehicle overseas. He took his tool box and a few personnel items boxed and sent them ahead, two days later they canceled the shipment altogether, poor Dave had lost his truck and his tools were on the way to the Bahamas, not to be seen for three weeks, he finally got his tools back but could not replace his truck, he had to settle for a Pontiac car instead.

Dave and I used to go to our trailer almost every morning to have a cup of coffee and work the crossword puzzles. There was a clue in the puzzle quite frequently, "the call of the bacchanals" when we finally got the answer, "evoe" we kind of adopted it as a call word when we would meet. You could hear us around the club as soon as one of us walked in and spotted the other it was "evoe" as loud as we could yell. About two years after I shipped out and was stationed at Mildenhall England, I was in the pub in West Row one night playing darts when I heard this loud yell "EVOE!" Sure as hell, there was Dave; he was being sent TDY to Germany and stopped over in Mildenhall for two days. Knowing I was stationed there he found out where I lived through the bases locater and went to the house where Joyce told him where to find me, boy did we ever get drunk that night.

Chapter Fifteen

My second tour to England

In 1959 I requested another tour in England. I found out this was not an accompanied tour, in other words, I could not take my family unless I could prove I had a residence established prior to being accepted. My wife, being from England did not take too well to that. Fortunately for us her mother worked on the base I was to be assigned so we contacted her right away, that woman could get where castor oil couldn't. She went to work using her influence; she wired back that we had residence established in a place called "The Mulberry Tree". I took the wire to the orderly room to my first sergeant. He read the wire, then looked up at me and said, "Sgt. Simmons, I've been stationed in England, this sounds like a Pub to me., I said, "So what, it's classified as a residence and they have accepted me and my family indefinitely." He just shook his head and said, "I'll give it to the old man". I was accepted and in three weeks we were on our way to Mildenhall RAF station in England. After we left Laredo, we went to Maryland to spend some time with my mother before going to England. Joyce's oldest sister, Rena and a gentleman friend of hers, who was preparing to go into a monastery, came to town to visit with us. Rena strongly disapproved of my drinking and she would have been very upset had she known I had taken her friend to the Rat Hole and tried to get him to drink a beer. He of course politely refused.

We went from my mother's house to Mcguire AFB in New Jersey for transportation to England; this was another trip from hell. Nearly as bad as my first trip over, this was aboard an air plane instead of a ship. They loaded us on an old 118 prop driven aircraft, they wouldn't even sit us all together. Joyce and I had Gary and Sheila with us and Ann was pushed to the rear of the plane with a couple of GI's. Sheila was nine months old and Joyce had given the stewardess milk for her bottles that somehow was given to other passengers. To make it worse, we flew to England via Greenland. This was in December; when we landed in Greenland we were told we had to get off the plane as they needed to change an engine. When the stewardess told Joyce she could not take a blanket off the plane that she had wrapped Ann in because she had thrown up on her coat, she hit a nerve. I have never seen Joyce so angry at anyone before, I thought she was going to throw the stewardess of the plane. Finally, I believe it was the pilot, said she could take the blanket. In 1959, military air transport planes did not pull up to the terminal as they do now, we had to disembark onto the frozen snow on the tarmac and walk some 100 yards or more to the terminal where we spent most of the night waiting for our plane to be repaired. This was not a pleasant trip.

When we arrived at Mildenhall, we were met by Joyce's mother who took us to the place she had gotten us lodgings. Sure enough as my first sergeant back in Laredo had said, it was a pub, which I had no problem with until we attempted to go to bed. The place had no heating except for a small fireplace downstairs in the bar that was of no use upstairs. We had to ask for extra blankets and everybody slept fully dressed, coats and all.

While I was assigned to the parachute shop, although I was in charge and was the senior NCO in charge of two other SSgt's and seven airmen, I was still only a five level and could not be promoted to Tsgt. without making a seven level. I went to my first sergeant that was one of my drinking pals at the NCO club and asked him to let me take the test for seven level. I was notified to report to the test room one morning, however I had not been given much advance notice and the morning I was to report, I was drunk. The test was scheduled to start at nine in the morning; I had already had a six pack and a few slugs of whiskey. I used my usual method of cleaning my breath by sucking on a lemon, (I had been told this was very effective, not true!) and I always carried a bottle of Listerine in my jacket pocket, so I figured I was prepared for any test. When the instructor started the test I raised my hand and started asking what he deemed stupid questions. After about five minutes of this, as others in the class started laughing at me, the instructor ordered me to leave the room. As he put it, I was not coherent enough to take the test. Instead of being embarrassed, as any sane person would have been, I got pissed off and stormed out of the room, swearing at the instructor, and slamming the door. I went to my first sergeant complaining to him about being thrown out of the class. He took one look at me and said, "What the hell did you expect Simmons, you are three sheets to the wind now, and I am about to throw you out of here". I told him to go to hell and went to the club, where I continued to drink. At about two in the afternoon I called my shop and asked one of my SSgt's to cover for me and I went home.

During this four-year tour I never attempted to get a car. I felt more comfortable, and I suppose safer, riding a bicycle but I had some narrow scrapes even here. I had a ten speed and I could make it from the parachute shop to the pub in about ten to twelve minutes, or the NCO club in about five, depending on the wind. My regular routine almost daily would start out with drinking enough to stop the shakes before leaving home, usually a six pack of beer or a water glass full of gin or vodka, sometimes, both. When I would get to work at seven a.m., I would give assignments to the six or eight airman working for me, either as parachutes riggers or fabric repairmen who operated the sewing machines, I worked alone in the survival shop. Around nine a.m. I would spread a parachute out on the rigging table, then go next door to the survival shop, inflate a few life rafts and some life vests making it look as though I had a lot of work going on. By then it would be around 09:45, the pub opened at 10:00. I would then go to the sign out board, sign out for two or three different places on base, some even fictitious, (there was no hanger 9 but no one ever questioned it) and head for the pub. I would stay usually until closing time at two pm then go back to the survival shop where I worked alone. Later in the afternoon I would go back to the parachute shop where I would finish packing the parachute I had spread out earlier, then go to my office and complete the day's paper work, close up the shop and head for the NCO club. Sometimes the routine would vary between the pub and the club, but always involved drinking, usually alone. Sometimes one or two the guys from the shop would join me. There was never a shortage of drinking buddies, however, I preferred drinking alone most of the time especially as my drinking got worse. As this type of drinking progressed, one thing I used to do was hide in toilets somewhere to drink beer, especially if I needed a "cure". I found out I could carry ten cans of beer in my field jacket: three in each of the side pockets, two in each of the top pockets. There were times when I needed this much to get me through the shakes and back to where I could function enough to appear to be what was considered normal. This was usually done in the early morning, after I had made some excuse for being away from my duty station.

One night when I was at the NCO club I started gambling. I was never very good at this, I mostly played slot machines, but this time a friend who was shipping out the next day got me in a poker game with about six other guys. As I started losing, he was covering my bets and slipping me money on the side. I must have lost quite a bit, I told the guy I would have the money for him the next morning, knowing very well that I could not. The next morning around nine thirty, when all my airmen were on coffee break, I was sitting in my office alone when saw this guy coming down the road towards my shop for his money. I knew I had to get out before he got there, but before going out of a window in my office I grabbed a bottle of whiskey I had hidden in the back of my office and stuck in my field jacket. I climbed out the window, as I slipped and the bottle must have cracked. I went next door to my survival shop where I locked myself in so the guy could not find me. When I pulled the bottle out of my field jacket I saw it was badly cracked and about to shatter. I took a piece of parachute material and spread it over a pail and let the whiskey strain into the pail and salvaged the most of it. The guy could not find me and finally left to catch his plane. I know what a rotten trick that was, but a desperate man has little conscience, especially a drinking man.

118

I realize how difficult it must be for some people to grasp or believe that someone in such a responsible position, an NCO in charge of parachute and survival shops, supervising eight to ten men, could manage to drink this much or more important, get away with it. The fact is I started drinking on a regular basis when I was fourteen years old, by the time I was fifteen, I was drinking on a daily basis. This pattern continued until I quit drinking some twenty-eight years later, at forty-two years of age. During this period, I can count on one hand the times I went without drinking daily. Once when I was in basic training from June until August 1951, (I even cheated there once), then the twelve days I was on the ship going over seas, once when I was hospitalized with an infected finger, again two weeks on our honey moon. One time while at Mildenhall, I had an accident while drunk and fell off my bike dislocating my shoulder. I was put in a hospital for three weeks where I suffered from the DT's. (Delirium tremens caused by drying out from alcoholic binges). I developed, very early in my life, a high tolerance for alcohol and was able to function satisfactorily after consuming large amounts of alcohol. In addition, our drinking was not discouraged in the military; rather, it was encouraged. An abundance of alcohol was everywhere and unless you did something that was going to effect or embarrass your superiors you were left alone. As I look back on those days now, I question the possibility myself, but believe me it is true. I was there and so was my poor wife, Joyce. I only bring up these facts, not for journalism or shock value, but if there is anyone out there, who might recognize themselves in these stories, know that there is hope, and I am living proof. A person has to first realize that no one can do it for them. Stopping drinking for someone else is just another futile effort. A person can only do this for him- or herself. Alcoholism is the only disease known to the medical profession that can only be cured by the patient; (cure is not the right term really, as there is no cure, only control. I am still an alcoholic, and always will be, just a non-drinker.) Some of my drinking experiences were humorous, some very sad, some downright scary and even mysterious. (Anyone finding these stories hard to believe, please just attend an open AA meeting, (the regular meetings are not open to just anyone), you will find similar or much worse stories, trust me.)

While we were at Mildenhall, Joyce's younger sister Stella was there as well as their mother. Stella married shortly after we arrived, her husband Bill and I worked on different places on the base but got together often while he was stationed there. Bill was with the 59th weather squadron. He was a crew chief on a WB-50 weather aircraft. He was a very good mechanic and was well respected by his peers and superiors for his work ethics but I knew another side of Bill, he could also be mischievous. One day he and I were walking on the flight line when we came upon this young airman working on an aircraft. We stopped and talked to him, Bill asked him about what he was doing. He was working on an engine and had parts, nuts and bolts spread very meticulously out on a piece of tarpaulin, each piece carefully placed. Bill nudged me in my side and winked. He distracted the airman for a minute, reached in his pocket and pulled out a handful of various size screws, bolts and some small parts. When the airman wasn't looking, Bill laid the things among the airman's parts then walked off. I asked, "What that was all about?" He said, "That guys going to go nuts trying to figure out where all those spare parts he has left over go." I said, "Bill, you're sick".

Although my duties were mostly administrative, I still from time to time packed chutes and inspected, repaired and repacked survival equipment. There was a procedure for all parachute riggers to maintain a logbook in a small pocket on the back of each parachute. This was to maintain a record of the date the chute was packed, and of course to identify the person who packed the chute in case of any investigation in the event of a malfunction. It also served another purpose, it was a tradition if anyone bailed out in a chute that you packed, they would bring the rigger a bottle of whiskey. I never had one of mine returned (I hope that was because one was not used) however one of my riggers did have a Major came in the office one day asking for the rigger who packed his chute. He had bailed out and was there to give him his bottle. The same airman that had packed the Major's chute met me at the shop door very excited one afternoon as I came back from lunch. He said, You'll never guess who was here." I of course had no idea. He said with a big grin, "I just sewed Brigadier General stars on Jimmy Stewart's flying suit." We later learned he had been up for promotion several times but there was a lady in congress that refused to promote a movie star to the rank of General. It seems she was out of the country on some fact-finding tour or something and the other members had approved it.

One of the stupidest things I did during this period was to get Joyce's allotment check out of the mail box on base, forge her name and cash the check, then go to the club with some buddy and proceed to get drunk(er). Of course when I did go home I had to tell Joyce what I had done and again beg her forgiveness. She was mad as hell at me but more so with the bank for allowing me to cash the check without her I.D. card. She approached the bank manager about it and he was very apologetic but the only thing he could do was to bring charges against me. She did not want to do that, nor could she afford to if she wanted to. As always, as so many times before, she had to suffer the consequences of my stupidity and forgave me once again.

There were so many ways to make money to cover my drinking expenses; the easiest was of course the black market in booze. I could get a forty-ounce bottle of gin or vodka for ninety cents and sell it for $2.80. Whiskey, cigarettes and cigars had about the same value, the problem was I was drinking gin and vodka at the time and dipping into my booze stash was cutting into my profits. I had also established myself at the two local pubs I frequented most to the point that I had a bar tab; unusual in pubs and not often done by the locals, I would run up a bar bill that I could not pay and then I would start bartering. Various items or stock would come up missing from one of my shops; the landlord of the pub would profit and my bar bill would diminish. One of pubs, The Pear Tree where I owed a fairly big bar bill, was in the process of redecorating the pub lounge. The pub owner's wife was looking at materials for some curtains. I had just received a large shipment of materials for my fabric shop. I asked her what color she favored. She hadn't made up her mind yet so I said I would bring her some samples. I took her about a half dozen different colors of some very expensive nylon and rayon materials, she picked out the colors she liked and I brought her plenty of material to make curtains, not only for the bar but for their apartment as well. My bar bill was cleared and I started another one. Later on without thinking, (I seldom did think) I took my boss to that pub one day for a game of darts. As we were enjoying our game and pints, he started to admire the lovely red curtains in the lounge. He said that material looked familiar, and asked if he had seen something similar in my shop. I said, "Hell man, we're in the north of England, where they make that material." He just ordered another round and looked puzzled.

Another way I would make money was betting on horse races with the local pub owner, although I was not too successful in this. My betting was mostly another excuse to leave the house to go to the pub to place my bets and continue to drink. I enjoyed betting on the steeplechase races, which were usually two or more miles over the jumps on turf. In England with a field of over twenty horses, they paid first, second, third and forth place as winning bets. I would bet what my brother Ross called "chicken bets"; this was across the board, or (win, place, show.) I could put down a two shilling each way bet for a total of six shillings (Around a dollar). Many times the long shot would finish in the money and with odds of anything from fifty to one to a hundred to one; I could pick up some good drinking money when I would win. As I said, however, I was not too good at this and usually lost my bets. The fun was having the kids and Joyce picks out their horses, you could bet as little as six pence each way for a total bet of about fifteen cents. I would spend the morning going over the horses racing history in the papers racing form, pick out my line-up then allow the family to pick theirs. Joyce and I noticed that Sheila, who would have been about four or five years old, was picking winners at an alarming rate. One Saturday while watching the races on TV, Joyce asked her what her secret to picking winners was. She just calmly and confidently said, "It's the one with the sheepskin nose band that always wins". It was amazing how often she was right and even today, when she picks out a winner while watching races with me, she still picks the ones with the white sheepskin nose band, and they often win. Gary, However, who was about six or seven years old, was the one who enjoyed it most watching my horse get beaten. One Saturday after I had placed our bets and came home to watch the races with the family (the pub closed at two in the afternoon), all the kids were watching for their horses to run. They do not use a starting gate with these cross-country races; they just have a tape across the track where the horses line up, when they are lined up, the tape goes up and "there off". Well I had a sure-fire winner in this five-mile, cross-country, steeplechase race, so I thought. When the tape went up the horses broke, my horse turned completely around and started running the wrong way around the track. I thought Gary would bust a gut; he rolled on the floor with laughter and kept laughing through the entire race, we still laugh about it today, even me.

At the other pub in the village, The White Horse, where I had another rather large tab, the landlord was pressuring me to pay the bill. I knew he and his brother, who owned a pub in another near by village, were fishermen. I asked him if he was interested in a life raft. He jumped at the idea. I found a raft that I had condemned for minor reasons and had not turned into supply yet. I faked the paper work and took the raft to him complete with a CO_2 bottle for him to inflate it with. I told him anytime he used it to give me the bottle and I would refill it for him. I was very popular in that village; I was even given the title of Honorary Mayor, and captain of the dart team. Unfortunately I shipped out owing one of the pub owners about a twenty pound bar bill, (approximately $56.00), but over the years I suppose he was really ahead.

Chapter Sixteen

Another crash recovery

While at Mildenhall, I was assigned to an aircraft tire shop that was also the reclamation and repair shop. We found a house in a village about three miles from the base. I purchased a bicycle from a shop near the pub where we had been staying and could make it from the house to my shop in about fifteen minutes.

I had only been on the base about two months. Early one morning as I was riding my bike to work, on a road that ran parallel with the runway. I heard this WB-50 from the weather squadron approaching the runway and as I watched there seemed to be something wrong. I stopped and got off my bike to get a better look. I realized he was coming in with wheels up. I couldn't believe what I was seeing. He just kept getting lower and lower, I knew he was going to crash. First I heard the props hit the runway, and then it looked like fireworks as the fuselage hit the concrete with fire bellowing out both sides and from behind. I got behind a large bush to avoid the blast but the darn thing just kept sliding down the runway until it came to a stop. Somehow it didn't catch on fire so I jumped on my bike and made my way to the shop as fast as I could. I knew this was going to be my first crash pick-up on this tour. I had been involved in several recoveries at my last base, but the biggest thing we had to deal was T-33s and once an old T-28 prop job, so I was prepared when I got to the shop and my NCOIC waiting for me in a pick-up. The rest of the crew had left already following the fire trucks out to the crash site.

The investigation was never made public to us, but as I had been working as a bartender at the NCO club since the first week I arrived, I got most of the story; some rumor some probably fact. The mission was routine, a tour around Alaska for weather check and back. One of the crew members I knew told me he was sitting right behind the pilot on takeoff when someone called out "fuel odor". It was normal procedure to return to base so they circled the base and approached the field. He said suddenly a very loud claxon horn sounded and the tower was trying to contact the air craft. He said the pilot was yelling "What's all that noise?" My friend told me when the flaps are lowered to a certain degree and the wheels are not down, the claxon sounds until the wheels are down. I don't know why the pilot never responded to the claxon or the warnings from the tower who had told him to go around, that his wheels were up. He could not have taken off again anyway, with the full load of fuel on board. Just why it never caught fire I'll never know, but I saw again just how lucky they were during the recovery operation we performed, after the fuel was off loaded, we had the task of getting the plane off the runway.

Another problem we encountered was this air craft was that it had been fitted with JATO (jet-assisted take off). This involved two large fuel tanks located on the outer end of each wing. After take off and the fuel was spent, these tanks were jettisoned by explosive bolts holding the tank to the wing. These were still armed and very dangerous, so our first task was to disarm the connecting bolts. This was a big aircraft, and flat on the concrete. We had to install four large flat rubber bags under each wing, and began to inflate them enough to get towing gear under the aircraft. I went under the aircraft to check the clearance and secure anything necessary when I saw where the skin under the aircraft was torn away exposing the main belly fuel tank, which held over 1,000 gallons of fuel. There was a pit cock that was bent to the point it was almost torn off, but did not break completely. If it had, there is no doubt a fuel leak it would have caused the plane to catch fire and all aboard would have been lost. The recovery work took the better part three days to get the plane off the runway so we could then begin the reclamation part.

Chapter Seventeen

The Christmas tree

After the first year in the crash recovery unit I was assigned as NCOIC of the parachute and fabric shops, this also included the survival shop where we tested and repaired life rafts, life vest, anti-exposure gear and anti-g suits. Our shop was set away from the other shops that were mostly in hangers, ours was two nice buildings on a large lot surrounded by some large pine trees and shrubbery. It was in December and fairly cold even for England, one day I was looking out of my office window admiring the nice green lawns and the pine trees, when I noticed an Englishman working in the yard, he was obviously one of the civil engineer workers, I had observed them working before and it was a base joke how slow they were on a job, milking every minute of the day, this gentleman was measuring off distances across the lawn for some unknown reason, he was digging a hole what appeared to be three or four inches across and about six or eight inches deep, he would carefully lay out a piece of tarpaulin, put his tool kit down on it, take out a small trowel type of tool, dig the hole and very carefully put the dirt into a neat pile, then inserted something in the hole and just as carefully filled in the hole again replacing the sod over the dirt so you couldn't tell he had disturbed the ground, then he would take out his measure, walk a short distance, some twenty or thirty feet then start the whole procedure again. I watched him for a while wondering what he was doing that took such precise work, as I watched it started to snow very lightly, suddenly I had an evil idea, one of my parachute riggers had an English friend who trimmed the tops off large pine trees each year and sold them as Christmas trees, the airman had acquired five or six of these trees for friends and had them stored in the survival shop, as I watched the worker in the yard it was coming up on ten a.m. "Tea-Time" as I looked out he had just finished a nice neat hole with the dirt mound next to it, he picked up his tool kit and tarpaulin and headed out for the café for his tea, knowing civil engineers I knew I had at least a ½ hour, I got the airman to pick out a tree that would fit snuggly in the hole, we then carefully picked up all the dirt, placing the tree in the hole, by now the snow was falling pretty heavy, lightly covering the grass. Well sure enough about a ½ later the worker came back to the area where he thought he was working, he walked around the area looking for the hole and the mound of dirt, he looked all around for about five minutes, walked back and forth then went back to where he made the last hole, looked back to where the hole should have been, shook his head, took out his measure and walked toward where the hole should have been, walking right up the tree we had placed there, looked back again to the last hole, in final disgust he threw his kit on the ground then his hat, then he stood upright as he heard our laughter coming out of the parachute shop, he realized, what ever was going on, those damn yanks had a hand in it; he headed straight toward the shop busting in the front door and with all the wrath he could muster gave us a good old tongue lashing, he would not even accept my apology, English humor !!!

Chapter Eighteen

A good assignment

After my second tour in England I finally got stationed in Florida. I had been trying to get stationed there ever since I had been in the service; I wanted to get back to my "big White City," Miami. I was assigned to MacDill AFB and was to work in the parachute and fabric shops. One of the airmen that had worked for me as a parachute rigger at my last base in England was stationed there and was assigned as my escort to the base. Since we had no place to live, Joyce and the kids stayed in a motel while this guy was supposed to be helping me find a place to live. We spent most of the time visiting bars or the NCO club; with no help from my escort we finally found a nice trailer in an upscale trailer park just outside the base. I was still a S/Sgt and level five; I had to be a seven level in order to be promoted to T/Sgt when I arrived there was no seven level assigned to the shop, so I thought this was my chance. After being there about three weeks, I was in the NCO club one night when the airman who had acted as my escort came into the club. He said, "You're not going to believe this, but come with me to the shop." The shop was about two blocks from the club. We went in and he showed me a large sign-in board and pointed to my name. I said, So what, I'm assigned to the parachute shop." He said, "Look closer at the top of the board." In great big letters it read ASSIGNMENTS FOR DAVIS MONTHAN AFB. I was being sent to Arizona! The next morning, I went straight to the hanger chief and said I wanted to see the old man. He said, Ok, but I can tell you he is in a bad mood this morning." I said, "Not half as bad as I am." The "old man" was a full colonel and wing commander. As it turned out his wife had kicked him out of the house and he had been sleeping in his office for the last few nights. I went into his office and reported to him. When he asked what I wanted I told him I had no desire to go to Arizona and asked permission to be relieved of the assignment. The Col. Said, "I'm taking these F-4's out there and I need parachute riggers and fabric men." I told the Colonel that this was the first time in over ten years I had the chance to make seven level and have the opportunity to make T/Sgt. He said, "Sgt. Simmons, if you will take one of those sewing machines out to Arizona, I will consider making you a seven level." I said, "Colonel, if you will give me the seven before we go I will fly that damn sewing machine out there." He glared at me and said, "I don't think you have much choice Sgt." I said, "I beg your pardon Colonel, but I think I have." (I had just learned from a friend who worked in personnel that my career field had came off the frozen list, meaning for the first time I could transfer out of it.) The colonel threw his hat across the room and yelled, "Get out of here!" When I walked out the hanger chief asked what the hell had happened in there. I said, "I think I just got fired, I believe I'll go look for another job."

I went straight from there to personnel and found my friend. I asked him if what he had told me was right about my career field being taken off the frozen list and if I could transfer to another field. He said sure, so I said put me in for anything you've got that is not in the survival or missal field. He said, "The 74 field is wide open now and they need people." I had no idea what it was and didn't care; I just wanted out of my field. He processed my papers and had them sent to the base commander for approval, that was Thursday. When I went back to the parachute shop the next day, my fellow workers could not believe what I had done. They said no one talks to the old man like that. I said, "Maybe it's time someone did".

My buddy from personnel called me that afternoon and told me to report to the Service Club on Monday at eight a.m. for briefing. I still had no idea what my job would be. When I got to the club that morning there was no one there except this nice looking young lady in some sort of a uniform I was not familiar with. Up until then I don't think I had set foot in a Service Club (they were not allowed to serve alcohol). This young lady asked if she could help me. I said, "I'm supposed to be here for a briefing." She said, "You must be Sgt. Simmons, I am the service club director, you are being assigned to work here with me." I could not believe what I was hearing. I had always heard the Service Club was for screw-ups and certain other types of people, but what the hell; I was out of the survival field and more important, I was not going to Arizona.

I came to like the job, as it had very little pressure and a lot of freedom, allowing me to pursue my drinking more freely. After all the years of packing parachutes and survival gear while half awake, if that, I felt I was lucky to get out without serious incidents. I suppose it was even luckier for those poor bastards that flew with the gear I had packed. I had a rather unpleasant event happen shortly after I started working at the club. I got a call from the base hospital to report to some doctor. When I got there I discovered he was a civilian psychiatrist. I wasn't too concerned at first, just puzzled. When I got to his office, there sat the most grotesquely overweight human I had ever seen, he weighed at least four hundred and seventy five pounds. I asked what he wanted with me. He had my records on his desk and told me he had the report concerning my hospitalization in England, when I had broken my shoulder and went into DT's while in the hospital. When he told me to sit down I saw him reach under his desk and I heard something click and then a whirring sound. I asked him if he was recording this meeting. He said it was procedure. I told him he could go to hell, and if he wanted to make a recording of himself to feel free but I had nothing more to say and refused to talk to him. After about a half-hour he turned his recorder off and told me to leave. I went straight to my new commander and discussed the matter with him. He asked me how I was doing with my drinking. I told him I had it well under control. I must have convinced him as I was due to re-enlist in two weeks and he said he would take care of things. I learned later that that damn quack, who as a civilian psychiatrist hired by the air force, had caused over a half dozen men to end their careers because of his investigations and reports, guess I lucked out again.

I got to be good friends with the Service Club director, Janet. We hit it off very well and she liked Joyce and my family. Janet was from Orlando; I told her how much I loved Miami and was anxious to return to my "White City". She asked how long it had been since I had been there and I told her not since 1950. She told me if I wanted to remember it as I knew it, I should not go back, as it had changed so much she felt I would be terribly disappointed. I took her advice and have never returned, I would rather remember it as I knew it. While working at the club I was able to take Joyce and the kids on several outings together with trips we scheduled for the service club. My oldest daughter Ann acted in a few plays we put on. Janet also allowed me to work spare time jobs to make extra money. At one time I was holding down four jobs at once. I would go to the Service Club from ten a.m. till six p.m., then go to the NCO Club to bartend from seven p.m. till one a.m. or so, then I had a janitorial job cleaning offices until around four a.m. then go home to get some sleep. On weekends I worked at the fishing camp on base where we had over twenty various size fishing boats, bait and fishing gear that we rented out, and to no one's surprise, we also sold beer. With these crazy hours, I went for weeks without seeing my kids and Joyce and I did not have what you might call much "quality" time together. I enjoyed my tour of duty at McDill as did Joyce and the kids. I was stationed at MacDill longer than any base I had been before, from 1963-1970. While I was stationed at MacDill there were several things that happened, some funny some not so funny. After my run in with my wing commander about going to Arizona and my getting assigned to the Service Club life got a lot better.

When we first moved into the trailer our youngest son Michael was around two years old. He was a wonderfully happy child and the apple of his mother's eye; however, he was constantly getting into something. He was not being bad or naughty, just curious. Every time Joyce would turn around he was into something else. Once we had just purchased a new couch and we were bringing in groceries from the commissary. We set the bags down and when we went to bring in more, Michael picked up a bottle of bleach and attempted to drink it, spilling it down his front all over the new couch. One of many trips to the emergency room at the base, he was constantly doing something that we had to take him to the hospital. Usually Joyce took him. One day I came in from work and Joyce was not home. I immediately called the emergency room and asked if they had a Michael Simmons there, they said they did so I said I'd be right there. When I arrived and asked to see him, it turned out to be an airman with the same name. Joyce and Michael were visiting a neighbor. Michael was a joy, but there were other times when he would just take our breath away. We had bought him a tricycle that he was very proud of and rode it all over the trailer park. One day he came in the trailer and told Joyce he was going to the commissary. She played along and thought nothing more of it, later a policeman came to the door and asked if this was her child. Joyce said, "Yes, why?" He said he found him on the road going to the base on his tricycle. She said, "Well, he did tell me he was going, I just never expected him to."

We were living in the trailer and I still had not gotten my drivers licenses back after losing it in a DWI in Texas. I found an old Vespa motor scooter on base for sale cheap. I learned in order to use it I needed to get an operating permit; I only had to pass a written test. I had my neighbor's wife take me down to the DMV office. I drank a few beers prior to going down, thinking no big deal, I'm not taking a driving test and no one would question me. When I got to the office I asked for the paperwork for the test, the patrolman asked me if I had been drinking. I said, "Yeah, but I'm not driving, so what's the harm?" He replied, "Look Sergeant, never mind driving, I should arrest you for walking in here in the first place, I suggest you go and sober up, then perhaps in a few days you may try again." For once I kept my mouth shut, asked our friend to take me back home. She laughed about it, but I did not see the humor. I did go back the following week, sober, and passed the test. I graduated from the scooter to a small motorcycle that I later wrecked coming home one night from the club and damn near killed myself. Finally I got my proper driving licenses back and started driving the car, while drinking of course; fortunately, I never got caught again driving while drinking.

133

An amusing event happened while we were living in the trailer park. One Thanksgiving Day our neighbor Audrey, who was a good friend of Joyce's, was cooking a turkey for their Thanksgiving dinner. She had placed about a twenty five-pound turkey in her oven early in the morning. As their family was going to be in church most of the morning she asked Joyce to keep an eye on her turkey. Her husband Ken was always open for a good joke, so he was in on this, although Audrey did not share his humor. Joyce had about half dozen Cornish Game hens, each about the size of a pigeon, which she was preparing for our dinner, as we were not that crazy about turkey. After Ken and Audrey left for church Joyce and I went into their trailer and exchanged Audrey's turkey for one of Joyce's Game hens. We placed the game hen in the same pan her turkey had been in. Then Joyce put Audrey's turkey in our oven to finish cooking it. Unfortunately we could not be in their trailer when they came back from church, but we were listening at our window as our trailers were next to each other we could hear Audrey scream. Her husband said the look on her face when she opened the oven door to check on her turkey was priceless; we still remained friends as long as we were there.

My own contribution to a similar event was at my expense. I had a friend of mine make me a bar-b-que pit out of a fifty-five gallon drum. I had a rotating spit on it, with a smokestack; I was the envy of the trailer park. One weekend I managed to get some time off and said I would cook dinner on my bar-b-que. I was not much into steaks, so I decided to try something new. I got a large goose from the commissary and fired up the bar-b-que. All was going fine until I guess I was into my second six pack of beer, not paying much attention to my goose. One of the children yelled to me, "Dad, your goose is on fire!" I had not realized how much grease there is in a goose; the fat had dripped down into the charcoals catching on fire. I had to get the garden hoses to put it out. Of course all of my neighbors in the trailer park had a field day with my bad luck. I was the talk of the base for weeks, every time I would walk into the club everyone would yell, "Hey Simmons, your goose is on fire".

While we were living at the trailer park Joyce's parents came to visit us. Her father was in awe of every thing in the states. He had visited Joyce's older sister first in California, but he really liked Florida, especially when we took him fishing. We also took him to Bush Gardens. I was a regular there. While working at the service club, we took tours there quite frequently. I used to also take the family there any weekend I had free. The children loved it; Joyce enjoyed the bird show and the grounds, and me? Hey, it was a brewery, free beer. The old gentleman who served the beer just stood there with the tap open while he passed one glass after another under the tap, then slid the glass of beer down the small bar to each person who was standing in a long line that just kept moving. I spent a lot of time in the line, the old man knew me almost by name, after seeing me there so often. He would just nod and slide me two glasses, as I would always take two at a time, as if I were getting one for me and one for someone else, drink both of them then get in line again. Yeah, he knew me well. Then one day during the week I called Joyce from my office and said to her, "Hey, how about taking your parents to Bush Gardens this afternoon?" as though it was a sudden inspiration. I didn't fool Joyce, but she agreed. I told my director I was taking my in-laws out for the day. She thought that was very nice of me, I didn't tell her where we were going. I loaded everyone in the car and we headed out to Bush Gardens. When we got there I naturally headed for my place in line. There was no line! I inquired from one of the attendants, who informed me it was Election Day, and no alcohol can be served in the state of Florida on Election Day. Joyce and her father had a good laugh about it; I had a miserable day at the park.

On my oldest son's eleventh birthday I took the day off. Without telling him what I was going to do, I called his school and talked to his teacher to ask for him to be excused from school that day while I took him out for his birthday. She agreed and I asked her not to say anything to him about it before I got there. I arrived at school around ten a.m. and had him paged to the front office where I asked him if he wanted to go fishing. He was totally surprised and delighted, as the teacher had not told him. When I loaded him on the back of my motorcycle and took him to the fish camp where I worked and took him out in one of our boats, he was thrilled more than I had ever seen him. I didn't think it was such a big deal myself; many years later, after he was married with children of his own, on my own birthday, I received a letter from him reminding me of the event. I would like to share with my readers the letter he sent to me on my birthday, I framed it and it hangs proudly on my office wall.

August 8 1994

Dad,

Of all the memories in my life as I was growing up there is one that stands out. Perhaps I could have shared it with you before but it's not clear to me why. On my eleventh birthday you picked me up from West Shore Elementary School on your motorcycle and took me fishing. The classmates were slack-jawed as you made your appearance in a military uniform and I was sprung from my teacher's wrath. I can still see them gathered by the second story window watching as we left. It was done in a grand fashion and I can tell you I earned a huge amount of respect that day. I had no idea what waited for us but I knew this was cool beyond my dreams. At the Fish Camp we boarded a humble boat that to me was a wonderful sturdy memory I would carry forever. As we loaded up what we needed I remember a tall crusty type of a man patted my head a bit harder than I would have liked and you stood up from the dock, seemingly taller than him, to let him know it bothered me. We didn't boat many fish that day and the tide took us beyond where we intended but I was with my dad on my birthday. The feeling of being so important that everything else in the world could wait, was by far the finest gift I will ever know.

My two sons have gained from this experience in my life and I thought it was time to let you know how that act of giving has carried on. A boy so small should not be answerable for all the problems in his life; this has helped me in my ways to make their life what it should be. That day in my memory is forever. Almost everything we do in life is insignificant, but it is necessary that we do them.

HAPPY BIRTHDAY DAD

Gary.

On one occasion at the club we had scheduled a bus tour to the coast, I believe it was St. Petersburg beach. When we made these tours I usually took my family. Joyce enjoyed these trips and usually came to the club to help Janet and me make up a picnic basket for all the people going on the tour. On this particular trip we had invited some visiting officers from Saudi Arabia. They were single officers stationed there for navigation training, they spoke English well and were excited about going to the coast, after all they were from Saudi and beaches are not so available to them (well, they do have the biggest beaches, just no water). When we got to the beach the water was beautiful, calm and warm. The beach at St. Petersburg has lovely white fine sand and you can walk a very long way out before you get into deep water, probably some one hundred yards or more. Well, these Arabs were like kids at Disneyland. They jumped and rolled in the water all day. Three or four of them decided to venture out into the deeper water. None of them could swim, so they just kept wading further out until they were almost out of sight. Suddenly they spotted a school of porpoise. They of course thought they were sharks. Well if anyone ever walked on water, these guys ran. They churned up the sea trying to get back to shore yelling. "Sharks!" all the way. After we explained to them what they were we all had a good laugh. Another time we made the mistake of taking them to "The Brown Bottle". This was the Schlitz brewery that had a courtesy room where they would invite guests from the base for a night of dining and dancing with live bands. It was very popular with the base personnel and we made the trip every month. I invited the Arab officers to one and the shock to them was when we started eating our dinners. We never took into consideration they were Moslems and they were serving ham for the main course and since it was a brewery, alcohol. Joyce and Jan the director of course were mortified and both apologized profusely. They offered to leave immediately but the officers refused, taking it all in stride and seemed to enjoy the music for the rest of the night. They thanked us for inviting them saying how much they enjoyed themselves.

One Sunday morning I had to go to work at the base marina and as usual had a bad hangover. I was not pleased when the guy running the marina told me I had to get one of the sixteen foot boats that has been in storage in the back of the marina ready for service. It was cold and the boat was under a bunch of trees and full of dead leaves. I threw my tool bag in the boat and started pulling the dead leaves out with my hands, suddenly I felt a sharp pain in my finger. I thought hell, a splinter, then I remembered this was a fiberglass boat, no splinters. I looked down in the bottom of the boat and there was a very large scorpion with his tail flipping around. Without thinking I grabbed my hammer and smashed it as hard as I could. Being in a fiberglass boat, this was not the smartest thing to do. I spent the most of the day repairing the hole I had made in the boat bottom, but the scorpion was dead. This was another one of the times I was drinking pretty heavily. I did almost anything to keep from taking money from the household funds. I was not working much at the clubs as bartender, so to help support my drinking one of the things I would do was to go to the big hospital in downtown Tampa and donate blood. They were giving I believe, twelve dollars for a pint of blood. I was surprised that they would take mine as much as I was drinking, but that didn't seem to matter to them. I made several trips for this with no ill effects. If there were any, they cleared up soon after I got back to the NCO club.

While we were living in the trailer park at Tampa Joyce and I were out driving around one week end and came upon a trailer sales lot, we went in to check out some of the units that Joyce had taken a fancy to. I had drunk the six-pack I had taken with me and was in the need of a drink but Joyce was not ready to leave until she had seen some more units. I caught the smell of whiskey on the salesman's breath, as it was not yet noon I figured this guy has a stash somewhere (drunks can sense these things). I asked to use to his bathroom. He showed me where it was and continued to talk to Joyce. When I got to the toilet I noticed an overhead storage area. I thought to myself, "That looks like a good place to stash a bottle." I got upon the stool to reach the overhead shelf, sure enough there was a fifth of Southern Comfort. I spent about ten or fifteen minutes in the toilet and helped myself to his whiskey. When I went back to join the salesman and Joyce he looked kind of suspiciously at me, but said nothing. We finished looking at his stock of trailers and went home telling him we might come back again and consider buying. We did go back the next weekend. Shortly after we got there I excused myself and went to his toilet again. I locked the door and went straight to his shelf to help myself to his bottle again but it was gone! I thought, what a rotten trick for him to move it. I went back and joined Joyce and him in the sales lot. He gave me the same strange look as before. We never bought his trailer, or went back again.

One day my name came up on the bulletin board in the squadron to report to the firing range to qualify on the M-16 rifle. I had tried several times to qualify with the old M-1 and other weapons and never could qualify. I was complaining about going to the firing range in the NCO club, when a friend of mine who was a regular at the marina, told me he was in charge of the range that week. I asked if he could help me out of a tough spot. He said it depended what I had to offer. I told him to meet me at the Marina the next day, Saturday. I opened the marina that day and he was one of my first customers. I managed to get him a case of beer and he told me to show up at the range on Monday afternoon. I just fired a few rounds to look as if I knew what I was doing. My friend later gave me the targets I was supposed to have taken my test on. I told him I didn't believe I had made all those bulls eyes. He said, "Are you going to question it?" Of course I said no, and took the targets and paper work to the orderly room. The First Sgt. was impressed; so was I when I was awarded a marksmanship medal, it was worth the price of a case of beer.

About two years after I was assigned to the service club a storm warning was announced, a large hurricane was due to hit that night. My officer called me to his office and told me that I needed to go to the base marina to help secure the boats. We had been through this before and learned the hard way that taking twenty-four fourteen-foot boats out of the water and securing them to the chain link fence was not the best way to secure them, and it would take too long. The guy in charge said it was best to pull the plug on the small boats and allow them to sink; they were still secured to the dock and would not blow all over the marina as they did the last storm. We were able to secure the larger boats in a large concrete building. After we secured the boats I reported back to my officer. He told me I would have to spend the night in the service club for security reasons. I asked permission to bring my family with me. He didn't think it was a good idea, that it may be unsafe. I said, "Major, my family is living in a trailer park a half mile from the base, you know as well as I do, they would be much safer in the club than they would be there." He finally agreed and gave me permission to bring them in. The storm was due to hit around midnight so I closed the club at six p.m. and Joyce brought the family in. The kids enjoyed it, Gary had the poolroom to himself and the others watched color T.V. while Joyce and I made some sandwiches and drinks. Around eight p.m. before the winds got too high, we walked a short distance over to the bay. It was weird, the bay was totally empty, and the tide had gone out farther than I had ever seen before. We expected there would be a flood on the base when the tide returned during the storm, but that never happened, it just looked strange. We went back to the club and watched T.V. until we lost power around eleven thirty p.m. We settled the kids in and made our own arrangements. The storm must have hit full force around two a.m. when a ping pong table I had stored against a wall by the ballroom dance floor blew over and woke everyone up. I thought the roof had blown off. It frightened the children, but they soon went back to sleep. We had a few hurricanes while we were there, the last one was not long before we left. We were living in base housing, half way between the NCO club and the base marina where I worked part time. The storm was due to hit in the night so the club director allowed me to take the night off to prepare for it, assigning one of the airmen to stay in the club during the storm. One of my neighbors, Al, and I had gone to the base civil engineers and picked up a bunch of burlap sacks to make sand bags out of, they were to be used to block the doors to keep the water out of our apartments. We were near the marina where we had a large beach, we went there to fill the sacks with sand. I had the largest car, an old 1954 Oldsmobile, and so we loaded the trunk up with all the sandbags and headed back to our quarters. We knew the rear end of the car was low and the front was high, we didn't realize just how high until at about twenty mph, I attempted to turn into our street, the car kept going straight, the front wheels were barely touching the ground. Al had to get out and push the front end of the car around while I drove. He steered from outside the rest of the way to our quarters, about six blocks away.

Anyone who has spent time in the military; and I'm sure similar events happen in civilian life, can appreciate an event I experienced at MacDill. I had been working at the service club for about five years when my director, Janet, said our coffee pot needed replacing and asked me to order a new one through supply channels. After thumbing through several supply catalogues I selected a thirty-cup stainless steel urn and placed an order for it. After about two weeks I checked with the supply clerk and was told it was on back order, I asked him to put a rush on it. After another two weeks it still had not arrived, I was getting impatient, as was my director; another call to supply received the same results. It had been over a month since I order the coffee pot when one morning an airman came into the service club asking for me. He wanted to know where I wanted the coffee pot located. I pointed to the kitchen area saying there of course. He said, "Perhaps you had better come out and have a look at what I am delivering." At the back door to the club he had a huge crate on a forklift. I asked what the hell he had, saying I never ordered anything that size. He handed me the paper work. I read the invoice; it was a thirty gallon, stainless steel coffee urn. I asked where in the world it came from and what was I supposed to do with one that large. Apparently, someone transposed some numbers. Clerks did not question the rational for the order, just shipped as the numbers indicated. The coffee urn was designed for use on a navy air craft carrier. I talked to my commander explaining what had happened, fortunately he saw the humor and had it returned to the navy. My director authorized me to go the Base Exchange to purchase a coffee pot. Later at the NCO club, I took a lot of ribbing over it, and the guy from supply came in one day and yelled to me across the club saying he had a backhoe for me to load my coffee pot with. I had seen a similar mix up with ordering supply's before, with numbers being transposed on an order. Once in the parachute shop I was working in on my first tour in England, one of the men in the parachute shop was told to order some rubber bands that we used in packing parachutes, we used a rubber band on each end of the strands of cords in packing a parachute; the rubber bands came in boxes of one hundred to a box, he was told to order one hundred boxes, the number he used ordered was one hundred gross, we still had plenty of rubber bands when I left two years later.

Another incident I thought at the time was hilarious, but ended as a sad event. There was a development company in Tampa that planned to build a large shopping mall about five or six miles from the base. The area was covered with hundreds of palm trees, the developer offered the trees for $1.00 each for anyone that would come and take them away. We had a base commander who most of us thought his actions at times were strange to say the least. This one proved to be even stranger. He offered to buy all the trees on the lot, and sent our civil engineers down with equipment to pull the trees up and trucks to haul them away. Now there was a happy developer, his land cleared and he probably made a few hundred bucks to boot. The plan was very impressive really; the commander wanted to plant the trees on each side of the road, stretching from gate one to the hospital, about a three-mile stretch that ran parallel with beautiful Tampa Bay. He wanted the trees placed about fifty feet apart. This was to improve the appearance of the base, which of course it did. The civil engineers pointed out to him however; palm trees take a lot of water to get them started, especially transplanted adult trees. He said no problem, and had them wrap each tree with burlap, bought miles of water hoses and had them wrapped around each tree with water dripping from the top. More trees were planted in various strategic points around the base, including in front of his office headquarters, with the same tender care. Now that was a lot of hoses, a lot of man hours for the engineers, but more important, that was using a lot of water pressure. MacDill had the last operating mess hall in the Air Force that was in the style of the old mess halls, as we knew them. It was to be preserved and kept intact for historical purpose. As fate would have it, the mess hall caught fire around midnight one night. The fire started out small, the fire department got there right away and hooked their hoses up to the hydrants, and they got a trickle that reached about two feet, no water pressure. By the time they got civil engineers to turn off the water to the commander's new palm trees, the mess hall had burned to the ground. Maybe I have a warped sense of humor, but I laughed about it.

Another time, the laugh was on me. I was closing up the NCO club and was in a hurry to get out to go to my other spare time job. After I had pulled my inventory on the bar I set all the barstools up for the cleaning crew, (it was in their contract). Not paying much attention to what I was doing, as I set one of the stools up it tipped over leaning on one of the beer taps forcing it open. It was a brand new keg that had only a few glasses out of it. By the time the cleaning crew got there it was empty, as soon as they saw what had happened they called the club manager and told him about it, of course I caught hell the next day from the club manager, who up until then had been a pretty good friend and drinking buddy of mine. The worst part was the rumor started by my fellow bartenders and waiters. The story was that I drank the entire keg then set the whole thing up, now I ask you, do I sound like the type of guy that would do something like that?

Chapter Nineteen

Burial detail

While stationed at MacDill AFB in Florida I was assigned to Special Services. I worked mainly in the service club, gymnasium, bowling alleys and other sports related areas. As part of our squadron's duties we were to serve as honor guards for funerals, body escort, prisoner escort, assist with USO shows, base functions, etc. Perhaps that is why it was called "Special Services". On one occasion a good friend of mine died after returning from Vietnam. He was sent home because he had cancer and lasted less than one year. I volunteered to be on the military burial detail as he was a good friend. We were in a team of twelve men, seven rifle bearers for the twenty-one gun salute, two as flag bearers, a bugler, a spare man in case someone fell ill and a M.Sgt. in charge of the detail to call orders. The M.Sgt was also a friend of mine and we both had worked with the deceased. It was sometime in July or August, and very hot and humid in Florida. We got on an old military bus, no air conditioning of course, and started about a two hour journey to the grave site. About half way to the gravesite the Sgt. in charge told the driver to pull into a small diner along a deserted road for coffee. We all trooped in and sat down at the counter. There was one black guy in our group. The guy behind the counter, a fat, unshaven seedy looking character, said in a voice loud enough for the other four or five customers to hear, "We don't serve blacks in here." We all looked at each other disbelieving what we heard in 1966. The black guy started to get up to leave when the M.Sgt stood up and put his hand on his shoulder, looked at the guy and said in a louder voice, "What did you say?" The guy behind the counter repeated, "We do not serve blacks in here." Without a word the Sgt pulled out his sidearm, a .38 revolver, and spun the cylinder. Holding the gun in plain view of everyone in the place and said in an even louder voice, "Say that one more time for every one to hear." The place went deadly silent. The guy picked up an empty cup in front of the black man and said, "Would you like cream and sugar with that sir?" We finished our drinks, the Sgt. Threw a five-dollar bill on the counter and we all walked out without another word and got back on the bus. At the gravesite two other incidents took place, one I was not proud to be a part of, the first was we were to stand prepared for the gun salute. The procedure is for the Sgt. to give us the orders: "attention", "present arms", "ready", "aim", "fire", "aim", "fire", "aim", "fire" then "order arms". Well I must have still been hung over or for some reason did not have my mind on the business at hand because after the first rounds were fired and he called "aim" the second time, I fired my weapon, prematurely. That had to be the loudest gun fire I have ever heard, but the team never missed a beat and went on to complete the orders in proper order, I felt like hell, to say the least. The bugler then played "Taps". As if that was not enough, when that part of the service was over the flag bearers proceeded to fold the flag and one of them took it to the gravesite to present it to the widow who was sitting in front of the grave. The poor guy got shook up I guess, and instead of presenting the flag, saluting, and saying, "The United States Air Force offers you it's condolences" he said, "The United States Air Force offers you it's congratulations". Realizing what he had done, he tried to regroup, stood at attention, apologized, stepped back to salute the widow, attempted to do an about face, and fell backward into the grave. This was not a good day, but I'll bet my friend who we had just buried had a good laugh about it all.

The prisoner escort was when a person was being held on an another base in the stockade, they would send a pair of NCOs to escort them back to our stockade, once another NCO and I was detailed as prisoner pickup, which meant picking up an AWOL who was imprisoned at another military facility, we were go to where they were and escort them back to our base, always in pairs. We had a guy from our base who had gone missing one time, they found his car with his shoes on the front seat, parked on the large Gandy Bridge between Tampa and St. Petersburg, they dragged the bay for him for about three days before giving him up for dead, about three months later he was picked up working on the docks in New Jersey, he was at an army post there in the stockade for us to pick up, another SSgt. And I got the detail, we had to report to the base commander for our orders, he instructed us to contact him personally if we encountered any problems, we reported to the Air Police to pick up our side arms before leaving, we were given four days to pick him up and return. When we got to Mcguire AFB my partner who was from Philadelphia asked if I minded if he went home to visit his family, I decided to spend the night in Atlantic City myself, we agreed to meet at the stockade the following afternoon, after making arrangements with the MP's I headed out for Atlantic City. When we picked the man up he was very accommodating, we explained to him that as long as he was in our custody we were required to have him in hand cuffs, except on the air craft, he said he expected that, the problem was he was over six feet tall and a pretty well built man, my partner was about five feet six, I was about three inches shorter, it was amusing to see me going through the air port with this guy on my arm, he laughed and said it looked like he was taking me in, except I had the side arm. As we boarded the air craft we turned our weapons over to the pilot as required, then sat back for the flight home uneventful, until we landed at Jacksonville, as we had no way of contacting the base at McDill I had made arrangements for the pilot to land there while I called ahead for transportation to meet us at Tampa air port, as our orders were not to spend time waiting around air ports any longer than necessary, the pilot kept the air craft running while I went to the terminal to find a pay phone and make the call, as I was instructed, I didn't have change so I called the base collect, when I asked the base operator to connect me to transportation, he said he was not allowed to take collect calls, I asked him to contact me with the base commander, he just laughed and said, "you must be kidding", I explained I was Sgt Simmons, on orders from the commander with a prisoner and was instructed to contact him, he said "I don't care if you are General Curtis Le'May, commander of SAC command , I'm not taking your collect call". I asked for his name and rank. I returned to the air craft; when we landed at Tampa I went to a local police officer in the terminal and explained our situation, he told us to wait in his patrol car with the prisoner while he contacted the base for me, our transportation finally showed up and we delivered the prisoner to the stockade and turned in our weapons. We then went to headquarters and reported to the base commander, "mission accomplished", when he asked if there were any problems, I told him about the base operator refusing my call to him, he saluted us and thanked us for a job well done, as I turned to leave, he said Sgt. Simmons, stop by the base telephone exchange and have that Sgt report to me, you've earned the pleasure, I am sure you will get from it. When I went into the exchange I asked for the Sgt I had spoken to, he was at the switchboard with a headset on, he looked up; he said, "Can I help you?" I said "yes, I'm General Curtis Le'May, take your head set off, the base commander wants a word with you", he looked a bit stunned; my partner laughed and said "you're wicked".

Once while I was stationed at Laredo there was one detail I am glad I was not selected for, it was a body escort. An airman had broken into a home near the base, raped and stabbed a fourteen year old girl, I knew the girl, as she was the daughter of a waitress at a bar I frequented, she was only fourteen, very attractive and could easily pass for eighteen or more, the airman thought he killed her, but the girl lived to identify him, he was arrested and placed in the stockade awaiting a general courts martial. Some how he managed to get out of his cell one Sunday night, stole a 38 revolver and escaped to downtown Laredo. Apparently when the local police attempted to arrest him he committed suicide with the gun he had stolen. As events turned out, there was a foul up in the paper work for his court martial and had been denied by headquarters in Washington, his status was changed to death while on duty, this made him eligible for a militarily funeral and an escort home to Louisiana, I met the guy who drew the detail at the NCO club later, he said he was also required to participate in the burial detail for the guy, he said he felt like a traitor.

Chapter Twenty

An untidy serviceman

On another occasion wile I was stationed at McDill I was assigned to go on duty as CQ which meant duty from five p.m. until seven a.m. the next morning, a duty no one held dear, I particularly didn't like it because it cut into my routine, as I was working other jobs after work it meant I could not bartend that night, or clean the offices I was doing at another job, but I guess mostly because it cut into my drinking time. I took off work from work early at the service club around two in the afternoon and spent a few hours at the NCO club before going home to change clothes prior to going on duty at headquarters to receive my orders of the day, The officer of the day gave me my briefing, telling me he had been flying all that day and intended to get some sleep that night and not to call him unless it was something I could not handle or something very important, I thought, you asshole, what do you think I've been doing all day, I did not have the option of sleeping, only the "officer of the day" had that privilege. Several things happened through out the night that interrupted his sleep though. First around ten p.m. an airman came in for an emergency leave, his father had just died, I could not approve it so I had to call the O.D. then around mid-night I got a call that a fire had broken out at the officers club, again I had to call him, then around two a.m. I got a call that there was an aircraft making an emergency landing, again I had to call him, on each occasion he

149

had to come into the headquarters office where I was to make out his report, by this time he was steamed, as he started to leave he turned to me and said I hope you can handle anything else that comes up Sgt. I said, "Captain, I have only called you on things that you had to deal with, I can't help it if you can't get any sleep, I can't even try," as he stormed out he said, "it had better be an emergency the next time you call me." Things got quiet, then around four fifteen a.m. I was reading a magazine and suddenly it seemed someone else was in the room, as I looked up there stood the most dirty, unshaven filthiest man I had ever seen, he was in fatigues with T/Sgt. Stripes, I said "what the hell are you supposed to be" he said very calmly, in a weak voice, " I need to talk to the commanding officer" I said "you had better talk to me first," he asked for a cigarette then started to talk in a very weak voice, he said "I am AWOL from my unit in Vietnam," I sat him down and got him some coffee and said "let me get this straight before I call that OD again," he said "I left my unit over a month ago, I caught several ships as a stowaway until I caught a tanker into Tampa then walked here and climbed through a hole in your fence, I am very tired and want to turn myself in." I picked up the phone and called the OD, when I identified myself to him he hit the roof and started to chew me out, I interrupted him saying, "you had better get down here before I call the base commander, which I am about to do, as I have a situation that he needs to be notified about and I think it would be in your best interest to be here when he arrives," he asked me what it was about, I told him he would find out when he got here, I could not discuss it over the phone, I hung up and called the base commander, telling him I had an urgent matter that required his immediate attention. The O.D made it to the office in about ten minutes and was still being briefed by me when the base commander came in; the OD was much more civil to me for the rest of the tour.

Chapter Twenty-One

Not all TDYs are good

While stationed at MacDill I was sent TDY to the Dominican Republic, it was in 1966 when there was an uprising against the president of the county who was assassinated by a rebel group. There were some American servicemen stationed there with dependents as well as American civilian guests in the city. The U.S sent the Army and Marines to evacuate them, I was sent as a recreation specialist, to entertain the troops mostly by showing movies and anything else I could dream up, the Army and Marines were stationed near the city of Santa Dominica while we were stationed at the far end of the island at a place called San Isadora, there were no building and we were put in large tents with about twenty men per tent, most of the shooting was over by the time we got there but there were still pockets of rebels we were warned to be on the look out for. At least once a week and sometimes more often we had to take the MSR (military supply route) in to the main city, early in the evacuation, just before I got there the rebels had changed the MSR route sign, directing three GI's in a jeep into a trap and one of the soldiers was killed, the rebels would not release his body and it took the army nearly a week of debating before they released his body. When we were shipped over there we were issued what was then the new military rifles, the M-16's with three clips of ammo. One of the stupidest orders I ever heard given was when we were going into town we were told if we armed the weapons we could be court marshaled, so we carried the weapon on our shoulder with the clips in our pocked, on about my third or fourth trip into town for supplies there was the driver, a 1st lt. riding shotgun, and two of us in the back of the open truck, there was a lot of tension around the city and the supply officer told us to keep our eyes open on the way back. About half way through the city on some very narrow crooked streets I was watching in every direction, when I looked up toward some of the little balconies over looking the street, there was this guy with what looked like a wine bottle in his hand and it seemed he was poking a rag into it, the first thing I thought of was a Molotov Cocktail, I pulled a clip out of my pocket and loaded the weapon, the other guy saw what I was doing and asked if he should load as well, I said not unless I have to fire, we were soon around the corner and on the way back to the base, when we arrived I jumped off and started toward the Lt. to explain what had happened as he got out of the truck , as I did I cleared my weapon ejecting a shell, he asked why I had armed my weapon, I told him I thought he was about to get a wine bottle full of gasoline down the back of his neck, he took me to the commander, I explained the situation to the Col. and he said I should have checked with the Lt. first, but he understood my position and said he would not take action but in future, check with the officer.

Although I was sent over there as a recreation specialist there was little I could offer in the way of entertainment outside of showing movies, however I was sent over with a rather large inventory of various equipment, in my supply room I had all sorts of equipment for base ball, soft ball, archery, fishing gear, golf clubs, tennis rackets and lots of other things that we had no use for, as there was no facilities to use any of these things in my shop on the area we were stationed, I even tried to set up an archery range with some bales of hay I had managed to get from the locals, but the commanding office was afraid some one would get drunk and shoot somebody, good thought, so being the entrepreneur I always have been, and knowing all the supplies and equipment I had shipped over was expendable, as we were under field conditions there was no way to turn damaged or surplus equipment back in, it was just to be disposed of more or less at my discretion . Now all of these guys were going to go back to their bases where they could use, say tennis racket, fishing gear, and a lot of the personnel equipment in my shop, also some of these guys were flying back and forth from our base to the naval base in Puerto Rico, where they could get me lots of that famous 150 proof rum, that stuff damn near killed me while I was there, but it did serve as a good medication when I injured my back.

The movie projector I was using I think was the first one ever made. It kept breaking down in the middle of a movie and I was getting a lot of flack from the troops, they were throwing beer cans at my projection booth and I got fed up with it, I went to the Col. and told him I needed another one, he made arrangement with the navy that had a ship anchored in Porto Rico and made arrangement for me to borrow one from them. I went over on a helicopter to pick it up, needless to say drinking was our main pass time and I had a belly full of beer when we left, one of the crew members managed to get a case of 150 proof Jamaican rum while we were there and we sampled it on the way back, as we were landing, I needed to get to a toilet in a hurry, I had the projector in my arms sitting in the doorway, when I thought we had landed, we hadn't, and I jumped out, just as gust of wind took us upward as I disembarked, what I thought was a few feet turned out to be a lot more so I landed with the projector and really screwed up my back, we did not have any medical facilities and I sure wasn't going to tell my boss what had happened as I was half snozzeled, I asked the crew members not to mention it, that I would take care of it, well the rough terrain around the camp didn't help and my back got worse, after about three days I could not get out of bed, the 1st Sgt. (he was the same MSgt that had been in charge of the burial detail I was in while at MacDill), came in my tent to see what was wrong, I just told him I had slipped on the rocks and twisted my back, I was about two weeks from rotating so he had me air evacuated back to the states. When I arrived in the states I landed at Fayetteville North Carolina, some Captain took me to an orderly room and asked why I was there and I explained I had been air-vaced out and he said there were no flights out for at least two days and he thought I should go to the hospital, well as much as I had been drinking, especially that damn rum, was afraid if I went to the hospital or spent even the night there, there was a good chance

I would go into D.T's. I asked permission to make a few phone calls and he said ok, first I called the Grey Hound bus station and asked if I could travel in fatigues, as I had no civilian clothes, he said he had no problem with that, then I told him I was carrying a weapon and he said as long I put it in with the luggage under the bus it was ok, just not to bring it on the bus, then I told the officer I would rather go to my base to get medical treatment and I could make my own way as I had made arrangements with Greyhound, he seemed relieved to get rid of me so he agreed, I caught a cab into town and got a room and ordered a six pack of beer to the room to "get better" with. I called Joyce and told her when I would get into Tampa so she could meet me at the bus station, I had managed to get a pint of whiskey to take on the bus with me to keep me going, when I arrived in Tampa I was in a good deal of pain but the whiskey helped, I got off the bus and the driver got my bag and weapon out of the bus for me, I thought nothing of walking into the station in fatigues with a weapon on my shoulder, but the local police had a different point of view, all of the sudden these two police officers were approaching me with great caution, and their hands on their pistols, one of them said very calmly, "hand me the weapon," I hesitated for a moment, give up my weapon, that is not what they trained me to do, but this guy looked serious and there were two of them, both armed and after all they were police officers so I handed it to him, the other one took my arm and said come with us, he took me to their patrol car, put me in the back seat, and my bag and weapon in the trunk and started off, talking as if I was not there one says to the other "he's probably AWOL from some base", I said "what the hell are you talking about, here are my orders," the officer that was driving pulled over and said "let me see them, I know something about military orders," he looked them over and told the other guy that they seemed legitimate, then asked me what I was doing here and I explained the whole situation, he seemed to understand and said he would take me to the base, I told him my wife was back at the station wondering where I was, so he agreed to take me back and talk to Joyce, in the mean time Joyce had arrived at the station and could not find me so she went to the information window and asked if anyone had seen me, and the guy asked if I was in fatigues, she said yes, he was returning from The

Dominican Republic, he said the police had taken me away, she said "why" and he asked why was he carrying a gun? She said "because they were shooting at him" by then I had arrived with the police and they talked to Joyce and she explained, I asked the officer if it would ease his mind if I called my First Sergeant to confirm my situation, he said that would be a good idea, I got the Sgt. On the phone and asked him to confirm it, he did and all was well.

Chapter Twenty-Two

A trip to the Far East

About two years after my trip to the Dominican Republic, I was enjoying my tour at MacDill when I was sent TDY again, this time to Japan and Korea, it was March 1968 when the North Koreans captured the USS Pueblo, we were rushed off and had very little time to prepare for anything, Joyce packed my duffel bag while I was getting my shots, I managed to take a brief case with me for my order and of course a fifth of whiskey, I always carried one with me when I flew, it was not that I was afraid of flying, I was afraid of flying sober, in any case I had my crutch and we boarded a civilian plane for San Francisco, I didn't realize just how much of a hurry we were in until when we landed in San Francisco, I headed for the nearest toilet so I could drink some more "nerve" when I came out everyone had gone, I asked someone at a desk where they had gone and they told me the group was at gate # something, and was about to depart, I ran to the gate and they were pulling the boarding ramp away, I ran up the ramp as they were closing the door and actually jumped aboard, I found out later had I missed that plane I would have been in serous trouble for missing a troop shipment, it was a long flight to Tokyo international and when we got there I headed again for a toilet for another break, when I returned the group I came with was standing in the middle of the air port wondering where to go, we were of course in fatigues and pretty obvious, there had been an officer on board and no one knew what happened to him, finally some Captain came over and asked where we were going and none of us knew, he asked who was in charge and we just looked at each other and said we did not know, there was myself and two other SSgt's. The Captain asked each of us our date of rank, I had the most time in grade, he said you are in charge of getting these troops to Itazoki, (sp) he called the nearest base and arrange transportation to the base and I managed to get us a flight that night, it was all very hectic, as President Johnson had ordered all available military from around the world to Japan and Korea, I met people there from Germany, England, France, Saudi Arabia, Alaska, all over the states and god knows where else, it was the biggest show of power I guess since WW-2, I suppose it was to intimidate the North Koreans that was holding our ship, it finally worked, and we got the boat back after a few months. While I was in Japan awaiting what our fate was, my back was killing me and I got to where I could hardly walk and the booze was not working very well, there were troops everywhere I looked. The lines at the chow halls were wrapped around each one I approached, the NCO club was packed to where it was impossible to find a place to sit, I had to elbow my way to the bar, the living quarters were the same, double bunks everywhere all crammed up against each other, the only time I had seen more men bunked together was on that damn troop ship I first went to England in 1951. And no one had any duties assigned, we were just to report to a certain place each morning for head count, no one was allowed off base, but I'm sure there were those that found there way to town, GI's are just that way, I had no interest in leaving my comfort zone, booze was plentiful, I think beer was fifteen cents a can, whiskey was about ninety cents for a forty ounce bottle, why would I want to go to town? To get mixed up with some sleazy women, get mugged or worse, wind up sober. Then we got orders we were going on to Korea, when I got up the next morning I had to get another guy to help me to the hospital, when I got in to see the doctor he took one look at me and said " oh another one trying to get out of the shipment huh? I tried to explain my situation but he refused to listen so I was put on a plane and sent to Osan Korea, we landed there in the middle of the night and it seemed every damn GI in the service was there, we were housed in tents, anyone who has been to Korea knows how cold it can be in March there, I had never been so cold in my life, after two days I was in such pain I could hardly walk, another guy helped me to the hospital and after the doctor examined me he asked what the hell I was doing there, I explained about the doctor in Japan, this Dr. was a full Colonel, where the other was a Captain, the Colonel got on the phone and gave the other Dr. hell for sending me there, he said I should have sent back to the states, as it turned out, that was not an option at this time, given the military situation, so he gave me some Valium to kill the pain, I already had some pain killer called Daravin I was given at MacDill before I left, it's a wonder I didn't kill myself, as I was taking both of these pain pills alternately and washing them down with beer or whiskey, but my back sure didn't hurt, or if it did, I didn't care, hell I don't think my dandruff was even falling, I was just floating around the base. The Doctor did however move me out of the tent and had me put in a barracks and had the civil engineers give me a sheet of ply-wood to put under my mattress, that helped a lot, between his medicine, the engineers help and the bartender at the club, I was starting to enjoy my tour, although I did miss Joyce and the kid's very much. One of the things that helped break the monotony, I was assigned to travel to other bases with a USO show, I had experience as an emcee and was glad to get away from the base and see some of the country, although most of our travel was at night, they put on some good shows the G.I's were grateful for the entertainment and expressed their gratitude by plying us with booze, not wanting to offend my hosts, I gladly obliged, accepting their hospitality.

I'll always remember going to the NCO club there, they served good food, but best of all they had oysters on the half shell for about a dollar fifty cents for a ½ dozen, I loved oysters and cold beer, both were plentiful, I used to get this same little waitress each time I went in, which was often, I kept ordering the oysters and beer, finally one night she said "you eat too many oyster's you go bong-bong," after giving me a rather graphic demonstration of what "Bong-Bong" meant, we had a good laugh and every time she saw me coming in she laughed and called me Sgt. Bong-Bong, you want more oysters?? Of course I said yes.

I was there about four months and they had got out ship back, so they started shipping us back, again it was a long flight back to the states, I first landed at Seattle Washington and spent two days there before I caught a plane back to MacDill.

I met a civilian on the plane who I really felt sorry for, he was sitting next to me and scared to death of flying, he was an engineer who had moved to Japan with his wife at the end of WW-ll and had not been back to the states since, every time the plane hit a small air pocket and bounced a little he would grab my arm and ask "what was that" I kept explaining everything was alright, but he would not have it, he said when "I get off this thing I'll never get on another," I asked him where he was going to when he got to MacDill? He said he was going upstate New York, when I asked how he planned on getting there, he said "I'm going to buy or rent a car and drive," I asked how long it had been since he had driven in the states, he said "before the war, in 1940, but I have driven some in Japan." I reminded him they drive on left hand side there, and they did not have the freeway system we had, he said I don't give a damn, I'll not get on another plane, I hope he made it out of Florida, let alone to upstate New York.

When I went through the airport at Seoul I found a small fishing pole with a rod and reel that was just the right size for Michael our youngest son who loved to go fishing, he was thrilled to death with it and could not wait to try it out, so that week-end we took him to Gandy Bridge near St. Petersburg where a lot of people fished from the bridge, Mike got baited up and cast his line out over the bridge about fifty feet above the water, unfortunately, he let go of the rod and it went sailing out into the bay; a bunch of fishermen attempted to retrieve it for him but it was lost, Mike never cried, just looked very disappointed.

In may 1970 my first Sgt. called me in the orderly room and said I had been selected for a shipment to England, I told him I had already been to England twice, he said he knew that and he also knew I had eighteen years in, I was eligible to retire in two years, however, they needed someone with my skills now and I had the option to reenlist and serve another four year term or I could decline and would be forced to retire in two years unless I made

TSgt. Joyce and I talked it over, we both liked it in Tampa, but she said she would like to go back home again, I realized I would have the opportunity to make Tsgt there, now that I had passed my seven level test and was eligible for promotion, but there were no openings at MacDill and no likelihood of ever being one anytime soon. So we decided it would be for the best, and the way I was abusing alcohol it was probably time for me to make the geographical change again, perhaps this time it would work, I hoped for the sake of Joyce and the kids, it would; if not for me. As most drinkers, I was going to have the geographical cure as we would always say. The last base was the worst and the next is going to be the best. Believe me, it doesn't work.

Chapter Twenty-Three

Third tour to England

In June 1970 I arrived at Bentwaters RAF Station in southern England. It was the first time we had a moved in decent weather; all of our other moves were in the winter. I started the tour off on the wrong foot. I was having a bad time with my drinking and had not had a chance to go anywhere I could get something to drink yet. The guy that was my escort to the base picked us up, I found out he was also my NCOIC. The first thing I had to do was sign in and fill out some forms. I was shaking so bad I could not sign my name, let alone fill out the forms. I told the guy I would fill them out later. I finally found the NCO club and "got well", from there I was able to take care of my self and I got back to the Quonset hut, temporary housing where we were staying while looking for a place to stay. I got there around three in the afternoon. Joyce and the kids were suffering from jet lag and we went to bed. We were awakened by a whole bunch of kids outside our hut making a lot of noise. I looked at the clock and it was six forty five. I jumped out of bed and ran out of the hut yelling at the kids. I said, "What do you think you are doing at seven o'clock in the morning making all this racket?" One of the mothers came over to me and said, "It's seven p.m. Sgt, what's your problem?" I apologized and went back into the hut to go back to sleep. I managed to get booze when I needed it and by this time I was a master at covering up.

We had no place to live as yet; the way we got concurrent travel in the first place was a friend of ours that was stationed with us at MacDill. He had a friend or relative who owned a pub in Ipswich, a town about ten miles from the base. They had the owner give us his address, saying he had quarters for us, this was not true. We told him we would find our own place when we got there, we just needed the statement and address for paper work, it worked and we got concurrent travel. When we arrived we already had a story made up about the pub owner having a heart attack and not being able to take us in. One of the civilians who worked in the gym where I was assigned said he had a friend who owned a pub in Framlingham, this was only about 5 miles from the base. He took us to meet the gentleman. The pub owner was of course thrilled at the idea of having yanks as paying tenants and said he would put us up until we found a house, which we thought would be a couple of weeks at the most. It turned out to be over four months. We also found a few other families in the same situation we were in and got them rooms, filling up the landlord's pub. He was very grateful and I got a lot of free booze from him, I made arrangements with him to leave me a bottle of gin or vodka available for me to get to in the mornings before I went to work, to stop my shakes. Joyce thought I was getting up early for work to go down stairs to have tea and scones before going to work, I was having the tea all right, but with vodka instead of scones. We were making good money from the per-diem we drew and Joyce was a master at controlling the money. We finally found a nice large house in a small village even closer to the base. It was a big old Tudor house called the "Black & White Cottage".

Joyce had done wonders at furnishing it with carpets and curtains. Our household goods were tied up in a dock strike and we had to go the base where they would lend families items they needed until their household goods arrived. They gave us a blanket each that you could read a paper through, a mattress each not much thicker, and a few utensils. The local preacher came to visit us and when he saw the state we were living in he was shocked. We explained that our furniture was tied up in the dock strike that had been going on for nearly 6 months. He clasped his hands together and said, "Father, please let these people's household goods be delivered." Finally they arrived the next week and we got settled in.

Black & White Cottage

Easton was a very small village with a church, a small post office that was also the local grocery store and not more than a few dozen homes. There were less than 400 people in the whole village, no police, and a PUB, just across the street from the house. I spent almost as much time there as I did at home. Well, being on the dart team, I had to make an appearance didn't I? One night when I was at the pub, I was playing darts with one of my newfound mates when he asked what kind of car I was driving. I said was driving a little old Austin I had gotten when we first arrived at Bentwaters. He asked if I was familiar with the Volvo. I said yes, they were very nice cars. He said he had one across the street he would sell me for twenty-five pounds (about sixty dollars). I asked if it was stolen or wrecked, he said neither, and it ran great. I thought it would be nice for us to have two cars, so Joyce could have her own. I was also fairly drunk when we went across the street to his house, the car was sitting in his front yard and it was very dark. Since we did not have streetlights in Easton, he brought out a flashlight (that was so dim you needed to strike a match to see if it was on). We looked around inside and out. It looked good to me, and the engine sounded fine as well. I went over to our house, which was only two doors down the street, and talked Joyce into letting me buy it without her seeing it. She liked the idea of having her own car. I told the guy I would take it home the next morning and paid him the money for it. When I went to get it the next day, I realized just how drunk I must have been. The car looked like it had been hand painted with a brush with the most horrible green paint I've ever seen. The doors and fenders had been badly dented, pounded out with a hammer and some kind of "Bondo" smeared over where the dents had been, then painted over, by hand. I was too ashamed to ask the man for my money back. I told Joyce it would make a good "work car" for me. She just shook he head and told me I deserved what I had gotten. I did drive it a few times to work and it did run pretty good, but every time I slammed the door to get it to close, a lump of the Bondo would fall off. Joyce would not ride in it as she thought it was unsafe, even for a Volvo. I tried a couple of times to sell it to some guys at the base, but they just laughed at me. I finally gave it to my daughter's boy friend before they were married. He thought I was a great guy, I thought he was a big as a sucker as I was, even if it was free.

Things went pretty well at work without anymore incidents that were noteworthy, for a while anyway, then about mid December my officer, a very young 1st. Lt. called me in and said he needed to send me TDY to Saudi Arabia. I of course challenged him on his choice, and told him so. I reminded him he had another S/Sgt in the same job as me, who was single. I had fifteen years in grade, eighteen years in the service, and this guy had less than 10 years in the service. He replied, "Yes Sgt. Simmons, but he is black, and they do not allow blacks in the country there," I remembered my brother Simon telling me when he was there in the early 60's this was a fact, and he had to wear civilian clothes as well. With all my arguments the Lt. would not back down, so Christmas Eve of 1970 Joyce and I was sitting in the American embassy in London getting my passport. I left shortly after that. I of course knew of the Moslem laws about no drinking of any kind of alcohol, so I thought this is going to be one hell of an assignment. Aboard the plane from London I figured I better make the most of it and I did, until I ordered another drink and the stewardess told me we were in Saudi air space and no alcohol could be served, and said she didn't think I needed anymore anyway.

When I arrived at the base at Dharan near Riyadh, I stumbled off the plane and was met by my escort. I thought I was seeing things, he was the blackest T/Sgt. I have ever seen. I said, "What the hell are you doing here? I was told they didn't allow blacks in this country." He laughed and said, "Is that what they told you? Boy, they are way out of date or someone pulled a slick one on you." He said that was true back in the fifty's and sixty's, but look what you have here, and there are plenty more of us here, then he laughed, picked up my bags and said, "Come on, I'll take you to your quarters."

I now realized what that damn 1st Lt. had done, he was sending me there to dry out; and boy did I have the last laugh. It is true you cannot drink in Saudi Arabia, however this was a U.S. military installation and not subject to those rules, but some very strict military rules. I was given my briefing the next morning where I learned why the guys in the barracks had all that booze the night before. I was told we had a ration of beer and whiskey (very liberal I learned). There was no canned beer, only bottles. NCO's were allowed either two cases of beer plus one bottle of whiskey every two weeks, or one case of beer and two bottles of whiskey, or various other mixes of the rations. In any case, there was no shortage of booze. There were regulations that went with the rations, if you were picked up off base by the local police, with any kind of alcohol, or drunk or especially driving drunk, you were on your own. The U.S government would do nothing to help you. This was a firm and fast rule for all base personnel, you would be turned over to the Saudi officials and most certainly go to jail. The rations were distributed in the barracks where I was living, the Khobar Towers. (This is the same building that was blown up by terrorists in 1996, my room was on the sixth floor, third room from right)

The rule was you had to bring in your empty bottles in order to get replacements. All bottles were accounted for. This was to make sure none got off base. There was a detail twice a week to destroy the bottles. In the basement of our barracks was a rock crusher. This was a huge machine that was actually for crushing rocks. Around three in the morning, two or three guys would go to the basement and throw the bottles in the crusher. They came out like sand, which it actually was, the "sand" was packed in large containers, loaded on a helicopter, taken out over the desert and scattered. The joke was not to go hiking barefooted in the desert.

The way we got the booze in was by helicopter that flew in from an aircraft carrier out in the Red Sea off the coast of Saudi. The local government had no problem with this, as long as it was kept on base. I enjoyed my tour in Saudi, except for the heat. I was sent there to inventory all recreation equipment throughout the country. Most of the military there was Army Communications and there were about 12 different locations. Some had only a dozen or less people stationed at the camps. My favorite trip was to Jeddah, a beautiful city on the coast of the Red Sea. I was well received everywhere I went. One reason for this was that in course of my inventory, I discovered some fifty or sixty kits for re-covering pool tables, complete with instructions on how to use the kits. I practiced on one in our own outfit and it worked out so well the Major I worked for had me take a large supply of materials with me to the sites I visited. There were pool tables at each of these sites and were all in bad need of repair. There were no locals that knew how to repair a pool table, apparently a game of pool is not in their culture. I was welcomed and treated very well, and in addition I was getting paid for each table I re-covered, I got very good at the job and took my skills back too England with me and continued this lucrative trade for the rest of my tour there.

Some of the things I found during my inventory were strange and some down right funny. In one supply room that had not been open for over a year, I found all sorts of items that just did not belong in this country. There were about thirty sets of brand new golf clubs (one hell of a sand trap), fishing rods and reels, tennis rackets, and bowling balls (we did not have a bowling alley). The most bizarre thing was forty unopened cases of softball gloves with twenty-four gloves per case. That was strange enough, but all of them were gloves for a left handed player. No one could explain this foul up so I went digging into past supply records and found that someone had used a reoccurring code when they ordered the initial items that should have been a one time issue. This was when they were using the old IBM punch cards for ordering items from supply. Computers do not question the order, they just send out what is on the card. Until I got there, no one knew how to stop the shipments, so they just kept warehousing them. The Major I worked for was very pleased with my work and gave me an outstanding report. There were numerous accounts like this all over the country at the bases that I visited. At a small base I flew into, there were only about twenty or thirty G.I.s there and it was even further out in the desert than we were at Dharan. Behind a building that had been used as an officers club, I found a 22-ft. fishing boat with a 45hp. Mercury motor under an old rotting canvas tarp. It looked as if it had never been used, and from the shape of it, never would be. One of the Arab civilian employees who worked for us in our library had a brother who worked with ARAMCO, a large oil company just a few miles from our base. He invited me to his house one evening for supper. I was amazed when we drove into the complex where the employees' housing was. This place was only about 15 miles from Riyadh, the capitol. It was in the middle of the desert; as soon as we went through the gates there were beautiful green grass lawns in front of these lovely big homes. I asked how they could grow grass In the middle of a desert. He calmly said if your water the ground, the grass will grow. My officer told me he was just as amazed when he first saw it. While talking to my friend's brother I learned that they had a gymnasium there for the employees, which included a lot of Americans, English, Irish and Italians, but they were having a hard time getting sporting equipment for their sports. I said I would have a word with my officer and see what I could do for them. The Major realized we had all this surplus equipment we would never use, so as a goodwill gesture he permitted me to let them have some of the basket balls, soccer balls, golf, soft ball, base ball and tennis equipment. I made points and benefited by getting a good supply of sadiki. This was a type of wine they made in their homes, similar to our home brew. I suppose they were not all practicing Moslems, and they did as we did, kept it on their compound. After I retired from the air force and was working at McClellan AFB, I answered a job announcement from their company about employment as a recreation specialist. They did not have an opening in Saudi Arabia at the time, but there was an opening in Iran. Although it was a very attractive offer, I declined. This was just before the Americans were taken captive by a rebel group.

I finished my TDY and went back to my base in England, where my first meeting was with a certain 1st Lt.

Chapter Twenty-Four

Vengeance is sweet

My trip back from Saudi was similar to my trip over. I met a gentleman on the plane who was apparently an executive from ARAMCO. He took a liking to me for some reason and invited me to join him in a drink. He was buying, so I went along. After several rounds, all on him, he said there was no need to wear the poor stewardess out, so he told her to bring us two bottles of Jack Daniels, one each. That got us to London and when we arrived, we were both feeling pretty good. He was on his way to the states and he went to meet his plane. Before he left he gave me his bottle and told me to keep them both and have a good trip home. I was at the airport in London without a clue as to how to get home to Easton, about 60 or 70 miles. I didn't know at the time how far it was. I found a cab driver and explained my situation and asked him how much he would charge to take me home. I cannot remember how much he said, but when I said I would throw in one of the bottles for him, he altered the fare. I gave him the one with the least in it and we proceeded to Easton, we both finished our bottles on the way. I didn't report back to work until Monday, where I immediately headed for the Lt.'s office. He was a young officer who didn't look old enough to shave yet, so my endearing title for him when ever I referred to him was "that little fuzzy faced bastard". When he saw me coming he made some fake gesture of welcome. I just blurted out, "What the hell did you send me over there for?" He came up with some lame excuse that he had been told I was the only one available to go. Rather than go off on him, risking becoming insubordinate, I laid a heavy guilt trip on him. I told him what a hardship he had caused my wife by leaving her there with four young kids in school and having to drive them in the snow to school with very little driving experience. He swallowed it hook line and sinker. I made him feel so guilty he offered to give me some extra time off. I refused and made plans to make his life miserable for the rest of my tour. I played many tricks on him, as he was so gullible. He came to dislike me as much as I did him. Once he had me make a sign for some reason. When I laid out the stencil I had reversed the "s" without noticing it. When he saw it he said, "Can't you do anything right? Look at that "s" it's backwards." Without missing a beat I said, "I did that on purpose to draw attention to the sign. It's and old advertising ploy." He said, "That's the dumbest thing I ever heard of." I said, "It got your attention didn't it?" He walked off without saying any more. Another time, he sent me into town to pick up something from the hardware store. There were two towns near us; Woodbridge in one direction and Wickam Market in the other. Small English villages have what is known as ½ day once a week, this means all shops are closed in the afternoon. Well, as it so happened, I knew I could get what I needed on base so I spent the most of the day in the NCO club. When I finally got back to the office around 4:00pm he asked where I had been. I said, "You sent me into Woodbridge for supplies didn't you?" He said, "Sgt. Simmons, it is ½ day in Woodbridge." Again, with out missing a beat, I said, "Yeah. I found out when I got there so I had to spend half the day going to Wickam Market looking for your damn stuff. He shook his head and said, "You always have an answer don't you?"

One of the best ones I got him on was a time he thought I had too much time on my hands so he decided to give me a task that would take a few days to complete. We were converting a building into what was to be a sound room for men to enjoy hi-fi music in. He wanted the room soundproofed and my task was to find out how much material was needed and what the cost would be. I had a good friend named Earl who ran the hobby shop on base. Earl was a retired M/Sgt who had married an English girl and had moved back to live there. He was a great mathematician. He was well known on base for his ability to do anything with numbers, so I went to see him first. He also knew of my rivalry with the Lt. and he didn't have much respect for him either. He told me to get him the measurements of the building, length, width and height. We took the information and headed for the NCO club. He had already obtained the size of the sound proofing tiles required and the cost of them, so he figured out just how many tiles were required. We spent the rest of the day at the club. The next morning, I walked into the Lt.'s office and threw the paperwork on his desk and said, "Here's the information for your sound room." He took the papers and looked at them for along time and said, "I'm impressed Sgt. Simmons, can you explain how you accomplished this in such short time?" I said yes, I went to the shop and measured the length, the width, height, measured the doors and windows, took the information over to Earl and had him work it out for me, ok?" He looked at me in complete disbelief shook his head and said, "Get out of here". It was no secret about my pet name for him, and I'm sure he was aware of it. If there were any doubt, I cleared it up one morning when Joyce and I were sitting in the car outside my office. She was dropping me off and taking the car. As we sat there talking, I had my window down and Joyce had asked me what the Lt. had me doing that day. In a loud voice I said, "I don't know but that little fuzzy faced bastard will think of something stupid". Just then a head appeared in my window and said, "Good morning Sgt. Simmons." Yeah, it was himself. I know he heard me but he never let on, he just said good morning to Joyce and went into the office.

After I came back from Saudi Arabia we were still living in the Black & White cottage. I got very much into repairing pool tables, a skill that I had learned in Saudi and became pretty good at it. We had pool tables all over the base. There were tables in about all of the barracks day rooms, clubs and in the fire department and hospital break rooms. I was getting the materials through our supply and I was repairing the tables for around $25.00 to $35.00 each. If they used the local economy, they would have charged at least $150.00 per table, so my bosses gave me pretty much a free hand with it and

I made very good money at it. I even got my children involved with my business, I would bring the rails from the table's home and Sheila, Gary and even young Michael would help me strip and recover them in the house. Sometimes my oldest son, Gary would go with me on jobs with me, usually after work. I even got to be known at other bases and they would ask me to come and repair their tables. I was asked to go to a base about twenty miles from Bentwaters called Greenham Common RAF Station. It was a very highly secure facility and required me to have special permission to get in. An air police escort met me at the gate and took me to the areas where I re-covered three tables for them, much to their commander's pleasure. He said morale had gotten to an all time low as the men were under lots of stress. He gave me a very nice commendation letter as well as my pay. The one down side of the trip was on my way back I was driving my precious old Rover car, I came to a cross-road where I had the right of way without a stop sign. There were stop signs for both roads on my left and right. I wasn't paying much attention, and probably had a beer in my lap. A car came through the stop sign, hitting me on my passenger's side. My car was an old 1954 and built like a tank. My door was damaged, but the lady that was driving the other car had a brand new car that did not enjoy the sturdiness of mine and did not fair well at all. The whole front end of her new car was destroyed. She was so upset, and the child with her was crying, I could not get angry about it. She said her insurance would cover my car but she was worried about how husband would react. The car had only about forty miles on it as she had just picked it up from the dealership.

Although I had been able to cover up my drinking for some time, it was getting out of hand again. I was getting as bad as I was my last trip to England when I was stationed at Mildenhall base. One particular night, I truly cannot remember a lot of what happened, but I was assigned base CQ (charge of quarters) one night, the tour of duty was from 5:00pm until 8:00am. I had been drinking all day and when I arrived for duty I had a fifth of whiskey in the back of my car along with a case of beer. I had a runner who was to assist me in my duties. By 11:00pm I must have passed out and the airman just let me sleep, I suppose he thought there was nothing he could do about it anyway. I believe I offered him some beer but he refused, he woke me up at 7:00am and told me I needed to take my report over to base headquarters. I was supposed to have made an hourly report throughout the night, when I handed my blank report to the Sgt. Major, he asked why I was giving him a blank report. Being a smart-ass, I said, "Nothing happened." I must have looked like hell. He told me to report to my commander. I honestly do not remember what happened for the next half-hour or so, the next thing I remember was I was standing at attention in front of my commanding officer. He had a book open in front of him on his desk reading the Articles of War to me. This was the same article 15 that I had been busted with in 1952. I just remember interrupting the commander asking if I was being disciplined. He looked at me with total puzzlement. He had an intercom on his desk and called for the First Sergeant, who was a good friend of mine, to come in. He asked him if I knew why I was there. The First Sergeant said, "I do not believe he does sir." The commander just shook his head and said, "Get him out of here." the First Sergeant took me outside and went with me to the café, gave me some coffee and told me to go home and sober up before coming back to work the following day. I must have been in a black out from the time I left base headquarters until I came to, after driving to the other side of the base to my commander's office. I never was punished for it and never heard another word about it, yes, they were enablers to the drinking crowd.

My drinking got so bad while I was stationed at Bentwaters I suppose my boss, a Tsgt. decided to hide me in an out of the way place. We had another base, Woodbridge RAF station about six miles away where all of the football games were played and all the equipment was stored. He assigned me to the equipment room, which was a building near the gymnasium beside the football field. This suited me just fine. There was no supervision; I just worked by myself in the equipment room. I would go to the shop around 08:00 with a case of beer in the back of my car and spend the day inventorying and making minor repairs and adjustments to the equipment and uniforms. I also took care of the football and baseball fields. I was up on a hill where I could see anyone coming long before they got there, so I could hide anything I didn't want seen. One day I guess I got brave (or stupid) and took a bottle of whiskey into the equipment room. I had been drinking beer most of the day, but I decided I would drink some whiskey while I worked the crossword puzzle. I would go to one of the lockers where I kept it stashed, have a drink then go back to the puzzle. I passed out sometime that afternoon. My boss decided to visit the equipment room along with the civilian in charge of the recreation department. He must have come in and found me passed out on the desk. When I woke up, the bottle of whiskey was on the desk in front of me. The lockers were all standing wide open with equipment and uniforms scattered all over the room, he had left a note under the bottle telling me to straighten up the room, then straighten myself up before coming to work the next day. He never said a word to me about any of it, he was shipping out for the states the next week and figured the civilian and the Lt. would deal with me. I never knew why but neither of them ever said a word to me about it. I went back to beer, for a while.

Around this time was when I had made my second attempt at sobriety; there were several events that lead up to it. The first was one night at the service club where I was working, I had been drinking heavily all day. It was around 5:00pm when my boss asked me to make the final urn of coffee for the night. I do not know if it was the coffee grounds, dust or what, I started sneezing and could not stop. Suddenly my nose started to bleed very badly. I had broken an artery, and was hemorrhaging. Everyone tried all they could to stop the bleeding, to no avail, my boss called an ambulance and they took me to the emergency room. The doctor worked with me for over an hour. I was getting weaker and passing out. The doctor told me later that he had to pack both sides of my nose from the inside by going down my nose to my throat and back up the other side of my nose, he said it was the worse case he had ever dealt with. While I was in recovery, the doctor came in to see me. He asked me if I had a drinking problem. Being the smart-ass, I said the only problem is getting enough. He was quiet for a minute, then he said, "I'm serious, Sgt. I believe you have a problem and perhaps I can help you. There is a group on the base that worked especially well for me. It is an AA group. Before you turn me down, I want you to know there are others who are aware of your problem and might not be so lenient." I said I would try it. I got out of the hospital the next day and my boss gave me the next three days off before the weekend. I attended the meeting and had a feeling it was time I straightened up. I did not drink anything for about ten days, Joyce was pleased and asked if there was anything she could do, I said to just pray for me.

I believe it was the tenth day when I went from Bentwaters to Woodbridge base to repair two pool tables. When I finished the last table, I threw my tool kit in my car and started home. I had the strangest feeling as I approached the NCO club, something just seemed to pull me into the parking lot at the club where I had spent so many nights. I knew then I was going to get drunk and there was nothing I could do to stop it. I walked in the bar and the bartender recognized me right away and said, "Have you been on leave?" I said, "No, believe it or not, I've been sober." He said "well we'll have to do something about that won't we", I went right back to where I had left off, and stayed that way until Friday 13th December 1973. Thanks to God, Joyce and Alcoholics Anonymous I remain sober thirty-one years later.

In January 1973, I finally made T/Sgt. after 17 years in grade. Instead of buying cigars, I went to the PX and got a bag of Bull Durham tobacco and some cigarette papers, stuck them on the bulletin board in the office with a copy of my orders and a note saying "Roll your own". The Lt. I worked with made Captain at the same time and chided me for being so cheap. He held out a box of cigars and said, "Here, this is how you celebrate a promotion." I said, "Captain, if you ever get as much time in grade, or the service as I have you might feel differently." I refused the cigar.

While stationed at Bentwaters, I had to do a good bit of traveling around from the base to towns, between bases and haul lots of equipment for the base teams. It was not practical to use my car and gas was rationed so I was assigned a staff car. It was like no other staff car on base. I was assigned a "cracker-box ambulance"

This was the big old thing like they use in the TV show MASH. It was like a tank, and on those little narrow English roads, with the way I was drinking, it is a wonder I never crashed the darn thing or worse yet killed anyone with it. I got to where I could handle it as well as my car, except one time when I had to take a bunch of football equipment up to Lakenheath for a game that week end. I did fine going up but spent a little too long in the NCO club and made matters worse by bringing a couple of six packs back with me. When I left I forgot to put the side step up on the side of the ambulance. The step protrudes out about 18 inches and on the roads I was traveling that was too much. I dug some ditches along the way back with that step. Fortunately, I didn't hit any cars with it but it sure tore that step up. Once before I was coming back from town where I had picked up some supplies and came to this very narrow road through a small village and met another vehicle. The ambulance had very large mirrors and I clipped the mirror on the other vehicle, cracking the mirror on the ambulance. I could see that I did not do much harm and was not about to stop as I had been drinking and in fact had a beer between my legs so I headed to the base which was only a mile or so away. I parked my truck in the hobby shop yard and got back to my office. The next morning, an Air Policeman came to my office and said a civilian was claiming I had hit his car and left the scene. I denied it and the airman asked where my vehicle was, I told him and he said let's have a look at it. I made some excuse about having to make an important call first. I called my friend Earl at the hobby shop and explained what was going on. He said to just play dumb and come over with the Air Police. When we got there, Earl asked the airman what the problem was and the airman told him what he had told me that my mirror had clipped the civilian's car and damaged it. Earl said, "You must be mistaken, that mirror has been broken ever since we got the vehicle over two years ago." The airman made out his report and left. I told Earl, "That's another case of beer I owe you." We went to the NCO club where Earl told me to watch my driving before I killed someone, I promised to do better. I really had an angel watching over me during this tour as well, they say God looks out for drunks and fools, I'm not sure about the fools but I know someone was watching over me.

One time someone found a safe in an old hanger that had not been used in years and no one had the combination to it. My little fuzzy faced friend told me to go to the hanger in my ambulance to pick it up and take it to Earl over at the hobby shop and see if he could open it with a cutting torch. When I got to the hanger I found the safe. It was about 4 feet square and must have weighed nearly a ton. An airman loaded it in the back of my vehicle with a forklift. Since I was going straight to the hobby shop, I never thought it necessary to tie it down. The hobby shop was clear across base and there was a fairly steep hill I had to maneuver. Of course I had a six pack of beer in the cab with me and had a can of beer in my lap as I came to this hill. I was ok until I came to a stop sign about ¾ of the way down the hill. I would have run the stop sign but there was a car coming and I had to break rather sharply. As I applied the brakes, I heard the safe starting to slide towards me. My first thought was for my beer. I grabbed the six pack from the floor boards just as the safe slammed into the dash board beside me, it smashed the dash board pretty good but only caused cosmetic damage, I never was able to use the glove compartment after that, but I salvaged my six pack. When I got to the hobby shop, Earl came out to see what I had. When he saw the safe buried in the dashboard he laughed. When he saw the six pack in my lap he said, "Well I see you saved the important stuff." We shared the beer then proceeded to remove the safe. We just pulled it to the back of the vehicle where he jokingly said, "After we retrieve the loot you can dump it in the swamp and tell them it was empty and you got rid of it." It took Earl over two hours to cut the safe open, there were only some crumpled up papers that were burnt from the torch, no jewels or coins. I gently drove to the salvage yard to unload the safe, returned my vehicle to the hobby shop for the night and headed for the club.

Chapter Twenty-Five

Final base in England

Just before I had completed my third year at Bentwaters, while we were still living at The Black & White Cottage in Easton, I finally got my request for base housing approved. This meant we could move into some new quarters near the base and have decent living quarters for the first time in many years. As a Staff Sergeant it was virtually impossible to get base quarters, but I had made Tech Sergeant and was authorized. Joyce was very pleased when we looked at the house; it was a nice four-bedroom townhouse. Being a new house it made it even more attractive. When we had been in the house about two weeks, Joyce had furnished it very comfortable and had hung full length curtains, a Gypsy woman came to the door offering Joyce some lace or something. This was usually how they started their pitch to hit you up for money and offer to tell your fortune. Joyce was very nice to her and bought some of her lace. The Gypsy lady smiled and said, "You are going to move soon." Joyce said, "No, we just moved in here." The lady smiled and again said, "You are going to move soon." Joyce explained this was our last move until we went back to the states. The Gypsy was adamant, "You will move soon." Joyce gave her some money for the lace and bid her goodbye. Well, things had happened at the base that day that Joyce was not aware of yet. I was told I was going to be transferred to Lakenheath RAF station about 45 miles north. I was so damn mad when that little fuzzy faced little bastard told me that I just stormed out of the office and went home. As soon as I got in the house, Joyce started telling me about the Gypsy. I handed her the copy of orders. She asked what I was going to do about it and I said I was going to fight it. I went in the next morning to talk to the Captain. He explained that they had lost the NCOIC for recreation at Lakenheath and could not get a replacement for 24 months. They wanted me to take over the position. I told him I had over 21 years in and could retire any time I chose. He agreed, but asked if I would consider it, or at least talk to the office in charge there. I agreed to drive up and talk to him. When I met him he said he was in a tough spot and would appreciate my help. I explained my situation and that I had just got base housing and was waiting for retirement. He said he was sure I could get adequate quarters on the local market. I told him I was very familiar with the local rental situation, as my last four-year tour was at Mildenhall, three miles away. I also knew that Lakenheath had recently built the very same base quarters we had at Bentwaters and the same contractors built them. The houses were identical to ours. I told him if he would assign me the same quarters I had at Bentwaters, I would finish my tour at Lakenheath for him He said, "Do you realize we have Chief Master sergeants who are E-9s waiting for those quarters? You're only an E-6." I said, "Yes, but do you have a NCOIC for recreation among them?" He said he didn't think he could get away with it. I told him to think it over and let me know when he decided whether to bump a Chief Master sergeant or get the Tech Sergeant he needed. I also told him if I was forced to make the move without getting what I wanted I would certainly put in for retirement. I went back to Bentwaters and went to my Captain. He asked how it went. I said, "It's up to the Captain at Lakenheath; if he gives me the housing I want he can have me." He said, "You mean you gave him an ultimatum? I said, "Captain, you should know me by now." He just shook his head and said good luck. Well, the officer from Lakenheath called me back later that week. He said, "I think I may have been able to pull this off by going through the base commander. You've got your house; but Sgt. Simmons, if were you I would stay clear of the NCO club. You are not very well liked there by some of the senior NCOs.

We had a black cat that belonged to my oldest daughter Ann that we called Woodstock. She was a quite a character. One beautiful spring day, she was laying in the living room basking in the sun, watching some birds out in the front lawn. The window she was laying in front of was a full-length window down to the floor. Suddenly, her tail started twitching, her lips quivered and she launched herself full force at the birds, smashing into the window. Just before I busted out laughing, she just turned and gave me a look as if to say, "I meant to do that" and walked off indignantly. Later on the next day or later, she was in the same position on the living room floor when one of the kid's white pet mouse, just very slowly, walked across the living room floor right in front of her. She looked just like a cartoon character doing a double take while the mouse causally disappeared behind a piece of furniture. After that, for some time as she would pass that piece of furniture, she would stop and snap her head toward the piece then walk away slowly. Now she was of course used to the house including the out side area where we had a large front lawn, as we were on the corner lot there were no houses directly across from us. When we moved to Lakenheath I followed the furniture truck up and Joyce brought the kids and cat later. The furniture was in place by the time Joyce got there. Since it was after dark when they brought Woodstock in the house in a carrier box she of course saw nothing different as the layout of the house was the same as the one we just left, and of course the furniture was familiar. The next morning I never thought anything about it when I opened the front door to let her out as usual. But as soon as she started out, she just froze in the doorway. There was no big front yard, and there were houses there that were not there the last time she went out. It took her a few days to get used to her new home.

My new job at Lakenheath was at the service club. Like the service club at Mac Dill, the club was a center for recreation and did not have a bar. The captain I worked for had a friend, another captain, who approached him about opening a pizza shop in one of the rooms of our service club. When my captain told me about it I hit the roof. I told him if the airmen wanted pizza and beer they could get it at the café or NCO club. He said he thought I was being territorial and hard headed; after all, he was the OIC. I argued, I was the NCOIC and spent more time in the toilet in one day than he had spent in the club his entire tour. However, my objections were over-ruled and the captain's friend got his pizza place and bar. This did not sit well with me. Hell yes, I was being territorial; this was my club and no damn officer was going to push me around. I let the man know he was not welcome and offered him no assistance in sitting up his place. I informed all my employees that they were not to assist him. I did make life miserable for him; the night of his opening he had a very large crowd in. I had a sign in the area that allowed a maximum of thirty-five persons in the room, approved by the fire department. He had closer to seventy-five people in there. The base fire chief was a good friend and drinking buddy of mine. I called him that night and had him pull an unannounced inspection. He closed the shop down for the night, the captain had made up several pizzas in advance and lost money the first night. I continued to harass him; one afternoon I called in the veterinarian's office (they inspected all food handling operations on base, another friend) and had the employees checked for food handlers certificates. None of them had one, so it was closed again that night. I also would take pleasure in going to a pay phone outside the club and call in a phony order then go back inside and watch the delivery boy steam when he came backing from a dry run. The captain was sure I was doing it but of course could not prove it. One night I went out to the phone and called in an order for about a half dozen various types of large pizzas and I don't know how much beer. I gave the name of Lt. Deadman in building so and so, then went back in and pretended to be doing some work in the club. The driver came storming back in yelling, "That son of a bitch did it again, that building is the base Morgue." I could hardly contain myself. I also helped myself to his English beer that he served in his place, I always closed up the club and naturally had to inspect all the rooms, including his bar. He always secured the kegs, but he was not very inventive and I was a bartender so it was not much of a challenge for me. After about four months he had lost more money than he made and closed up shop. I didn't feel guilty about what I had done. I was just following the instincts I had learned earlier on the track: don't get mad, get even. I got my club back anyway.

184

My oldest daughter had met an English fellow shortly after we arrived at Bentwaters. They courted all the time we were there, eventually becoming engaged. They decided to get married while we were at Lakenheath base about a year before we were to leave for the states. Joyce had made all the arrangements for a big wedding, being a friend of the NCO club manager and a bartender I hired the club for the reception, with full bar naturally. The wedding and reception were a great success, except for me. The morning of the wedding I was hung over and had to sneak out about 8:00 am to get a bottle to get well. When I came back, I decided to prepare our car for the wedding. I spent the morning washing and waxing it. The car was a very nice old 1954 English Rover, an English luxury car, affectionately referred to as the working man's Rolls Royce. After polishing it, I hung a big sign over the grill that a girl who worked for me in my art shop had made. In great big red letters it read "JUST ABOUT MARRIED". After finishing with car I went into the house to get ready for the wedding. Joyce asked me to control my drinking for the day; of course I promised I would. I continued to drink the pint of whiskey I got earlier that morning and was pretty much in control of myself for the wedding. At the reception however, I continued to drink, against Joyce's wishes. The longer the reception lasted the worse I got. There were a lot of Joyce's relatives and friends there; her mother, cousins, uncles and aunts. I continued to embarrass her throughout the day, especially when I attempted to dance with one of the bride's maids and fell flat on my face in the middle of the dance floor on top of the poor girl. But Joyce managed to uphold her dignity and control the situation, until it was time for us to leave and I was attempting to drive her and some of the guest home. She flatly refused to let me drive, not that I could have anyway. One of her cousins took us back where we lived in base housing, when we got in the house she broke down, I just passed out.

Another incident I am deeply ashamed of was also during my time at Lakenheath. I had gotten my oldest son Gary a job at the NCO club washing dishes and doing janitorial work. He had worked there during the summer and was preparing to go back to school in the fall, he had received his last check, or so he thought. One day the club manager told me he had Gary's final check, to have him come by and pick it up. I said I would take it to him, the cashier gave me the check and I asked her to cash it for me, as I didn't know when he could get down to the club. I just signed his name and she cashed the check. I don't know how much it was, probably $25.00 or so, but that was a lot of money for him. He never knew about it as far as I know (sorry Gary). These are the stupid things an alcoholic will do for a drink. We always seem to take from, and hurt the ones we love most, probably because we know anyone else would beat the crap out of us.

Chapter Twenty-Six

The beginning of yet another life

During my last tour in England, and at times much earlier, my drinking had really become a serious problem. There were many humorous events, but more important was the damage I was doing, mainly to my family, myself and jeopardizing my career. There is much of my drinking time that I cannot remember. Some, I do not want to remember and/or quite honestly, I'm ashamed of and do not care to talk or write about. Anyone who has been in my position knows what I mean and I know there are many of you out there. Rather than go into a lot of tales reminiscing about my drinking days, I think it is more important to talk about my getting sober. I was stationed at Lakenheath RAF station until 1974, my last tour prior to retirement. When I look back and realize how much I was drinking, from the time I got up until I went to bed, usually passed out, I am amazed. But I still was functional, doing my job as NCOIC of Special Services, although I was in charge of the bowling alleys, theaters, swimming pools, gymnasium and clubs, most of my work was running the service club. As much as I drank, I was able to cover it well, or at least I thought so. In those days these things were over looked or just ignored, there was no longer a draft with an endless line of replacements and it seemed our drinking was actually encouraged. I was working as a bartender in the NCO club and spent more time there than at my assigned station, the service club which

187

was next door. My boss was an English lady who was at ease the way things were, I suspect she was somewhat intimidated by me. I seldom saw the officer in charge of me, so I was pretty much left alone. On paper I was doing a great job. My officer did get word I was absent from my job quite often and called me in to question me. I was pretty high when I reported to him but he didn't say anything then, and he was apparently satisfied with my explanations. A few days later he came into the NCO club on unannounced inspection at around 10:30 am and I was behind the bar. He asked me why I was there and I made some lame excuse that the regular bartender was ill and asked me to cover for him. I didn't tell him that I had opened the bar at 07:00am, which was normal. He appeared to accept it; a few days later he came into the service club around noon. I was high again, or rather, still. He asked me to come to his office. I reported to him that afternoon and his first question was "Have you been drinking Sgt. Simmons?" Being the smart-ass I was I said, "Since I was about 13." He was not amused and he asked me if I intended to retire as a Tech Sergeant. Thinking he was prompting me to re-enlist with the offer of a promotion, I said, "Yes, there is no way I would stay in even if you were to offer to promote me to Master Sergeant today. He looked at me and said, "I was thinking of a lower grade." I said something stupid like others better than him had tried and failed. I saluted and left; why he didn't punish me right there I didn't know. I found out later though.

My wife's mother had been staying with us and was getting ready to go back to the states. We were going to take her to Heathrow Air Port, we had an old 1954 Rover car at the time. It was large for an English car, and had a stick shift. Joyce could drive it as well as I but she did not want to drive to London, so we started out. It was a Friday; actually Friday the 13th December 1973. Joyce hated to ride with me when I was drinking, but on many occasions she had no choice and this was one. She asked me not to drink so much with her mother in the car. I of course agreed and started the some 80 mile journey. Now there was no way I could go that long with out a drink, so I made sure I had a couple of six packs in the car. As usual, we hadn't gone far when I started in on the first one. Joyce put up with it yet again. After about ¾ of the way, I was getting pretty drunk again.

I always had an excuse; I was tired, my back hurt, my eyes hurt or some excuse to get Joyce to drive before I wrecked the car. She took over and very nervously drove to the airport.

That night something happened I have never understood, or could ever explain. After we got our rooms and had settled in, I found myself out of drink. I wandered down the hallway and found one of these machines where you could purchase these small bottles of whiskey like the little ones you get on a plane. I purchased a few and went back to the room. We were watching TV when a show came on with Dick Van Dyke who was my idol along with Mary Tyler Moore. He was telling for the first time publicly that he was an alcoholic. I was dumbfounded and I listened to every word he said. After about a half-hour, I turned to Joyce and announced if Dick Van Dyke with his fame, could stop drinking then I had a great desire to stop. Joyce drove us back home I believe. We arrived home and went to bed. The next morning I was hung over as usual, but somehow different; there was calmness within me I did not understand. I really do not remember much about that Sunday but on Monday morning, I don't remember if I told Joyce what I was doing or not, I made a call to the base hospital. Lakenheath had just opened a clinic for alcoholism; it was the only one in England and only one of two in Europe, the other being in Wiesbaden, in Germany. I made an appointment for 09:00 that morning, then I called the Captain I worked for and told I was turning myself into the hospital. He asked me to come by his office before I went. When I got to his office and reported to him he asked me to sit down and asked if I wanted to talk about it. I said, "Captain, I now realize how much of a problem my drinking has become and I want to stop. I understand this program at the hospital may be the answer." I also told him about my experience in London. He said, "Sgt. Simmons I am very relieved to hear this, and I wish you all the luck and help you need. But before you go, the reason I asked you to come in this morning was to let you know you already had an appointment at the hospital. I made it for you. Since you have made this decision on your own; and I respect you for it, I will cancel the appointment I made." Had I not made that appointment, there is a good chance I would have been busted or worse. This program was just getting started. The way it was set up was, if a person turned himself in there would be no repercussions. But if the commander recommended you, you were subject to court marshal charges. I'm not sure if it was my Irish luck or someone above was looking out for me again, I think more than likely, the later.

Chapter Twenty-Seven

A hard and sad trip home

I got out of the recovery program just after new years 1974. It was supposed to be a 30-day program with no breaks. I was doing very well and Joyce talked them into letting me out for Christmas. Later when they saw how I was improving, they let me out about a week earlier than planned. I was a very lucky person in my recovery, most of the people I met had a real hard time adjusting and many suffered relapses. I had a friend I met later in an AA meeting who told me of his fear of returning to drinking. He said one day he walked into a grocery store and suddenly found himself in an aisle full of wine, whiskey and beer. He said he panicked, and said it was the worst day he had since he had stopped drinking three years earlier. Another fellow, with eighteen years sobriety, got on a train from somewhere in the mid-west to Sacramento. He said it was the same journey he had taken on his last binge, he told us later that he knew as soon as he got on that train that he was going to drink. He said he could not understand the urge to drink but he went straight to the club car and proceeded to get drunk. (this is the same thing that happened to me at Bentwaters when I attempted to sober up and it lasted only ten days) It took him two years to get sober again, losing his eighteen years. It can happen anytime to anyone.

As I say, I was fortunate. That night in the hotel in London, I lost all desire for alcohol. To this day, 31 years later, I still feel the same way. It would only take one drink and I would be right back where I left off. I attended AA meetings regularly for probably the first 10 years, then for no special reason, I just attended less and less. I still have the same feelings about the things we stood for in the meetings. I always said there and I still believe my program would get others drunk, but it works for me, and that is the important thing.

My mother had been suffering from stomach cancer for a few years and was getting worse. She had moved in with my oldest sister Marie, who by then had become the matriarch to the rest of us in the family, and still is today. Marie called me shortly after I got out of recovery and told me Mom was getting worse and was not sure how long she would last. I went to my First Sergeant, who was a good friend of mine, and explained my situation. He said he had some contacts on the flight line and would see what he could do. He called me at home that night and told me there was a KC-135 on the hard stand that was ready for a state side flight when I needed it. My leave was approved in advance. Three days later Marie called to tell me Mom had passed away and I told her I was on my way. I called the First Sergeant and told him I was leaving, he had my paperwork sent to the terminal and I was on the next plane. I don't know how many readers may be familiar with the passenger arrangement in the tail section of a KC-135, but I was put in where there is only room for I believe 4 passengers at the most. There was only one other person on board with me, a sailor who had hitched a ride to the states. This guy had a hangover like I have seldom seen, other than my own. Only heaven only knows what this guy had been eating or drinking but as the aircraft took off this guy let go some of the foulest air I had experienced in many years and there was no escape. If I could have I believe I would bailed out, and he never apologized, maybe he never even noticed. I could relate to that.

When I got to Mcguire AFB in New Jersey I took a train to Aberdeen Maryland. My two brothers, Ross and Simon who I had not seen in a few years met me there. These two were always heavy drinkers and both knew I was too. We came to the first liquor store where Bud pulled over and said, "Lets get something to drink on the way to Marie's." I said no thanks and they both looked at me like I was crazy and asked what was wrong with me. I said, "Nothing, I just don't drink anymore." Of course they laughed. I said, "It's true, but you guy's go ahead and do your thing, don't mind me." Ross was more sympathetic and let it go but Bud just kept at me to have one until Ross told him to leave me alone, we did not speak much for the rest of the journey.

When we got to Marie's she of course was glad to see me and when I told her I had stopped drinking, she was very pleased. My oldest brother Sam was there from Denver and of course Marie's husband Harold. Marie made it quite clear to Ross and Bud that she would put up with their drinking while there as long as it did not get out of hand. But they were to leave me out of it and not pester me or even try to offer me anything to drink. She made quite sure that they understood she was serious.

The funeral was two days later, it was a very nice service. I really felt sorry for Ross; he was having a very hard time with his drinking.

He could not even get through the service without a drink, which he brought with him. I fully understood and did not question him about it; I knew what he was going through and could only sympathize with him. I stayed another 10 days with Marie and Harold. My First Sergeant had told me to take as long as I needed due to the fact I was retiring in June of that year anyway. On the flight back to England, I could not get the thought out of my mind that the one thing I regretted most was the fact I had not got the chance to tell my mother that I had quit drinking. This really hurt and bothered me, as I knew how much it would have meant to her if I could have told her before she died. I told Joyce about this that night when I got back as we were going to bed. She took my hand and looked me in the eyes and said, "She knew Rick, I told her before you got out of the hospital". Mom always thought the world of Joyce, and this was typical of her, she has always been such a wonderful person through out our marriage of over 50 years, I put that woman through pure hell, and she always stood by me. Thank you again Joyce.

Chapter Twenty-Eight

First attempt at retirement

We left Lakenheath early June 1974 for my retirement. I chose Mather AFB as a retirement base mostly because Joyce's sister Stella was living in Orangevale, about seven miles from the base with her husband Bill She had sent us the local papers and telling us how the area would make a good place to retire. I also liked it because I wanted to live near a base without living on it, here we would be between two bases, Mather on one side and McClellan AFB about ten miles in the other direction. I also wanted to live in a small town but still have access to a larger city. Orangevale was twenty miles from Sacramento, so it sounded ideal. We moved in with Bill and Stella, they had a very nice four bed room house. One of the many problems was they had six children and Stella was pregnant with her seventh. We had three of our four children with us, as Ann had married an Englishman the year before we left and they stayed in England for the time. Things were of course crowded but we were glad to be together and things looked good for us for the first time in twenty some years. I was seven months sober and feeling better than I can ever remember. One of the first thing I did when I checked in at Mather AFB for retirement was to find an AA meeting. I was directed to a barracks where the meetings would be held. I talked to a M.Sgt. In charge of the building, he said they were trying to get a group started and would welcome me as a member. At the first meeting he introduced me to Henry L. and Jeanie M. We were the only attendants for some time, eventually we build the group up to as many as 35 or 40 guest at times. We also added a group for spouses of alcoholics, ALANON, with sometimes more attendees than we had in AA. I was very active for the first eight or ten years, then I suppose with my schedule at the post office and my schooling at CSUS, I started missing meetings. It had no effect on my sobriety, although I would caution anyone else from practicing my program, it worked for me. I was very comfortable with the AA groups; they were sincere and honest, something that had eluded me most of my life.

My experience with AA was different the first time I went to a meeting. I remember my first attempt at trying to get sober, it was when I was stationed at Laredo AFB in the late 50's. I felt so bad and guilty about the way I was treating Joyce that one night when I was drunk in down town Laredo, I went to a pay phone and found an ad for Alcoholics Anonymous in the phone book. I called and told the man that answered that I wanted to get sober. He said he would not try to talk to me while I was drinking but to come the next day to an address he gave me. I told Joyce about it and she was very pleased and said she would support me in anyway she could. When I arrived at the address it was someone's home. I was invited in and introduced to other people. I was quite hung over and badly in need of a drink. As I sat there, listening to what I soon deemed to be a bunch of old farts telling drinking stories, I wondered what the hell I was thinking. I did not belong here, it just didn't take. I was not ready, and I was doing this for all the wrong reasons. I was doing it to please my wife and perhaps other people, or to get myself out of trouble, but I was not doing it for my self. The fact was, I had not "hit my bottom" yet. As bad off as I was and would be for many years to come, I was not ready.

That is the sad truth about anyone who wishes to stop drinking and doesn't know where to turn. There has to be a self-evaluation and an honest desire to improve oneself. Each person has their own "Bottom" and only they can know what it is. A benchmark is when your drinking starts to interfere with your work or your home life; that can be a red flag. Some people are only weekend drunks and can function very well the rest of the week, but if it is affecting their lives and depriving them of peace of mind, there is a problem. Others are, as I was, knee-walking drunks who develop a high tolerance for the stuff and can also still function. It is truly a personal thing. Anyway, I was grateful for finding a way for me to sober up and am still grateful for the support I received through Alcoholics Anonymous and the love and support I received from them and my family, who got back the husband and father that alcohol had deprived them all those years.

Joyce was very savvy in researching real estate properties and went to work finding a place. She found a four-bedroom house in Folsom. The house was only six months old and the owner's company was sending him to Arizona so he had to sell the house. We did not have enough for a down payment and I of course was unemployed. She managed to talk the owner into allowing us to rent with option to buy. He said he would give us a year to manage the down payment and take over payments. Folsom seemed the perfect place for us, it was near every thing we needed. At the time we moved here, Folsom had a population of around 5,000 including the prison. The joke of the town was half of our population was in the penitentiary. (now, thirty years later the population is closer to 50,000)

I had managed to get a 10% disability from the Air Force for my back injury which gave me preference on government registers for job applications. I really didn't look for work for the first six months, just enjoyed my sobriety and retirement. Then I took every test I could get, mostly for the Postal Service, but none of them were successful. Then I found an opening at McClellan AFB for a Recreation Specialist for the civilian employees. I got a new suit and went for the interview. The club director was a retired Air Force Chief Master Sergeant. Liking my potential, he hired me right away. This gave us hope for buying the house; then we found out in order to qualify for the loan I had to be employed permanently. At the time we were applying for the loan I had only been working three months and was still under probation for the first year. When I explained my situation to the man who hired me he said he thought I would make a good employee and gave me permanent status which qualified us for the loan. Things were beginning to look better all the time.

After we moved out of Bill and Stella's and had moved into our house in Folsom, Bill took us to Tahoe for the first time one day. It was in the winter and although we had nice weather where we were, the mountains were covered in snow and ice. Just about 100 miles up the road, when we got to one of the casino parking lots, as I started to get out I found the parking lot had about a foot of snow and was frozen over with a sheet of ice. As everyone else started towards the casino I was still getting out of the car. Bill came back and asked me what was wrong. I said, "Hell Bill, I just realized I have not walked on snow and ice sober for nearly thirty years." He laughed and took my arm and led me into the casino.

Joyce's talents did not only include the purchase of our house, she has constantly made improvements to it, in the past 30 years she has knocked our walls, extended closets, and bathrooms, painted, wallpapered, and had new carpet throughout the house. Where we had purchased a four-bedroom house, thanks to her we now have a very comfortable three bedroom home, with a very large master bed room. We each have our own offices (we each took one of the spare bedrooms) with desks, computer and all office necessities, she has had a very nice glassed-in large back room with attractive furnishings. She is presently in the process of completely remodeling our entire kitchen and living room. Again, I am very fortunate to have met her and enjoy her company over these years.

I really enjoyed the position I had at McClellan and worked very hard at it. I became very well known around the base and made a lot of friends. After just over a year, my boss decided to leave and bought a home out in Utah. I missed him as he was a good boss and friend. His assistant took over and we got along fine until in about a year or more he too decided to leave and take a job in Yosemite as a park ranger. The shop I was running offered various tours to places like Tahoe, Reno, Napa Valley and cruise ship bookings. It also included the rental of sports equipment, fishing boats, skiing equipment and camping gear. I had added five camping trailers that became very popular and increased the revenue from my section considerably. I had also created a twelve team soft ball league, a ten team bowling league and was offering a lot of special events. I invited "THE KING AND HIS COURT" to the base, this was a three man soft ball team with Eddie Fiegner as the pitcher, a catcher, and an out fielder. Eddie was world renown during the sixties, he would take on a regular full team and beat them every time. I had him at the base three years in a row and each time was a great success. I also set up a donkey softball game. This is an hilarious game, where the batter hits an over size soft ball then jumps on a donkey and tries to make the bases before the other team gets him out while they are also on donkeys. I pitted the top-ranking officers of the base, including a two star general, against the top civilian directors of the base. This was also a great success. At the time I was working there, the base employed over 14,000 civilians and about 3,000 military personnel. During this period I had been trying unsuccessfully to get a promotion. I was hired as a EA-5, I believe the lowest level in management in civil service. Instead of promotions, they would give me a new title. First I was a Recreation Specialist, then Program/Sports Director, then before my last boss left I approached him about a promotion and he made me Recreation Director. This is where I started off on the wrong foot with my next boss, that was supposed to be his title.

My next boss turned out to be a real A.H. and we bucked heads from the first day he came into the unit. Here I was stuck with another fuzzy faced bastard. This one was a bit older, but still much younger than me. I found out he was just as gullible as the Captain I left at Bentwaters and made for some great stories as I made his life miserable as I possibly could. I was never really disrespectful to my superiors, I just spoke my mind a bit more than others. Well, maybe one time at MacDill AFB; a 2nd Lt. was giving me a hard time and I told him he was full of s---. He said he was going to charge me with insubordination, I told him in order to do that, I would have to be subordinate to him and no way in hell did I feel that was the case. He of course reported me to the Major I worked for, who liked me and told me in so many words to get off the Lt.'s butt and avoid contact with him until he got some experience.

But this new boss didn't even offer me a challenge, he just fell for it then come back for more. Once he walked into my office and

I was working a cross word puzzle with a ball point pen. He said, "I guess you think you are pretty good huh?" I said yes, he said, "And what if you make a mistake?" I just calmly said, "I don't make mistakes". He walked out of the office. Later that day I found a paper with a crossword puzzle and the answers in a back page. I carefully put the puzzle in a typewriter, and patiently typed all the answers in (it took me about an hour) then I took it over to his office and tossed it on his desk and said, "this is how you do a crossword when you are as good as I am." He wasn't amused.

Another time he decided to make some shelves from a sheet of ¾ inch plywood. When he approached me about it I reminded him I had a bad back and could not saw the board. He said he had seen a jig saw in my shop, and told me to go get it, he would do it himself. It was about 90 some degrees outside and this guy always wore a three piece suit. We got the plywood out on the back loading dock and he told me to stand on it to keep it still. He took the small jig saw and proceeded to cut the wood into four shelves, it must have taken him the best part of an hour and he was pouring with sweat. When he finished he asked, "How's that?" I said it was a bit crooked and he asked if I thought I could have done better. I said of course I could have. He said, "How do you figure that?" I said, "Well in the first place I would not have attempted to do it with a jig saw, I would have used a proper rip saw." He said, "where in heavens name do you think you would have got that?" I said, "In my shop, right beside where I got the jig saw." He almost exploded and said, "You mean you had a rip saw over there all this time and you let me do this with a little jig saw?" I said, "That's what you asked for, and that's what I got." I never even said anything to him when he threw the jig saw down and broke it.

Another time he made an attempt to discipline me for taking time off. I had asked his assistant if I could have the afternoon off as I had no equipment due in or out and needed some personal time. He said fine, when the boss came in the next day he called me in and said he was going to dock me for the time. I could not go to a union representative as I was in management, however, we came under military jurisdiction and the base Inspector General and a good customer of mine. He and his wife both skied and got their equipment from my shop, so I went to see him and explain what was happening. The result was the IG called my boss and told him not to touch my pay or he would answer to him. This rivalry continued until he decided he could do better somewhere else. When he left they put a guy in charge who used to be the bartender in the NCO club. We got along ok but this guy had no clue how to run the section, his background was civil engineers in the military and he was lost in administration. I later learned there was rumor of the base closing and things got very political. I didn't know it at the time but they wanted my section to lose money so they would have an excuse to close it and appear to be saving money. My unit was making a better profit than any other unit, so they started denying my requests for equipment or supplies. Finally it got so bad I could not offer a lot of my programs. I could see the writing on the wall and decided to protect myself. I again went to the post office and talked to the guy who did the testing and recommendations for hiring. The only tests available were for part-time carriers, I knew I needed a full time job. The guy asked if I were a disabled veteran I said that I was. He explained that the post office had a policy where there were three jobs reserved for disabled veterans. These jobs were elevator operators, security guards and custodial workers. He said the only one available in Sacramento was the custodian position and there was an opening, would I mind that as a full time position. I told him to sign me up. I took the test on a Wednesday and was called in for an interview the next day, I never said anything to anyone at work about my plans. After the interview I went back to work and made some excuse for where I had been. The next day was Friday, I was called to post office personnel and the lady there swore me in. I asked, "Am I hired?" She smiled and said, "You are now a full-time employee of the U.S.P.S, report to work at 10:00 pm Monday night." I was put on graveyard shift and had to make a 90 day probation period. It was about two in the afternoon when I got back to the shop. I went straight in the club where my boss was working in the kitchen. When he saw me he asked where I had been. I said, "I just felt like taking a few hours off, as the matter of fact I think I will take off for good." He asked, "Rick are you quitting?" I said, "You're not as dumb as you look are you?" He got mad and came towards me shaking his finger at me saying, "You know that shop has to be inventoried and you will be responsible for all the equipment." I said, "I put the stuff there, you inventory it". I tossed the shop keys to him and walked out. Damn, that felt good.

Chapter Twenty-Nine

Another career

The job at the post office was just what I needed at the time, no pressure and I was able to pursue my education. After I was at McClellan for about a year I decided to try using the GI bill to go to college. I didn't think I stood a chance of getting anywhere but what the heck, I could get paid for going to school; even though I didn't have as much as a fifth grade education. I was able to get my GED through the military. On my first tour to England, I applied to the University of Maryland to take the test. They just gave us a generic test, I never heard of anyone failing. It made the service look good to have more high school graduates. This allowed me to enroll at American River Community College. It was difficult, but I had some very good tutors and they carried me through. To my surprise, more than anyone else's, I was the first one in my family to graduate from college. My oldest sister Marie had gone one year to the University of Delaware in Wilmington on a scholarship, but I had graduated from college. The counselor who had helped me the most asked if I would like to continue my education at CSUS. I said, "You cannot be serious; you know I have less than a fifth grade education and you expect me to go to a university?" He said "Richard, you just graduated from college, don't sell yourself short." He said he had friends over at Sacramento State University, that could do the same for me that he had done at American River

College. I thought what the heck, I still have a few years on my GI bill and have nothing to lose and every thing to gain. I won't say it was easy, working full time from ten p.m. until six thirty a.m. and going to school full time carrying 12 or 14 units per semester. I had to work my school schedule to where I had three classes after I got off work in the morning, then home to sleep, get up around five p.m. have supper, make it to classes from six thirty p.m. until nine thirty p.m. then make it to work for ten p.m. Yes it was hard, but I graduated with a Bachelors Degree June 1983, not bad for an uneducated, unsophisticated, alcoholic race track bum.

There were many humorous stories to tell, I had a lot of fun with the guys I worked with, they were all ex-military and we had much in common. One incident I recall was one of the men was a young man who had been put out on a medical discharge. He was much younger than the rest of us. He was an Italian lover, or so he thought. He was dating a very attractive girl who would pick him up in the morning after work in her convertible BMW. We noticed as soon as he left the dock he would take his ID badge off before he got in her car, we asked him why and he made the mistake of telling us. He did not want her to know he was a janitor, he had told her he worked with mail processing. One morning as we were all crossing the parking lot, as he was getting in her car, one of the guys yelled out to him, "Hey Tony, did you empty your mop bucket and hang up your mop?" He just hung his head and wouldn't speak to any of us for a week. After that he was seen catching the bus home.

Another one of my coworkers named Robin, I was particularly fond of. We became very good friends. She was a very attractive young lady about eighteen years old, just out of high school. She came to work with us early in 1983; I had been working as a custodian for about two years when she joined our crew. Robin was very shy and did not seem to be comfortable with the other workers, she seemed to trust me and I kind of took her under my wing so to speak. Our group leader assigned me as her trainer, I soon learned she was a very dedicated worker and took pride in doing the best job every day. She was very easy to train, and we became good friends. We would always take our breaks and lunches together. There was a time shortly after she started working with us that she began to think about quitting; she said she felt she could not do satisfactory work and was insecure with the job. I had many talks with her explaining the benefits of making a career of the Postal Service; I tried to assure her that the custodial craft was not her only option, that there were many other avenues she could take and offered to help her in finding other positions that were offered. We were working the gaveyard shift at the time and it was difficult for both of us. Being so young, it was hard for her to stay up all night and try to sleep in the day. For me it was also difficult, as I was still going to school full time at Sacramento State University. Although I was in my senior year and had worked my schedule where I was only caring three units, it was harder on her than me. Robin and I used to make it a regular thing to stop off for coffee on our way home to relax and discuss the day's events. We usually had a few good laughs over the events of the day. We continued this friendship even after I went into management, not so much at work, but we would often meet for lunch or coffee either before or after work, I always enjoyed her company and we shared many stories. After I went into management, it was a while before I became her supervisor. It was at this time I was giving my employees special achievement awards. I was putting Robin in for a five hundred dollar award, when she found out, she came to me and asked me not to put her in for it, she did not feel she deserved it. Although I tried to assure her she did, she did not want the attention it would give her. I of course honored her wishes, against my better judgment, as I felt she was the most deserving of all the workers. Even after I left the shift she was on, we continued to enjoy each others company. She enjoyed taking me to her favorite restaurants where she introduced me to Asian food, and she would take me to a Thai or Chinese restaurant and try to get me to try various types of foods, although she tried hard to get me to try sushi, I just could not force myself to try it. I still see her every once in a while when I go back to the Post Office to visit old friends, she hasn't changed, still the hard working, smiling, attractive person I have always known, I feel much richer for knowing her and still admire her very much.

When I first started as a custodian we were warned about picking up things off the floor that resembled money, checks, change or such items. We were to first contact a supervisor so he could tell us if it was ok. We were shown the little windows up near the top of the building, they were about ten to fifteen feet apart and all around the facility. These were windows where the postal inspectors had a view of the entire facility, we were only permitted access to the inspectors galley for custodial work the last two days of the month when we cleaned an vacuumed the areas. They set their own trash out for us and the doors were locked, any access had to be by escort only. This made new people like me very nervous, especially when told all kinds of ghost stories by the old timers. I remember going in the coffee shop one day on break to use one of the vending machines for coffee or something. When I pulled my change out of my pocket, I dropped some on the floor, I automatically looked up towards the inspectors windows, of course they were one way glass, they could see out but you could not see in. No way in hell was I going to pick up that change I had dropped. Years later, when I was a supervisor myself, I learned the inspectors were only up there when they suspected illegal activities. I have seen them in action and they are very fast and efficient in their duties, they could suddenly appear from the small door leading onto the workroom floor and have someone off the floor before you knew they were there. Once an employee was suspected of "popping coins", she could feel the coins in the envelope, she would swing the envelope causing the coin to pop our, pick it up and put it in her pocket, what she didn't know was the inspectors were not only watching her, but filming her on camera as well, it was well known that if an inspector pulled you off the floor, do not waste money on a lawyer, they have you on tape and enough evidence to convict you before they grab you. I also learned when I was attending the US Postal Academy, which is also the training facility for postal inspectors and that they are the oldest law enforcement agency in the country.

On the rare occasion we would see an inspector, they would usually be in a dark, three-piece suit. One night when I was working as the night supervisor of Building Services I received a call from one of the inspectors, he asked me to meet him in a certain place in the facility. When I arrived at the arranged place, there stood this little man in a black three piece suit. He asked if I had master keys to the facility, I said I did. He said he had been locked out of his office and asked if would I let him back in. I said, "I'm sorry inspector. I have keys to every place in the building except there." I explained to him that the key to the inspectors' galley was secured in a safe in the registry office. He asked if I had a key to the registry office, I again said I did, but the key he wanted was in the safe, this was after midnight on Friday; no one would be in until after 08:00 Monday morning. He said, "You mean there is no way I can get back in my office? I explained the Postal Inspectors policy, was that we were only permitted access on the last two days of the month; this was the first week of the month. He looked defeated, and asked to use my office phone. He had to call his supervisor in San Francisco, over a hundred miles away. As I was leaving after my shift, I saw him sitting in his car with his head on the steering wheel, waiting for his boss; I was glad I was not in his shoes. I never saw him around after that.

I always got restless after being with a job for a while. I wanted more, to advance, have other challenges to meet; I think this was fueled by my sobriety and the fact I had graduated from college. I felt like I could do more with my life and was determined to prove it, not so much to other people, but more for myself. I felt that I could succeed in anything I put my mind to if I really applied myself; this determination made me a better person and an effective supervisor throughout the rest of my Postal career.

I worked as a custodian from 1981 until 1985, when I was promoted to Supervisor of custodians. I got a lot of support from most of my former fellow workers, there were a few who held it against me but they were hard line union men who disliked anyone in management, it never bothered me and I became very successful in my job, receiving numerous awards and citations. My employees respected me as I did them, of the three tours I had the highest morale on my tour, I treated my employees as I wanted to be treated when I was in their position, never forgetting where I came from. A method of supervision that is often talked about and even taught in management courses, but seldom implemented, is to treat employees as you would like to be treated. I not only practiced this philosophy, but also used it effectively and consistently. Soon after I was assigned as Supervisor of Building Services, I found myself in charge of fourteen former military NCOs. Most of these men had held rank either equal to me in the service or higher. They, like me, had taken jobs as custodians to improve their military retirement income. Also like myself, I knew these men had demanded or earned the respect of their subordinates during their previous careers so I planned to earn theirs. One of the first things I would do was make an appointment with each of them, separately. This was to get to know them individually, and for them to get know me more, and to let them know just what I expected of them as employees. One tactic I found to be very effective was to tell each employee there was no harm if a person made a first mistake (unless it was stealing or fighting); I explained my method of dealing with mistakes. I would tell them the first time they committed an infraction, I would approach them and explain what was wrong about it, and how it should or should not have been done, then caution them not to repeat the action. I would then tell them if it was repeated, that I would call them into the office for a formal discussion, explain the repercussions to expect, and mete out any disciplinary action I deemed necessary at the time. I would then explain, should they repeat the same offence the third time, the punishment would be severe; and that if they had any doubt, they could ask (I would give a fictitious name). I would then purposely hesitate. After a brief pause I would calmly state, "Oh that's right, you can't ask him, he's no longer with us". It had a sobering effect on my employees. I never abused my position, I was respected for that, I practiced this philosophy throughout my managerial career, I found it especially effective while supervising in mail processing, where the employees were much younger, and did not have supervisory experience themselves. I never abused it and always respected the employee, giving them an opportunity to explain their actions. I also had a good relationship with the union representatives. In over sixteen years as a supervisor, I had only two grievances filed against me, and both were deemed frivolous.

I looked into a Post Office program for rewarding employees for meritorious service, I found there had only been about three awards made in the past several years. When I questioned my boss about it he didn't seem to think there were many deserving of awards, they just did their jobs and got paid well for it. I disagreed. Shortly after I was promoted I was sent to the Postal Service Academy in Maryland for managers and supervisors. I learned that the awards program was separate from our station's budget and was told rewarding deserving employees with monetary awards was a great incentive for employees to improve their work habits. It increased productivity and was encouraged by the academy as well as the US Postal service. To implement the program, when I got back I started making notes on all my employees.

There were four of us supervisors and one superintendent in the building services section and I was the only white guy. One day our superintendent called us all in for a special briefing. As he was giving his talk he was using a flip chart to explain his plans and operations. To make his point, he was making a statement about where he was finding difficulties from the higher ups. As he pointed to the chart with his stick he said, "Someone in their "white" wisdom wants it done this way." He immediately stopped and looked at me sitting at my desk right in front of him. I don't know how black men blush, but he seemed to, and apologized. I said, "No problem Bob, I was always considered the white sheep of the family." We all had a good laugh and got on with the business at hand, there never was conflict among us.

Once when we were preparing to move into the new facility in West Sacramento I had a custodial crew preparing the floors in the new maintenance areas. We had spent three days scrubbing, waxing, and polishing the new tile floors. As we just laid the last coat of wax on a long strip of floor running by what was to be the new office for our Manager of Maintenance, this big galoot of a maintenance supervisor started to open the door and go across the floor. I yelled at him not to walk on the wet wax. He said, "I'll just walk lightly up to my office." Although I cautioned him several times as others did, he just kept walking making big track marks in the wet wax. I followed him into his office and told him he could explain to the Manager about the tracks in front of his office. I told the men to pack up their equipment and gave them other work to do until the end of the tour leaving the floor as it was, when the Manager came in the next morning he called me at home. I explained what had happened and said the supervisor responsible owed him about 32 man-hours of work, plus the inconvenience to him until we completed the work. He assured me he would deal with him; I understand he did rather severely. In the next three years I worked all three tours at different times, on tour two (day shift) I had fourteen employees, on tour three (swing shift) twenty two and on tour one (graveyard shift) sixteen. I alternated between these shifts for several years, although most of my time was graveyard. In a three-year period I gave out seven $500.00 awards, plus several smaller ones, as well as letters of commendations. This was more monetary awards than had ever been given out in our department. This action was not to gain favor from my employees, but to reward them for outstanding achievements and earn their respect, and it worked.

The tour superintendent of mail processing approached me one evening on the work floor asking to discuss an ongoing problem he was having. He explained the supervisors were getting complaints from employees about handling what they considered hazardous materials. I found out that vials of blood and urine samples were being sent through the mails not properly packaged. Many of these products were coming from the prison in Folsom and medical facilities. Many times these packages were found to be leaking, causing justifiable concern. I asked him to accompany me to my superintendent to discuss the matter. My boss asked me to prepare a report for us to take to the new post-master. After the meeting we were asked to form and train a hazardous material team to control the shipments. I had been to several classes on various safety measures including hazardous material handling, my boss assigned me the task of forming and training the team. With the help of the safety office, I formed a group with four on each team. This work was in addition to their assigned custodial duties. I also visited each of our branch offices and trained personnel at the stations. I designed a special area to be used for the storage of hazardous materials in the event we had to store anything that needed to be handed by the Sacramento Hazardous Materials team. I was given a meritorious award for creating the team and a $100.00 suggestion award for the storage area.

An event I enjoyed during my efforts for upward mobility, was to promote the Postal Service in the city of Folsom where I live.

Each year, a fund-raising event is held to benefit charities such as Make-A-Wish Foundation, Aid For Polio Victims, Cancer Research, Sacramento Burn Unit and several other organizations. I do not know if people outside of Northern California, or even the Sacramento area, are familiar with this beneficial event; it is the annual "Folsom Snail Race". Basically, people or organizations donate an entry fee in order to enter a "snail" in the race. The money goes to benefit the various charities. The event is held in one of our large parks. There are usually twenty or thirty entries. We actually use live snails, about twelve people serve as "jockeys" representing their organization. They set the snail at the bottom of a twelve inch pole; when the bell rings for the "gates" to open, the jockey must encourage his/her snail to climb the pole without touching it. They can blow on it, wave a piece of paper, or offer a piece of lettuce at the top of the pole to encourage the snail to move upward, the first snail to reach the top is declared the winner. There are lots of preparations that go into this event and it is taken very seriously by us locals. There is a lot of publicity and the event raises thousands of dollars each year. One year I persuaded our Postmaster to post an entry; he agreed and put me in charge of the event. I named our entry "Mr. Zip+ Four". I made arrangements with our Folsom Postmaster to have the snail delivered in one of his Special Delivery mail vans to the park, along with my daughter Sheila, dressed in a pair of racing silks I borrowed from a racing stable at the Sacramento fair grounds. Sheila finished 3rd on "Mr. Zip + Four", but we received 1st place for best delivery. Another post office entry came in on horse back as "The Pony Express" and got 2nd place for delivery. I attempted to get Bill Shoemaker to make a guest appearance but he had a previous engagement, and could not make it. When I called him at the jockey's room at Santa Anita racetrack, Laffit Pincay answered the phone, I heard him call to Bill saying, "Hey Shoe, they caught up with you, someone from Folsom Prison wants to talk to you". When Bill came on I explained who I was and what I was calling about, he laughed as I explained about the race, he said it sounded like it would be fun, but unfortunately, he was scheduled to ride three races that day. I told him I understood and wished him luck. That was the first time I had spoken to him in over twenty years, and unfortunately, the last time I would have the opportunity to talk with him.

After a few years I got restless again and wanted a more challenging job, I requested to be assigned to mail processing. I was accepted and again worked all three tours. tour three had the most employees and at the time processed the most mail and I requested to be assigned there. After about four months my tour superintendent called me in and said he thought I had gotten enough training and was sending me back to my regular job in building services. I asked if he would give me more time and permit me to work in every operation he had. He asked what that would do for him. I said it would give him a supervisor who was familiar with both upstream and downstream operations; a more informed, more productive supervisor. He thought it over and agreed to give me a try, I worked another six months for him before I was needed back in my own job. I worked every position except one unit, 010, where mail was first received. This unit required a more experienced supervisor, but I know in time, I would have mastered that too. After I left mail processing I noticed in about six months the superintendent began moving all his supervisors around to different units, where before, they would spend years on the same tour, doing the same job many times being totally ignorant of what was going on in other operations, I felt I contributed to the betterment of the service.

During this period there were several job openings that came up and I applied for many of them, there was one in particular I wanted, it was a training position that led to higher grade levels. I knew I had the qualifications, but I needed approval of our Director of Personnel. He and I had bumped heads before, but I had dealt with other hard heads before, from grouchy owners and over-zealous trainers during my racing career, to several officers that would make this guy look like a rookie. So I made an appointment with him. He acted like he was doing me a great favor by even granting me an interview. He immediately challenged my qualifications; I met every challenge with a quick and accurate answer. He was sniffing and rubbing his nose throughout the interview, I assumed he either had a head cold or a bad illegal habit. His arrogance came through even stronger when, half way through the interview, he reached in his back pocket, pulled out a handkerchief, blew his nose very aggressively. Then leaned back in his big chair and proceeded to "read" his handkerchief with great intent. If I had reverted back to my racetrack character, I would have flicked a booger onto his glasses and walked out; but no, I wanted this job, and instead I thought, "I am a promoted supervisor, sober, and a graduate of California State University, I will not stoop to his level". He attempted to discourage me by saying this position required me to attend several classes and seminars away from our district and would require me to be away from home frequently. I politely reminded him I was a retired NCO, with over twenty three years of military service, which at times required me to be away from home, usually overseas, for sometimes from six months to a year, without any hope or chance of advancement. I assured him my wife would support me in the little time I would be away from home improving my status in management. He reminded me of some of our previous encounters and his displeasure of my attitude toward him. I felt that he was implying, without actually making the statement, that I was not going anywhere as long as he was in this position. He appeared to be bored, so I ended the interview for him. I could tell I was not going to get any support from him and he more than likely would black-ball me; which I'm sure he did. I suppose the nail in my coffin was as I stood up, wearing a three-piece suit, I reached in my inside pocket, as if to adjust something. He suddenly looked very pale and nervous; he asked me, "Mr. Simmons, have you been taping this session?" I calmly looked at him and responded, "Haven't you?" and walked out letting him believe I had been. I of course did not get that job or any of the others I applied for.

Then I was given the opportunity to work as a relief Postmaster at a small office in a settlement in the foothills about 12 miles from Folsom, I eagerly accepted and again was successful in that position. Next I was assigned as supervisor of delivery in Folsom, this was great, as it was only about six blocks from my house, I hoped to get the job on a permanent basis, but it was not to be. As it turned out, it was fortunate I did not get the job. Soon I was assigned my final position, Mail Flow Controller, where I stayed until I retired; it turned out to be the best job I ever had.

A few humorous events took place while I was at the Folsom station. I was the early supervisor and I had to open up the facility at 2:00 am. This meant turning off the alarm that was hooked up to the local Folsom police station and the postal inspectors in San Francisco. I was trained only one day on the procedures for disarming the alarm. When I opened the side door I had less than two minutes to punch in the code to disarm it, this was no problem the first two days. When I opened the door on the third morning I found that someone had turned off the light over the alarm system and I could not find the panel. I had to cross the building to turn on the lights then go back and punch in the code. This took longer than the required time. Since it was a silent alarm, I never heard any warning noise. In about five minutes one of the early workers came from the dock door I had just opened and said there are some police on the dock. I went out to see them and as they approached me I asked if I could be of service. One of them said, "we are responding to the alarm." I said yeah, that was me and proceeded to explain what had happened. Although I had my postal badge in my inside pocket, it was not required to be displayed. the officers took a step back. Cautiously, one asked if I had any I.D. I thought he said "any idea".

I said I haven't a ------- clue. He came a bit closer, his hand on his hip, and repeated, "Do you have any kind of identification?" Then I pulled out my badge, slowly, and showed it to them. We discussed what had happened and they said they would notify the inspectors for me.

Another time the guards from Folsom Prison came in on their daily run to pick up mail for the prison. You could always tell when we had mail for the prison, the women that wrote to these convicts would soak the letters with some of the strongest, cheap perfume I have ever known. The area where their mail was stored reeked of the smell. I was talking to one of the guards while we drank a cup of coffee as the other one was collecting the mail. He started talking about his partner. He said, "That guy has a warped sense of humor and is going to die a horrible death." I asked why, he told me his partner was always pulling dirty tricks on the prisoners. He said there was one guy in the prison who was doing three life sentences that would total about two hundred and fifty years. He said his partner told this prisoner to do something for him one day; saying he would do a favor in return for him, implying he would get him extra cigarettes rations or magazines. After the prisoner completed the task and was back in his cell, the guard said, "I'm going to talk to the warden and get six months knocked off of your sentence." Then he roared with laughter as he had the cell door closed. The guard said, "Yeah, he's going to die a horrible death."

The reason I was in these other jobs was that the positions of Supervisor of Building Service had being abolished, as were a lot of other positions in one of the postal reorganization plans. The affected supervisors were assigned various positions until they could find us a permanent position. I had applied for over thirty five positions in the past few years I thought I had a good chance now to get one of them. Being who I am however, and one to speak his mind openly, I had stepped on some big toes and ruffled the feathers of several chiefs. This included the Manager of Personnel who was so rude in my last interview with him. I later learned that a lot of the positions I applied for and should have gotten were given to unaffected, less qualified or junior employees. When I challenged these things, I was pushed off into some other slot. Out of some fifty or sixty affected supervisors I was the very last one to be placed, although my position was the first one to be abolished. It was obvious when I was assigned the position of Mail Flow Controller, it was an effort to get me to retire. This position required very technical skills. The other eleven employees that had been selected for the position had been given extensive technical training that I had not been given the opportunity to receive, and was no longer available. Fortunately for me, two of the men I was to work with, Joe Hartman and his colleague Wayne, took me under their wings and gave me the training I needed. I was then, and still am, very grateful to them, especially Joe, for their patience and ability to train such an inexperienced newcomer and accept me as one of their own I really enjoyed the job and spent the next nine years there until I retired in 2001.

The three of us were assigned to the graveyard shift; we came in at ten at night, working until six thirty in the morning. I was intimidated when I first started, after all this was called "CCR",

(The Computer Control Room.) My experience with computers was limited to college classes that mostly consisted of computer literacy classes. But I was determined to make a success of this job; I had met challenges before and never yet walked away from one. I explained my ignorance to Joe, he said he would teach me all he could, and he felt between him and Wayne, they could make a Mail Flow Controller out of me, and I felt more confident after talking to him. True to his word, Joe made me his personal project and after about two or three months, I asked him to be honest with me and let me know how I was doing. He told me I was making great progress, if I would be patient he felt I would be successful. Well it was Joe who needed the patience; I can recall one night when we were the only ones on the shift, as Wayne was on his day off. There was a malfunction on the tray line around two o'clock in the morning. Joe had to go out to check it. He called back to me on the two way radio, instructing me to type in the particular command on one of the computers to correct the malfunction. after about a half a dozen tries, failing to correct the problem, Joe would have to come back in the office and show me how to initiate the proper command. This happened on several occasions, but Joe persevered and eventually, I did become a full fledged Mail Flow Controller. I loved the job and stayed with it until I retired with twenty years of Postal Service.

Shortly after I started working in CCR, we were alone in the unit again one night. There had been some major changes and modifications made to the system by the company who had initially installed the equipment. There had been numerous tests run and many malfunctions. The atmosphere in our unit was tense, as it was out on the floor, and tempers were short. There was a team from our headquarters in Washington D.C. overseeing the operations and doing some statistical evaluations. They still had the system down from the previous tour. Joe asked how long it would be before we could use the tray line, and they could not give him a definitive answer. After about an hour into our tour, Joe notified maintenance that he was starting the system up. In about five minutes, this very large gentleman in charge of the team from headquarters came storming into the office. He demanded to know who had started the system and Joe told him that he had. The man became very red faced and approached Joe sitting at his console, yelling that he had just ruined all of his work for the past hour. I didn't realize just how tall Joe was until he came up out of that seat. He must have stood over six foot four, with his face just as red as the gentleman's. Joe stood toe to toe with the man, their noses almost touching, and shouted back at him, "I have over thirty workers out there on the floor, costing us thousands of dollars for every hour you are holding them up, twiddling their thumbs, awaiting for mail to run on their machines, while you and your team are playing with your figures. Whether you realize it or not, we have thousands of feet of mail to get out on the street to our customers, who don't give a damn about your statistics." I was surprised when the man turned and walked out. As he was a pretty high-ranking person. I was afraid Joe was going to get into trouble, if for nothing else, insubordination. About three o'clock in the morning, the man came back into our office looking much calmer. He walked up to Joe and said, " I'm sorry, I owe you an apology. You were right and I was wrong; you had a job to do and I was interfering. I admire you for your loyalty and dedication to your duties. Perhaps we can work together from now on." Joe shook his hand and they became very compatible. I was proud of Joe and thought that seemed like something I would have done; however, there was a time I would not have been as gentle.

While I was working at the Folsom post office in 1992, I was diagnosed with prostate cancer. I was sent to Sutter Memorial Hospital where I was given radiation treatment. I was told by my doctor to expect some bad side effects toward the end of the treatment. I volunteered to work the early shift at the post office which meant opening up at 2:00am, getting the office ready for incoming trucks and assign work for the first crew that came in at 2:30am. This allowed me to go for my treatments before noon after I got off work. Once the initial treatment was done the follow up radiation work only took about ½ hour so I went every day for 6 weeks and never missed an hour of work, although I had over 1500 hours of sick leave. The treatment was successful, it has been 12 years since I was first diagnosed, although I have some minor ongoing treatment. I have suffered no serious ill effects from it, well almost none, the treatment I am getting involves quarterly shots of a medicine called

Lupron, this is a type of woman's hormone known as estrogen. This is what causes women to have the hot flashes during menopause, and yes I do have hot flashes, and yes it can be embarrassing at times. My colleague at work, Laura had a lot of fun with me over it and teased me about it, even buying me a fan, and from time to time call me "bitch". But as I would tell her, "It beats the hell out of the alternative." I consider myself very lucky. For some reason I never had a lot of concern about the cancer. I'm not being frivolous about it, of course I knew it was serious, after all I had lost both my parents, and three brothers from various types of cancer over the years. Neither was I in denial about it, I think I just felt, if the good lord could see me through my alcoholism, this would be a cake walk for Him. I have no doubt that had I not stopped drinking when I did, I would probably not have lived to my first retirement, let alone my second one. I really was that bad off. Again, it is true, God looks after fools and drunks, even us non practicing ones.

Chapter Thirty

More than a brother

My brother Ross and I were always very close, not only in age but we were also very good friends. Ross was just over nine months older than me and even as kids we ran around together, played together and hung out together at school as much as possible. I really cannot remember us fighting, nothing like any mixture of the other brothers, it seems I was always fighting with my other two brothers, Sam and Simon. Ross could get along with Simon most of the time, but they fought at times. But Ross and I just got along well, especially as we got older. He of course saved my butt from the truant officers when I ran away from school and he got me on the race track. He got me out of several scrapes in various towns. We were even known around the track as the gold dust twins, we just seemed to have more things in common.

Ross always had my best interest at heart; I remember when my drinking starting being a problem I was living with him and his wife Evelyn on our owner's farm where his horses were raised. We stayed there about nine months; Ross and I were both breaking yearlings and grooming some of the brood mares. I was coming home drunk every night and although Ross never complained about it, one day I got an envelope in the mail. When I opened it there were some brochures from Alcoholics Anonymous. When I questioned him about it he admitted he had sent off for them for me as it seemed

I was getting out of hand. I ignored them and we went back to the track later that month and things returned to normal. He never mentioned it again and we continued to drink together. I suppose it was because of his wife and new baby that he was concerned. His wife stayed in Maryland most of the time we were traveling around with the track.

When Ross would get drunk he was a real comic, I can remember one night there were about four of five of us sitting up in our quarters above the stables playing cards, around midnight Ross decided to go to sleep and leave us playing cards. Around two in the morning the rest of us were still playing, when Ross sat upright on the top bunk swinging his legs, we thought he was awake because his eyes were wide open. He suddenly started singing "Old Black Magic" (a song he hated). He sang the entire song, then just laid back down and was sound asleep. He never believed us in the morning when every one was making fun of him for it but I convinced him it was true. He often talked in his sleep, as a matter of fact, Bob Flowers and I found out when he started talking, if we would just hold his hand or finger he would carry on a conversation with us. We did this many times but our laughter would finally wake him up and he would get mad at us.

He was the hardest person I ever knew to wake up, he was always late for work and the trainer was constantly on him about it. One time in Bel-Air he overslept three mornings in a row and the trainer really got on him. When we were going to bed that night, he and I were the only ones in this room and he told me, "Dick, make damn sure I'm awake in the morning, Fred is really getting tired of me being late for work." I assured him that I would. When I called him the next morning he got up with me and started getting dressed. As I started out I asked if he was coming. He said, "Yes, I'll be right down." I was in the shed row when the trainer came and asked where Ross was. I lied and told him he had to go back upstairs for something. When the trainer took a horse out I ran back up stairs and there Ross sat with one boot on holding the other in his hand. I shook him to wake him up and told him Fred was looking for him, he got dressed and was getting his horse out when Fred came back from the track, he asked Ross if he had overslept and Ross told him no. That night I told him he had to start getting up when I called him. He said, "Make sure I'm awake before you go down in the morning. Hell, slap me if you have to." Well, I got up and shook him awake he started getting dressed, as I started out I asked, "Are you awake?" He said, "Yeah, you go on down, I'm coming." As I started out the door I hesitated and looked back; he had one boot on and was staring in the other, just sitting on the end of the bed. I walked back over and slapped him on the side of the head. He jumped up and yelled, "What the hell is the matter with you? Are you crazy?" He was wide-awake, just checking his boot. We laughed about it later. When we went to town that night he went into the drug store and bought one of those old alarms with two big bells on top. He sat it next to his bed that night but woke up around midnight swearing at it. I asked him what was wrong and he said it was making so much noise ticking that he couldn't sleep so he put it in one of his drawers under a pile of clothes. I guess I relied on it to wake me, we never heard it in the morning and were both late for work. We found a better, quieter clock and all was well.

After I retired from the Air Force and we were living in Folsom, Ross and his wife came to visit us. He refused to stay with us and insisted they stay at a motel down the street from us. He was drinking very heavily at the time and was embarrassed about coming to the house drunk. I assured him I was only concerned for him not his actions, and that Joyce understood, but he went to the motel anyway. He was shaking a lot one morning when he and his wife came to our house from the motel. I took him out and got him a six pack to "get well" I was very familiar with the situation. I told him not to fear anything he might think I would feel, we went to a quiet place to let him drink his beer. The strangest thing happened. As we were reminiscing about the time we spent on the track, I mentioned something about Bob Flowers. Ross said he could not remember him, I could not believe it, after all, they had spent many more years together after I left the track and those two were never separated, they were nearly as close as Ross and I were. I kept telling him stories about the things they had done but he said he just could not remember him. I can only think that the alcohol had destroyed parts of his memory. Ross's wife Evelyn told me before he died he had begun to read the bible every day. I suppose he went back to the roots we were brought up with and embraced the religion we were taught; anyway she said he was at peace in the end, and for that I am grateful. I learned years later that Bob had left the track shortly after Ross had and was working in the coal mines in Pennsylvania where he was killed in a cave in. I still think, how sad, as much fun we had together, Ross could not remember him and I never got to say goodbye to him.

Chapter Thirty-One

My wonderful children

We have four children, two boys and two girls. I really cannot take credit for their upbringing as I was not there most of the time for Joyce and them. I was either in the NCO club or some bar when each of them was born. This is one of the facts I am most ashamed of about my drinking days, the way I treated Joyce throughout our marriage. I loved her and the kids very much, it was just that I had an illness that I refused to accept, or knew how to accept and could not control. I knew inside I was treating them wrongly. It was eating me up but the more I ached, the more I drank. It is a vicious cycle. I would not accept that it was the booze or that I even had a problem, but still Joyce stood by me. She couldn't understand it either but somehow she knew it was not my fault and she protected me through it all, those are some very sad memories.

Our children have given us great pleasure. The oldest, Ann Marie was born nine months and two weeks after we got married. Joyce's mother was doing the hand count as soon as we told her Joyce was pregnant, after all it was she who brought this yank into her home and introduced her daughter to him. She knew of the G.I.s who shipped back to the states leaving wives and children to never hear from them again. A lot of this happened during and after the war so there good was reason for her concern. I was paged in the NCO club the night Joyce went into the hospital and by the time I got there on my bicycle Ann was already born. We had been living with Joyce's great aunt during her pregnancy but she developed an infection and we moved in with her parents, in a very small house. We stayed with them until I had to ship out before her and leave her to fend on her own with a six month baby, until we got to my mother's place in Bel-Air, Maryland.

In December 1954 we moved to San Marcos Texas first to Gary AFB. They later changed the name of the base from Gary AFB to Edward Gary AFB. The next year our first son was born, again Joyce went to hospital on her own. This is where I named our first son after the base. We stayed there until they closed the base in 1957 and I was sent to Laredo AFB about 200 miles south.

After we were there about a year, our second daughter Sheila Marie was born. Again no support for Joyce; when she called me from the hospital to be brought home she asked me to bring her some clothes. I took a dress, no underwear or necessities. We were living in a trailer at the end of the run way and the screaming T-33 jets nearly drove Joyce crazy. In December 1959 I requested my second tour to England and was accepted, we were being stationed at Mildenhall RAF Station, this was some of my worst drinking periods, so a lot of that tour is a blur.

For our fourth child, a boy named Michael William, Joyce took a taxi to the base hospital, again alone. When Mike was about six month old we shipped out again, this time to a decent assignment, MacDill AFB Florida.

We are very proud of all of our children and the way they have grown up, all of them have become successful in their careers, Ann is now a Registered nurse at U.C.Davis Hospital in Sacramento, Gary has his own plumbing business on Long Island in New York, (he is the only one to be away from us). Sheila worked for several years in the medical field as a pharmacy technician. She now works as a computer analyst for a large optical company near us. Michael also has had several various positions, mostly mechanical. He is a master machinist, and now works with his cousin Mark in his business of installation of high end appliances. We consider ourselves very fortunate that none of them ever gave us major problems. For that I again I commend Joyce's teaching and leadership abilities.

Chapter Thirty-Two

Final postal position

When I first started work in the Computer Control Room (CCR) as a Mail Flow Controller, I was intimated and overwhelmed by the concept of what we were doing, controlling the flow of the mail. This was in our new facility and at the time it was the most modern facility in the country. After Joe Hartman, the guy who was training me, showed me around the equipment we were to be working with and the importance of what we were doing, I became more impressed than intimated. I thought back to my drinking days and thought boy am I ever glad I am sober, no way could I have grasped the concept of this technical world in my drinking days. As good as I was at it, all my "Irish bull" would not have got me through this. Joe was a very good trainer, I know I tried his patience at times, but he stayed with me and got me through. We became friends and I still go back to the office once in a while with some Donuts or just to visit him and my other old cronies, including the people in Building Service, still not forgetting where I first got my start. The job in CCR was ideal for me, I was still in management without having anyone to supervise and required very little supervision ourselves. We were mostly answerable only to the Tour Superintendent of our tour. Most of the supervisors didn't have a clue what we were doing so they never questioned us. They needed us more than we needed them and that felt good. I soon mastered the most difficult tasks and soon was able to run the unit on my own on weekends The only down side of the position was I was back on graveyard shift again, 10:00 pm-06: 30am. Although I did not like the shift, I got used to it as I had before but it was hard on Joyce. I wasn't able to help out around the house much as I was sleeping most of the day, but what else is new for her. At least I was sober and I think that was some compensation for her.

After about three years on graveyard I finally convinced my Tour Superintendent that I was needed on tour 3, 2:00pm to 10:30pm. This suited Joyce much more and I loved it, the other guy on that shift had been working many days by himself or with minimal relief. He was glad to see me and we got along very well. Still, with our days off there were four days a week that there would only be one of us in the shop. I requested a full time relief and it was granted, we had several persons accept the position but more permanent positions came up and they would move on. Until one day I approached a young lady named Laura Garrard, working in the manual units. I had observed her for some time and admired her work habits; she seemed dedicated to her work. Although I had never spoken to her she seemed a pleasant person. (I later learned she was the daughter of a friend of mine) I introduced myself and asked if she would like to work with me in CCR. She said yes without asking what her duties were (most people knew of our unit and were envious). I took her into the office to show her the operations. She was very impressed and enthusiastic about working there. I had trained many employees during my career so I laid out a training period of 90 days. She was very intelligent, took copious notes and progressed rapidly. Half way through her training she was competent enough to run the operation with out assistance. I was very impressed at her ability to grasp the most technical problems.

Although our work was serious we managed to find humor in many things. We were both working on different computers beside each other one day when she started talking about a friend of hers and something about her new baby. She said she felt so sorry for the little one and I asked why. She said that the baby had just been circumcised and was crying a lot. Without looking up I just calmly said, "Yeah, I used to be circumcised." She let out a big gasp and said, "What the hell do you mean you used to be circumcised?" The look of complete disbelief and surprise on her face was priceless, when I started laughing she nearly knocked me out of my chair. When I was training her on the "green monster", a large machine with conveyer belts that carried the mail sacks and large to medium size packages across the building, approximately 100 yards to a section where the mail was keyed onto another conveyer belt then diverted into slides allotted to various zip codes. We had cameras throughout the building so we could track the mail in any given part of the facility. We had seven monitors and seventeen cameras where we could switch to various parts of the mail tray lines or conveyer belts to watch for malfunctions. I was showing her on one of the cameras displaying an area of the green monster where a mail sack was hanging up on a corner of the chute it was supposed to drop into. I explained that it would cause a huge jam as subsequent sacks and parcels arrived at that point and could damage the machine if it was not cleared. She asked what to do and I told her to notify maintenance of a pending malfunction, which she did. I explained to her if they took too long we would have to shut the machine down as a last option as this would delay the mail, as we watched the sack on the monitor I said "just a moment, let me try something" I grabbed the monitor with both hands and shook it, just as I shook the monitor, gravity caused the sack to break loose and fall into the proper slot, she was in total shock, and said, "How did you do that?" as soon as I started laughing she realized I had nothing to do with the sack falling and punched me in the arm, we laughed about that often. There were many other good times, she turned out to be one of the best employees I had the pleasure working with in my postal career.

I always enjoyed playing tricks on my colleagues; once one of my coworkers and I were discussing something about the microwave oven in our office. I nonchalantly mentioned how well I could do a boiled egg in the microwave. He immediately challenged me saying you could not boil an egg in a microwave. I said, "Of course you can, all you have to do is carefully place a rubber band around it." He argued it would explode. I said, "I do it all the time. Just make sure the rubber band is snug, not tight, lay it on the rotating plate for thirty three seconds, and viola, you have a perfect boiled three minute egg." He huffed expressing his disbelief and let it go. The next day when he came in the office, he came straight to me and said, "You got me in a lot of trouble with that damn boiled egg in the microwave." I asked him what happened. He said it had exploded. I asked him to show me how he had placed the band on the egg. He said he just put it around the egg. I said, "Well no wonder, you need to put it oblong around the egg." He said he didn't believe me, I just said, "Ok have it your way, but I still enjoy my egg every morning" and let it go. As he left at the end of the shift I told him to try it again, that he would enjoy it once he got the hang of it, he just huffed again. The next day he busted into the office yelling at me, "You so-and-so, you got me in trouble again, my wife made me clean the whole kitchen." I asked again what had happened and he said, "You know damn well what happened, that egg exploded again." I put my hand on his shoulder and asked, "What color rubber band did you use?" He jerked away saying, "Go to hell. I've heard enough of your Irish bull!"

Chapter Thirty-Three

Time to hang up my tack

My plans were to work until I was seventy years old before I retired which would have been in August 2001. My boss had inquired a few times, without actually asking, when I thought I might retire. I told her whenever she or someone pissed me off enough. Well it happened in April. Certain events happened and work no longer was a pleasure, instead it was becoming a burden. I would have liked to stay, as it would have been economically beneficial. After President Clinton dropped the top cap on wages for people drawing social security. Before, had I retired and put in for social security a portion of my retirement pay would have been deducted from it. When this law was passed, I put in for SS and started drawing that plus my full postal pay. The law was retroactive; I was also back paid from the 1st of January. I could have kept on drawing my full pay plus my maximum social security until I would have retired in August. I am not complaining, I have done very well. I was lucky really; my race track pay, fees, bonus, and percentage of purse for races I had ridden and won paid into my social security fund so the necessary four quarters required to draw the maximum was paid before I even joined the Air Force. Just as well too, as the military stopped taking SS out after 1954 I believe, so that would have only been about three years. I did pay into it again at McClellan AFB while with civil service for seven years; however, my twenty years with the Postal

Service paid nothing into it. So after twenty three years of military service, plus seven years with civil service and twenty years with the USPS, I figured fifty years of government service was enough and I should hang up my tack.

Our first priority was to travel. Joyce and I both love to travel on our own terms. Although we traveled quite a bit while in the service, our choices were extremely limited. There is some very nice country right here in California we take advantage of and visit often. We always enjoy visiting our son Gary on Long Island in New York. While I was working we didn't have the opportunities we now have, so we go there as often as possible also. The first year I retired we had planned a long stay with them in the fall, as that is the nicest time of the year to go there. The Hamptons are always crowded in the summer. It's just too damn cold in the winter so we decided to go after the kids were back in school and the summer vacationers have gone back to the city. We had our trip planned out and plane reservations made, we had our bags packed and arranged for one of our nephews to take us to the air port on the morning of 09/11/2001. Our flight out of Sacramento was scheduled for around noon. I got up early and was reading the paper, drinking my coffee when the phone rang. It was my son Gary in New York. He asked if I had the TV on, I said no. He said, "Dad, put it on. There is something going on in the city that may interrupt your travel plans." I put the TV on and saw one of the twin towers in Manhattan burning. I called Joyce who was just getting up. She came in just as the second plane went into the second tower. We spent the rest of that day and most of the week in total disbelief, watching along with the rest of the country and world as it was shown over and over again. Joyce immediately called and canceled our flights, although we knew we were not going anywhere for a while. Joyce said we should not try to travel until other people who were stranded had first chance to get flights to where they needed to go. It is typical of her to think of others first.

We finally got off on our visit to the Hamptons about three weeks later. We had a wonderful visit and also drove down to Pennsylvania to visit my oldest sister Marie. We had an especially good time as we went back to all the places we had lived as kids. Marie could not remember where they all were but between the two of us we found them all. It took us all day but it brought back many memories for both of us. We spent the most time at our birthplace where our father ran the farm and where he died. The people who now own the place were very gracious hosts and were genuinely pleased to see us as we gave them much more information about the place than they knew. We have been back to see them once and they have given us an open invitation to return, I know we will.

We return to Europe as often as possible. We belong to an organization that is affiliated with the first base I was stationed at in England, Burtonwood. The base has long closed but we have a reunion yearly, every other year it is in England, but each year it is held at various cities around the United States. We attend as often as possible and always have a good time. When we go back to England we try to visit as many places as possible. We stay in England with some of Joyce's relatives then visit Scotland, Wales, Ireland and our most favorite place, The Isle Of Mann. What I enjoyed most about this place, other than it's natural beauty, is that this is where they hold the famous TT motorcycle races. They are held around the last week of June. There are no motor vehicles allowed on the roads during the time of the races, the motorcyclists take over the main roads of the island. Which is only approximately 25 miles long and about 17 miles across, these roads are very narrow and the racers reach speeds well in excess of 200 mph. I have not seen the races other than on TV and have a complete video of the race in 2001. But the most exciting thing for me was while we were in Douglas, the main city, we rented a car and I drove the entire racecourse. I bragged about driving the course, sometimes reaching speeds in excess of 45 mph. Another thing that impressed me about The Isle of Mann was how clean it is. There is no homeless people, no unemployment and you never see anyone pan-handling. If you are found to be homeless or unemployed, you are simply asked to leave. It is not easy to purchase a home there either, you must have some kind of connection with the island, such as being Manx. It seemed somehow harsh, but it certainly keeps the riff-raff out. I'm all for it if it keeps it like it is. Another place I enjoyed of course was Ireland, as this is where my mothers people came from it has a natural draw for me. I enjoyed Dublin but it is so crowded, it was as bad as San

Francisco, and I never realized how many different nationalities there are there. It is a very large city. We plan to go back for two or three weeks to the country side and stay in a Bed & Breakfast inn, renting a car and touring the island, I hope soon. Another neat thing we do is house swap with Joyce's relatives. We coordinate our vacation times, they come over here and take over our house as a base and we go over there and take over theirs. We use each other's cars and everything as if it were ours. It works out great for everyone and is very economical.

Chapter Thirty-Four

Postal highs and lows

When I first started work at the Post Office as a custodian I had no great goals to aim for, I was just glad to get out of the situation I had been in at McClellan AFB. Of course I was going to school full time at CSUS as well but other than getting a degree, was satisfied with the achievements I had made so far. Quite frankly, I was really amazed at how much I had going for me. I considered myself a very lucky person; first I suppose that I was even alive, then there was my sobriety that I truly believe is the reason I was alive, my wonderful supportive wife and my children that were doing so well. The fact I was able to retire from the air force, that I was able to get the job at McClellan making it possible to get our house. That I could leave one job and step into another more secure position. With my limited educational background, I had graduated from college and was attending a university nearing graduation again. I really was a very lucky person, I felt I had been blessed and I was flying high.

For the first two or three years I had no ambitions for advancement, but it seems to be in my nature to seek challenges and prove to myself I could do more. As I observed the people who were supervising me I thought to myself, I had been an NCO for twenty years, mostly in a supervisory position, at times with as many as ten subordinates, surely I could do their job. I applied several times for the position but there were no openings. Then one of the supervisors retired and another transferred. There were several applicants. I was accepted along with one of my co-workers, Theo James. One of the positions were on tour three, 2:00pm -10:30pm and the other on tour one, 10: pm -6:30am, graveyard. I was given the graveyard shift, I was back in management. This kept me happy for the first few years, then again I felt the need to prove to myself once again that I could go farther yet. I observed the mail processing supervisors and again and thought, what the heck, I can do that. I applied for several positions but was not taken seriously, perhaps because of where I was coming from, the custodial craft. So I thought I needed another strategy. I applied for every school I could that would give me knowledge in the field of mail processing. I went to classes for supervisor of mails, supervisor of deliveries, and supervisor of carriers, plus extra classes in communications, safety and computers. I attended the Postal Academy in Washington D.C. for supervisory training when I was initially promoted, but I requested to attend again as a mail-processing supervisor. I was accepted for this and was also sent to Los Angeles to the Postal Management Academy. Our postmaster at the time was not approachable, however I had always admired his second in command, Mr. Tom Dunbar, I had spoken to him on several occasions. One morning as he was coming to work I met him on the dock and asked him for an appointment regarding upward mobility. He asked me to bring a resume and see him the next morning. We talked for about an hour and I told him my desire to advance into mail processing and asked his advice on procedures to accomplish my goal. He sent me to see Mr. Mark Meske, the supervisor of automation. This particular part of the postal service was then in its infancy and fortunately for me that Mark had been appointed the overall supervisor of automation. Mark was very knowledgeable in the field; he had been appointed to oversee and implement improvements to the overall automation department. He was very good and was "looking for a few good men".(where had I heard that before?) Mark took me under his wing. I was inexperienced in the actual mail processing functions, but he walked me through each operation explaining the functions and how each affected the other. After about two weeks of training he selected me as one of the first Automation Readability Specialists. There were three of us assigned to this new position. With me were another recently promoted supervisor of mails and a young lady window clerk from a near by small post office. Our task was to assist in finding reasons for the mail being rejected by the new automation machines using OCR, (Optical Character Recognition.) One problem was that the machines could not read hand written addresses. We found that envelopes that had various printed designs, windows or skewed address would be rejected. These machines have long been replaced with much more sophisticated equipment; these were akin to the first computers I suppose. We would pull mail from the rejection bins to study reasons for the rejection, we would visit the firm sending the mail and explain how we could work with them to improve the acceptance rate of their mail pieces. Assuring them a more rapid response from their customers by improving methods of addressing their mail pieces, we were very well received at some of the largest companies and mailers. It was a very gratifying job and again I felt blessed and enjoyed my new position. I had hoped to get the position permanently but it was not to be. After three months I was sent back to my assigned position as custodial supervisor, this was the first of many disappointments in my attempts at upward mobility.

Now that I had all these schools and training behind me plus the experience I had just completed in Automation I felt secure in applying for other positions. Over the next few years I applied for every opening I could find. I made many interviews but always with the same result, "We found your qualifications were very impressive, however…" At first I took it as an experience in the process of upward mobility but then it got personal. The rejections were affecting my home life; I was letting it get to me and neglecting my family again without realizing it. One day when I got yet another rejection letter I flew off the handle and when Joyce tried to comfort me I rudely walked out and started to work. As I drove I suddenly had a sinking feeling, "What the hell am I thinking? I just left my wife in tears again through my selfishness." I turned the car around and went back home to find her crying. I called in and asked for the day off, I apologized and we went for a long walk along the American River bike trail.

There were many more disappointments in the following months and years. I now realize these were things that were not meant to be. As hard as it was to understand then, I do now and I am grateful for the way things worked out. Joyce has often said, "God always answers our prayers, he just doesn't always say yes, or he answers them in ways that we never expected or hoped for."

While working with the postal service in the late 1980s, I experienced of the biggest disappointments in dealing with people. It involved a young lady, and I use the term lady loosely. At the time I was very much involved with Toastmasters International. I was the treasurer of our district at the time and part of my duties was recruitment for new memberships. I had met this lady from time to time on the workroom floor in my duties as Supervisor of Building Services, she seemed a nice person, and very shy. During a conversation one day, she mentioned her difficulty in talking to people and overcoming her bashfulness. She told me she had just gotten out of a very abusive marriage to a postal worker. I explained how beneficial Toastmaster International could be for her, she seemed interested and we discussed it on several occasions. I usually talked to her with one of her friends around. One day she said she was interested in learning more about toastmasters, she had previously given me her phone number, this day she gave me her address and said I could bring some pamphlets to her home. When I arrived later in the week she was not home. I did not see her at work for a while so I called her, she said her mother was ill and she had to stay off work and care for her and it was putting her under a lot of stress. I found a friendship card in a shop and sent it to her as a good will gesture, later that month I got a call from someone in personnel telling me I was being named In a sexual harassment suit against the postal service and several other persons. I was told to cease and all contact with her. I was dumbfounded and approached several of my superiors inquiring what the hell was going on. It seems the lawyer that took this girl's case had named everyone she had ever came in contact with while working at the post office, including me. This thing drug out for over three years. I was called in for interviews numerous times, having to fill out affidavits and make sworn depositions giving statements to her lawyers. Anytime I attempted to ask any questions I was shunted off. During all of this, I was never permitted to approach or challenge my accuser. There were even upper level managers in personnel who had given sworn depositions that they had interviewed me in taped statements regarding my involvement with her. I denied then, and still do, that the interview ever took place. When asked to produce the tapes, they said they had been lost. Even after I produced official clock rings from the payroll section proving I was not even on duty for two weeks before and after the times they swore they had interviewed me, they swore the interview took place late in the afternoon. I proved I was working day shift, getting off at 2:00pm and still I received no backing from my superiors. This all happened during the postal re-organization process when my job as custodial supervisor had been abolished. I was refused promotion or transfers to at least fourteen positions, being the last person to be reassigned from the many affected by the re-organization. This is when I was finally assigned to the position of Mail Flow Controller, a position certain people in upper management was sure I would fail in and ultimately retire from the postal service (nice try). Although I worked another ten years before I did retire, on my own terms, I was never given an explanation, apology, or even the results of the lawsuit. I learned much later the postal service had made a very large settlement on her behalf. She claimed she was so traumatized over the events she could not associate with anything to do with the postal service, that she could not even open her mail, yet after the settlement, she married another postal worker. I was deeply disappointed in my superiors, that they would treat one of their supervisors with such disrespect. It took a long time for me to let go of this. It had been hard on Joyce as well, seeing me suffer under the pressure, but then I practiced some of my AA training. Some of the prominent sayings are "Let go and let God", and "This too will pass". Not that I am gloating about it, but I learned later that everyone of the people who could have helped me, but chose to desert me had much worse things happen to them. There were divorces, loss of families, disgraces, several sexual harassment cases, loss of prominent positions and opportunities. Now I look back at the way things turned out, I believe the situation made me a better person.

237

My decision to retire was made mostly due to an unpleasant event that happened in the Computer Control Room one evening while I was out of the office for lunch break. A lower level supervisor came into the office and got into and argument with my colleague Laura. Apparently she made some very disrespectful remarks to her, it resulted in the acting superintendent telling Laura she had to go back to her old job in mail processing, taking away her much loved status as a Mail Flow Controller. That was the last straw for me, the work environment had become so political and hostile I wanted nothing more to do with it. After sending my resignation to my supervisor the next day by e-mail with courtesy copies to all of my superiors in upper management, I went to human resources and asked a lady how much notice I was required to give. After looking over my records she said, "Richard you could walk out of here today if you wish." That was on a Thursday, around the 20th of the month. I said I would stay until the end of the month. When my big boss called me in for the traditional final briefing he asked me if I was going to give the regular thirty-day notice. I said, "How about the end of the pay period?" When he asked my reasons for leaving I let him know in no uncertain terms. It was not only the work environment but the style of management in general, the lack of respect for not only the employees but for supervisors and lower management workers as well. He was not pleased with my answers but accepted my resignation. On the day before my last day I was called into the main office and given a token going away party, cold pizza and warm coke. I think that in their minds it was more of a "go-away" party. My big boss was there and gave me the traditional thank you for fifty years of government service plaque and others gave me good luck cards.

The next evening was my last day at work. At the end of the shift I went to turn in my walkie-talkie radio. Just before turning it off, I switched to the maintenance channel calling, "Attention all maintenance personnel, thank you for twenty years of support and friendship. Richard has left the building." I got response from all over the building, saying good-bye and good luck. I then switched to the mail processing channel and gave the same message and got similar responses, it felt even better than when I left McClellan AFB.

Chapter Thirty-Five

Retirement rocks

My retirement from the U.S. Postal service was April 30, 2001. Although I would have preferred to keep working until my seventieth birthday in August, circumstances dictated otherwise. I am however, very pleased with the way things turned out for me and Joyce. I was actually thirty-six days short of working fifty years for the U.S. Government,

June 6, 1951 to April 30, 2001 but I do not feel I would have benefited by serving out the shortage and it would have made no difference to my pension. Anyway, I figured the time I spent working overtime during my 23 years of military service without compensation, 7 years with civil service at McClellan AFB and 20 years with the USPS, 1500 hours unused sick leave, extra days working during my military career and volunteer work more than made up for the shortage.

My first wish for our retirement life was to travel. Although we had traveled extensively during my military career and I did see quite a bit of the states during my racetrack career, still I wanted us to travel on our itinerary, and we have. We started soon after my retirement, first to southern California, where we visited our niece Paula. We are very proud of her. I have a special attachment to her as we were in college at CSUS at the same time for a few semesters. She is a Major stationed at Vandenberg AFB, and very successful in her career. It is a beautiful area and we have been back several times. Then we were scheduled to visit our son Gary and his family at Hampton Bays on Long Island New York. That trip was scheduled on the morning of September 11th 2001, but was delayed for three weeks because of the twin towers tragedy. But we did make it later and as usual had a wonderful trip. One the perks of visiting Gary is that he always generously gives us the use of one of his automobiles so we can drive down to Pennsylvania to visit my eldest sister Marie. We can go from her place a short distance down into Maryland and visit Bel-Air and places we used to live. We also return to England as often as we can. While there, we enjoy staying with and visiting Joyce's relatives. We try to make the reunions of my old base at Burtonwood, we also try to visit London when we go. Joyce has a cousin who is a Nun and the superintendent of a school there. She and two of her colleagues, with the aid of the church were able to purchase a very large apartment building that they have turned in to a place for visiting priests, nuns and other church officials. When we are expecting to be in London, we make arrangements with Sister Margaret and she schedules a room for us. We are grateful, it is handy and of course economical. One of the things I enjoy when we visit her is there is a bookie just a few blocks from the apartment. They make fun of me sneaking out of the "nunnery" to go to the bookies, but it is all in fun. She is a wonderful person, as are her colleagues.

Another little perk I enjoy is the privilege we have of visiting the Royal Mews at Buckingham Palace. My oldest daughter Ann has an ex sister-in-law who is married to one of the drivers for the royal family. They live in an apartment over "the mews" which is an area where all the royal family cars and horses are kept. We visit them sometimes when we go, if he is not out of town on duty with the royal family. When Joyce and her sister Stella stayed with them they enjoyed catching a taxi from downtown London and telling the driver to take them to Buckingham Palace. The driver assumed they were going somewhere near the palace using it as a landmark, and he would get near he would ask where they were going. They told him the palace, then watch the drivers face when they produced their pass to gain admission through the gates to the palace, that's neat.

After Ann's first husband died she married again and some time in the early 90's her sister-in-law and her husband came to visit us. Ann and her husband Ron were going to San Francisco to meet them. I was driving a 1986 Lincoln Town Car at the time. The car was in showroom condition and Ron loved to drive it. He asked me if he could borrow it to pick Karen and Keith up, he said he thought Keith would be impressed. I said "Ron, Keith drives Princess Anne around in Rolls Royce's and Bentleys, do you think you are going to impress him with an 86 Lincoln?"

We did not do much traveling in 2003, as Joyce was ill for a good part of the year we stayed home and did some minor repairs and decorating. A couple of sad events occurred the year of 2003. One was the death of Bill Shoemaker. He died in October that year after years of being paralyzed from the neck down due to the automobile accident after he retired from the racetrack. I admired him for the stamina and strength he showed during the time he was wheel chair bound. I watched the memorial service that was put on for him in the winner's circle at Santa Anita racetrack, a place he was very fond of and rode many of his winners. I regret I could not attend, Joyce was not well and I did not want to leave her alone. I just sent a sympathy card to his daughter Amanda and her mother Cindy. I will also miss him and his famous smile. Another great rider whom I admired and had the privilege to meet and work with, Johnny Longden also died that year.

Sometime after the first of the year in 2004 Joyce was reading some brochures when she came across one with an article about the new Queen Mary 2. Although I never knew it, it had always been a dream of Joyce's to go on one of the big luxury liners. I had never given it a second thought, as a poor old country boy it was way out of my class. Joyce has a friend in a travel agency so she and her sister Stella, who often travels with us, went to see her. She found out it was not only something we could afford but found many attractive amenities that could be added. We found out this was to be the last trip to England for the Queen Elizabeth 2. The new Queen Mary 2 would be taking over the US to England route while the Queen Elizabeth 2 would be used around the islands and through the Panama canal (the QM2 is to big to go through it). We had the option of taking the last trip on the Queen Elizabeth 2 or the maiden voyage to England on the Queen Mary 2, the largest ship in the world. It is twice as big as the QE 2 and there was very little difference in the cost, it was a no-brainer. We used our frequent flyer miles to New York, stayed three days in Manhattan. Our son and his wife from Long Island spent time with us before we departed, boarding the Queen Mary2 for a six-day cruise.

QM 2 & QE 2

I stood on deck the night of the departure with Joyce and my oldest daughter Ann, who had joined us on the tour with a friend. I watched as between our ship and the skyline of New York City as a large barge loaded with fireworks was positioned. There were news helicopters and all kinds of security boats and helicopters all around us. After dark, around nine o'clock, we watched the most spectacular display of fire works we had ever witnessed. The display must have gone on for at least an hour, it was breathtaking. In addition to all the fireworks, we looked at the skyline with all the skyscrapers in the background. Every window was flashing with flash bulbs from people taking pictures of the Queen Mary2 with the Queen Elisabeth just ahead of us, with the statue of liberty in between the two ships.

As I stood there in the cold wind, with hundreds of people around me, I suddenly realized where I was. I thought to myself My God; I am on board the Queen Mary2, the largest ship in the world. So many thoughts rushed through my mind; thoughts from my childhood, times at the racetrack, all of the years I had wasted drinking. I thought, did I deserve to have all of this? Then as I looked at Joyce and Ann I thought, Yes, I have earned this. It has been a long hard ride. Now it is time to stop beating myself up, forgive myself, accept and enjoy my sobriety. I'm going to enjoy every minute of this; and I did. I am glad it was dark and crowded; for as I pondered these thoughts and experienced these feelings, I'm not sure I didn't shed a tear, of joy of course.

As you may recall, my last trip on a ship in 1951 was 12 days and not quite as luxurious. After docking in South Hampton, we were taken by bus to make connections for a trip on the Orient Express. We enjoyed dinner on the Express, then a tour of some cities and magnificent castles, then on to London where we stayed for five days with Joyce's cousin in the "nunnery". Ann and her friend had to take a flight back to California, as they had to get back to work.

We spent a day at Buckingham Palace, where I again visited the Mews, getting some great pictures for our scrap books.

Then we traveled up north for five weeks, four weeks with Joyce's cousin, then one week in Liverpool with my reunion. We then returned to London for a ten-hour flight to San Francisco and a stretch limousine ride home to Folsom. That was the trip of a lifetime. The Queen Mary2 was beyond all expectations, the food alone was indescribable. There were restaurants or food courts open 24 hours a day, a planetarium, a library that would rival most city's library, casinos, ballroom dancing, theaters, night club acts with top entertainers, art shows, over one million dollars worth of art displayed in strategic places around the ship. Various college courses from Oxford and Cambridge Universities were offered, including computer classes. We had a computer in our compartment with our own e-mail address, and again, I must mention the food. I managed to lose 15 pounds before leaving so I could get into my tuxedo that was required at many of the dinners. I gained 12 of those pounds back during the trip as did my daughter Ann. If I have any regrets at all, it would be that it had to end.

We attended my reunion again in October 2004 in southern California. My next hope is to make the trip back east perhaps in the spring and maybe, if I'm lucky, make that much desired two or three week trip to Ireland and of course visit merry old England, and attend my reunion again.

Now that I am retired and enjoying my life, I try to stay as healthy and fit as I can. I had a gym in one of the rooms of our house for a while but it got boring and I was not getting the benefit I had hoped to so I sold the equipment and joined a large gym near home. That too became a hassle, so now I just walk about 4 to 4 1/2 miles a day, mostly around one of the very nice parks we have near our house. As I walk around the park, I see all the young school children playing soccer, softball, and tennis or shooting hoops. I sometimes stop and watch with envy. I never had such a childhood, I see these high school kids playing and I think how lucky you are. When I was your age I was riding horses, making a living and destroying my life with drinking and carousing. I hope they take advantage of the opportunities offered them by today's modern education system, opportunities that I never had. I wonder if my father had lived, would I have had those opportunities, and if so, would I have taken advantage of them? I suppose we all have the tendency to wonder "what if". I am sorry for many of the things I did in my life, but if that is what it took to get me where I am today, I look at what I now have; and I truly believe it was worth it. One hell of a finish! But I'm not finished; as Jimmy Buffet puts it, "I've got boats to build".

Joyce has not yet read much of my writings, she started on some of the earlier chapters while I was on the race track, when she got to the chapters after I met her, she could not read more, it was too painful. I understood. A lot about my earlier life she never knew, when I first met her, I thought of her being such a sophisticated lady that she would have nothing to do with the type of person I had been, at first I never elaborated on my life on the track, and later on I was so deep into my drinking, I was just ashamed of the most of my previous life and kept it to myself. These were feelings and memories I was just too ashamed of and did not wish to share, especially with someone I loved so much and wanted to protect from my sordid past. One night recently she was going through some old photographs, she showed me some of her after I retired, of her with our first grand children, she looked so happy and bright eyed, so alive; then she showed me some of her when we were in Florida and others when we were in England during my heavy drinking, she looked so unhappy, her eye's were so dead and sad, it brought back so many unhappy memories, I could only apologize again and tell her how sorry I was for the hurt I had caused her, she of course forgave me again saying she knew I was ill and that she understood how I must have suffered myself.

My reasons for writing this book are many, first it brought back many pleasant memories, along with some unpleasant memories and issues that until now, I do not feel I have really dealt with. Now that I have, it somehow gives a sense of relief. I found it to be therapeutic. But I feel the most important reason is that it may somehow benefit some of the many poor souls who are out there suffering, as I did. Perhaps they may see themselves in these stories and find the hope that I found. They just need to realize, the help they need is within, and only takes a true desire to find it. And I sincerely hope that even though they too may find life a long hard ride, it can also have a great finish.

To be continued…not the book …… ***the Ride!***

Epilogue - A tribute to my mother

The following are the memoir my mother wrote of her own life many years ago. My sister Marie typed her hand-written notes in the style that mom wrote them. Neither Marie or I have made changes to the original writings or style. I feel it is appropriate to include these writings in this book as she wrote them, unedited.

"REFLECTIONS"

Life is real, life is earnest
And the grave is not its goal.
"Dust thou are - to dust returneth"
Was not spoken of the Soul

Life was created by love - God is love,
Life was created for love -God wanted love.
Since the beginning, life has been the results of love.

My own simple life began when I was born - March 18 1900. Whether it was morning, noon or night, I do not know. Perhaps the hour of my death will tell, since it is said, one, one leaves this life on the same hour of the day on which our life began. Whether this is true or not it really doesn't matter.

My memory goes back only to the time I was about five or six years old.

I had one sister and two brothers, all older than I. It was a normal routine life. We played together and some times had fights. Being the youngest, I escaped most to the fights.

We lived on farmland, mostly pasture fields. There were horses, which would chase us, so we stayed out of their way. My father worked away from home and could not farm. We had only a garden and perhaps a truck patch until later. The house, as I can remember, was a quaint weather beaten frame house, perhaps one time a log house. It had typical wood shingles on the roof, they stood the test of time, they lever leaked.

There was the living room and a big roomy kitchen. The safest place in the world for kids, there were three bedrooms and I'm sure the boys had their usual pillow fights in their room.

Plenty of grassy fields and tall trees, many flowers surrounded the house in summer, red roses, peonies, and snapdragons and hollyhocks, there were plenty of fields to roam and woodland to investigate.

The one of the fields stood an old apple tree, it produced only hard, knotty apples, but my brother, two years my senior, and I thought they were good so we often climbed the tree. We had heard that sometimes Gypsies came along and carried children off. One day while up in the tree, we saw a horse and buggy coming up the road, we were sure the driver was a Gypsy, terrified, we made a hurried descent. My brother reached the aground ahead of me; I caught my elbow in the fork of a limb. I could not get down or up enough to extricate my arm, my bother gave me a boost and my arm was freed, we made a hasty retreat home and never returned for more apples. I guess I was somewhat of a tomboy. We liked to climb the small "saplings" in the woods, we would climb until our weight would bend them over and we would drop to the ground, one day I climbed one that did not bend so well, I was left hanging between heaven and earth several feet from the ground, my brother had to climb up and ad his weight so we both dropped to the ground.

Beyond the field and highway, then a dirt road, stood an old log church, built in the year 1877, and known as "the old log church" it stands yet today and is used on special occasions as immemorial services, many old fashioned revival meetings were held there, I can remember hearing the happy singing and shouting of the old saints of that day.

Back at our house, we had no old fashioned pump, our water supply was from a waterfall that tumbled down the mountain side, over stones and under shade of trees, to from a large saucer shaped body of water, before continuing on down another hill, this was where we carried all our water for drinking, cooking and laundry and baths, so cool and clear you could see the pebbles, the crayfish, and little black fish shaped creatures that hid back in the mud when we dipped our bucket in for water, we had not head the work "pollution". The water came right out of the ground, clear and pure.

A tree had fallen, partially uprooted but still green in the summer, it was arched over and a few feet above the stream, we would climb out on a large limb and holding on tightly to smaller branches for reins, we bounced up and down, this was our daily horseback ride, to us, this was a real wild bucking bronco.

In the evening sunset we looked out over the tops of mighty oaks and stately pines that pointed toward heaven like great church steeples and would see the golden sunset tinged with purple shadows, we loved this peaceful place and were happy with our lot. Then one day we were told we were moving to a new home, Father had gone earlier, cleared the ground and built a hoe for us. The household goods were taken by wagon, we had to walk, we got very tired, it seemed like miles and miles, and, in fact it was.

We finally reached our new home, it seemed like a wilderness to us, there were trees every where, our uncle had told us kids that there were bears in these woods, kidding us of course, but children tend to believe adults, this was worse than gypsies, at least the gypsies wouldn't eat us.

By spring father had cleared more ground for crops, he also had a large well digging rig come in and drill for water, we children were fascinated watching the big machine drill a big hole deep in the ground, it was necessary to drill 150 feet down and through solid slate to find a good stream of water, when it was finished and the pump installed we had a good supply of clear cold water but it took strong arms to man the pump. My mother planted a silver maple tree near the well platform; it was a beautiful sight when the wind stirred the silver leaves.

My father was a very ingenious man, he had received certificates for patents that he had invented, he was a carpenter-farmer, I guess in a sense, an engineer, he dug an underground cellar with double walls which he filled with earth to serve as insulation and over this he built a second story where he hung our supply of cured meat. He also built a very modern corn crib and usually had it filled with corn, there were also plenty of mice, one day I decided to see how many I could catch by hand, I wasn't afraid of anything except bears and wildcats, and perhaps Gypsies, so one day I went hunting, I had caught four and had them hanging by their tails, trying to catch my fifth when one I was holding bit my finger and I lost all my game.

This seems silly and unbelievable, consider Charles Darwin trying to catch beetles, he had one in each fist when he spied the third that he must have, he put one of the captured beetles in his mouth, it squirted acid down his throat and in a fit of coughing, he lost all of his beetles, at least I didn't put one of my captured mice in my mouth.

Being of a different age group, I had to invent entertainment for myself, I was always looking for something new, birds, flowers, plants, even frogs, usually after a rain there were many toads hopping around, knowing they were afraid of snakes, I would get a stick and push it through the grass behind the frog, I chased a number of them to certain corner corralled them and then leave them on their own.

Father also built a large barn with stalls for horses, cows, and even a yoke of oxen, named Buck and Bright. They were strong sturdy animals, it was amazing the amount of heavy loads they could pull. Father built up quite a farm all by himself with all kinds of fruit trees and berries, he also had about four kinds of grapes, large fields of corn and wheat and a big field of buckwheat that gave off a sweet smell when in bloom, it looked like ocean waves when the wind blew across it, this is also where the honey bee got it's sweetest nectar for making honey.

All of the crops meant a lot of work for the older children while I took to the fields and woodlands to look for wild flowers and watch the birds build their nests. I watched a robin guild her nest in the fork of a large honeysuckle branch that leaned over a stream where many wild flowers bloomed on the banks. First she laid sticks, twigs, and straws for a foundation, then she took clay from the bank of the stream and used it to reinforce her nest, she filled it with bits of string, horsehair and feathers and other soft materials. Sitting and turning she fashioned it like a bowl, I watched her daily and then one day there was a little blue egg, then there were four, in a few weeks thee were four baby robins. Each day I watched her bring food, they had such big yellow mouths I wondered how she ever got them filled. It seemed they grew so fast, eventually climbing to the edge of the nest, then one day they were gone. I missed my little brown-feathered friends.

In the evening I listened to the croak of the frogs and the call of the whippoorwill and watched the swallows and chimney sweep as they darted about. In the fall it was the chirp of the lonely cricket and the katydid which foretold of the coming Autumn, after the first frost the chestnut burrs would burst and the squirrels would cause them to fall like hail, while the rest of the family ate breakfast, I took a bucket and went out under my favorite tree and picked up chestnuts, it was a huge tree about three feet thick. Every time I hear "under the spreading chestnut tree, a mighty smitty stood" I think of my favorite chestnut tree.

In the fall we are all getting ready for school, new shoes, clothing fit for the occasion, I was anxious to get started, my brothers did not share my enthusiasm, I remember one winter morning the snow was about fourteen inches deep and we had about two and a half miles to walk to school, my mother did not want me to go that day but I begged and she said ok and I went, during the day the snow stopped falling but it turned cold and the snow had a crust on top, when school was out we started home my older brother decided to try a shorter route, it was all uphill, we really had two hills to climb, the first one we made without much effort, buy the second was much steeper and I was already tired and cold, I almost didn't make it, the only way I could make it up this steep hill was to place my hands in the footsteps of my brothers where they had broken the crust of the snow, I had no gloves and by the time I reached the fence at the top of the hill, I could not move my fingers, my brother tried to put his gloves on my hands but my hands were so cold I could not use them, after trudging through an open field we reached my grandmothers house, I staggered in like a drunken person, she knew my plight and immediately placed my hands in cold water. My grandfather had fought in the civil war and remembered how the troops used scrapped potatoes for frostbite, they tried everything, and finally, feeling returned to my fingers but for years my fingers would peel and have always been very sensitive to cold. I spent a week at grandmother's house before I went home, needless to say, I never returned to school.

Summer came again, long days, so much longer than they seem today, cooler evenings and the repeated hoot of the owl at night. One evening mother came out into the lawn to see the stars with me, occasionally a flying cloud passed over the moon, as mother stood looking toward heaven, I saw her lips moving, I was sure she was saying a prayer. Her life had not been an easy one, with the care of four or five children, she had the same problems that every mother has, like the time I climbed upon a chair and turned the old fashioned coffee pot over, it went all over me, it left its scars on my arms, they told me about it later, I have just a faint memory of the incident. My mother was a very quiet person but a heart full of love and grace. No youngster can go through life successfully without knowing God and a patient's mother's love. Had it not been for his love and her prayers, my life would have been quite different. She loved me, cared and prayed for me, the only sad thing, she ever did to me was to die and leave me.

It was a mild September morning, we children were aroused from our beds, fed and hustled out of the house, I didn't see my mother that morning, there was a strange mystery about it all, we could not understand it, at least I didn't. My grandmother and aunt came, their coming so early seemed so strange and unexpected, and there was a seriousness on their faces, it fell my lot to care for my two younger sisters while it seemed my older sister stayed over the wash tub and strangely silent, we were not allowed to go back into the house, even our lunch was served outside.

My paternal grandmother came later, never before had both my grandmothers come at the same time then someone told us Mother was sick, I wanted to go in and see her but was told I could not disturb her now. Later we were told we had a baby sister, the doctor was called but because of the long distance, he was late. When my brother returned form calling the doctor, he was sent back to tell the doctor he was too late. My mother had died, in those days doctors were not called to pronounce the cause of death or perform and autopsy.

That day my whole world collapsed, I had a numb feeling, I could not cry, somehow, somehow I didn't want to, I looked at my smaller brothers and sisters and wondered what would become of us now. The baby lived only three weeks, maybe mother asked God to let the baby come home to her.

I thought of the love and security I had enjoyed, my happy childhood, how we children played together in summer, making snow forts and sledding in winter, our long walks to school together on cold frosty mornings, now it seemed we had nothing left. The long day passed somehow, I just walked, trying to find solace somewhere. I came upon a mother cat washing her kitten's face, I thought "you fortunate little kitten, I had a mother who used to wash my face, but that mother is gone".

As evening came, the rosy sky faded, dark clouds formed, a few rain drops fell, warm like tears, in the distance I heard a dull rumbling sound like clods of earth falling on an empty box, I don't remember going to bed but the morning broke bright and clear, I never saw the sun shine so brightly on so early a September morning, there seemed to be a peace and quiet, it must have been Heaven's welcome to my mother's home coming. In a way it brought peace to my troubled heart.

As I passed where she lay, so silent and cold, (I did not get to tell her goodbye or how much I loved her, I'm sure she knew) I touched the feet that had walked miles for my sake and it saddened me to know that those dear feet would never walk with me again. I did not go to see her buried, I'm glad that I was spared that last sad scene; I stayed home to help my aunt care for the smaller sisters. In the spring our home was broken up and we children went to different homes, my youngest sister went to our maternal grandparents where she stayed until in her teens. Some of my brothers and sisters I did not see for twelve and seventeen years, now I know what is meant by the statement, "When father and mother forsake you, then the Lord will take you up". My mother left me by death; father felt he could not do for us what would be required, so we went our different ways. I cannot remember how many different homes I had. I went from place to place, as I was needed as a babysitter or household maid.

During this time I missed about two years of school, no one seemed to be interested in my future, I had strong beliefs in all that was good and determined to stick to my convections it wasn't easy, the world is big, bold and cruel to children of broken homes, I learned that if you strive to do the right things, you have a lot of oppositions, but somewhere in the shadows God is keeping watch over his own, I could see the wide margin between how I felt and how the people were living, I wanted something more solid and secure, I just wanted to leave it all behind. One evening in September, I was so discouraged and discontent I could not stay in one place I walked out to the edge of the trees, looking back over the house top, the sky seemed to be all ablaze, I had heard that the world would be destroyed by fire the next time, it filled me with fear, I thought, "maybe this is it". Returning to my room, I could not stay there, I went back to the trees, I heard a voice, it seemed to be coming from the branches, I turned to find where the voice was coming from, never before had I heard a voice like this one, so soft and compassionate, this voice said to me,"Daughter, give me thy heart." I had never heard these words before, but it did something to me, it changed my life completely, not knowing what to do, I simply said, "Lord the first chance I have I will". Really, I did not need another chance, I did not know it then, but I felt a great relief, my fears and all left me and I felt safe and secure.

The next week I was staying with a good aunt, she was a kind quiet, Christian woman, those I had been staying with were exactly opposite, they were more detrimental than helpful to me, the fact that I had a change in homes proved that God was thinking of me and making a way for my escape from a life of wrong. A week later a revival meeting began in a little church that was one time a garage for farm machinery, the church was at least three miles form where I lived, over a country road with a sticky clay base that made walking or any kind of transportation difficult. Two of our aunts about my age, a girl friend and a brother came by one evening to walk with me to church, I don't remember who the preacher was for the evening, but when the altar call was made a girl friend I once went to school with to me and asked me to go to the altar for prayer, I really felt I should go but said no, and promised I would go tomorrow night, all the way home I remembered the promise I had made under those trees, I had been given that chance and didn't take it, again, I promised tomorrow night I'll go.

The next afternoon about 3:00 pm it started to rain, it seemed like torrents, I thought of that long muddy road and wondered if we would be able to get back to church, I felt I must keep that promise, I went to my room and knelt to pray, I simply asked God to stop the rain so it would be possible for us to get to church, there are many who would not believe this, but when I looked out, the rain had stopped and the sun was shining brightly, the bluest sky I had ever seen, who can doubt a God like that? We made it to church, I kept my promise, my life was changed that night, and I have had a different outlook on life ever since. He always keeps his promise too.

Sometime later a good lady from this church whose name was Ada and who was at one time my schoolteacher, found a good home for me with a preacher and his mother His name was Naf Morrison, he had a been a pastor in another county, His mother was alone and became ill and sent for him, he gave up his church and came home. She recovered but he never went back as pastor. However, he helped in the two local churches and accepted calls to others, he was a very humble and devout man, his life was a great inspiration to me, we went to the two local churches every Sunday. A good Christian family lived near by, they had a son about my age, we often walked to church together and I guess were secretly interested in each other, but being a little shy, kept our thoughts to our selves, I guess in a way our eyes communicated even though our lips were silent.

When Christmas came he wanted t give me a present but didn't have money of his own, they owned a farm and every one shared in the labor without wages, he went to his mother with his problem as he had always done before, she understood and gave him the money, he got me a long, very thin scarf, very popular in that day, it had bright red flowers, green leaves, and shiny beads all over it, very pretty. Being timid about having a girl friend, he did not want his brothers to know about it until he could give it to me, trying to keep it a secret, he hid the gift in the wood pile until Christmas morning, I kept the scarf for years until it fell apart with age, years after his death. We both took a lot of kidding when the secret was revealed, they called it my wedding veil, after that we did not mind being kidded and our friendship grew and never died, even though we were separated for several years by circumstances.

That same Christmas, I got my first Bible from "Santa" by my preacher friend, it has been one of my most cherished possessions, through my Bible, morning and evening devotions and the devoted life of this good minister, I learned what a consecrated life could mean. The courage and faith to meet all odds, and I met plenty of the odds in the days that followed, but like David, I was prepared. Young people today don't necessarily need David's slingshot and a stone, but they do need what he had to give them the strength and courage to stand and fight for the right, I felt that I was a little short on these qualities and prayed that I might obtain them, one day as I came downstairs, there seemed to fall over me an illuminating light, similar to Paul's experience on the road to Damascus, I did not learn of his experience until later, from then on I was sure I could stand on his promises and trust in his grace.

When world war l came along, very few men, including ministers were exempt from serving in the armed forces, this good minister had to sell his home and answer his country's call, of course this meant another new home for me, his elderly mother went to live with another son, the lady who found this home for me found another place for me, I had a room in the same home where she was rooming in college, this was another city and county.

My minister friend took me to this city by train, on our way we had to spend the night in another city, he got a room for me next to his and we went for a walk to see the sights, this was a new experience for me as I had never been in a city before, when we returned he made sure I would be safe, he told me to lock my door and leave the key in the lock. The next day we arrived at my new home, a very lovely college town, this would be my home now for another two short years, Neff went back home to settle affairs before going to training camp, Fort Oglethorpe Georgia. He wrote me from there saying he did not mind the training so much, but he did not like working on Sunday, something he never did before, after his basic training, he was sent to France for a year or more, When the Armistice was signed he came home, somewhat broken in health, I never saw or heard from him again. Fate can be cruel, it separates friends and families, however, his example of a real Christian left its impression on me, someday, and I hope to meet him again.

I made a lot of friends in my new home, some of them were college students, I was grateful for their friendship, and I attended many of their Christian training meetings. I shall never forget "Fanny", what a friend, she was studying journalism, she also wrote poetry, one poem she dedicated to our friendship. Fate or fortune separated us also, me to another state, she to her journalistic work.

Since I was working my way through school, I took jobs that gave me room and board and a little spending money, it was little, the homes I had included doctors, lawyers and senators, the last one in the college town was a lawyer's home, his name was Ulysses Grant Young, he had served three terms as a U.S. Senator, defeated in his attempt for a fourth term, he went back to law practice. They were fine people, taking an active part in community affairs, his wife Millie, was like a mother to me, there were four children, two boys and two girls, the oldest daughter, married to a service man, had come back home to await the birth of their baby when her husband was sent over seas. The baby was born in December and the grandparents kept the baby when the daughter went to Zanesville Ohio to be with her husband who had been discharged and set up in real estate business by his father. The grandmother kept the baby until my school was out in June; she then took the baby to its mother and me as a baby sitter.

New homes, new friends and new schools became a way of life for me by now, my new home was in a pretty residential section of the city, I liked my new school, it was one of the first consolidated schools, eleven hundred students, black and white, catholic, Protestant, and Jews, a well organized school, disciplined by principal and faculty of long experience, my best girlfriend was Catherine, we shared many experiences together, we met one gray frosty morning on our way to school, she was a new student, I saw her coming and waited for her, she seemed like a lonely girl, I waited for after school too, her father was manager of the Woolworth 5&10 cent store. He became ill and one day Catherine was absent from school, on my way home from school alone that afternoon, as I crossed the ridge spanning the wide Muskingum River, I seemed to hear Catherine say, "Father died this afternoon", the moment I got in the house the phone rang, the first words Catherine said was, "Father died this afternoon," I inquired what time and she said "about three o'clock, almost the exact time I had heard those same worked as I crossed the bridge.

The family left the city for Lancaster, Pennsylvania but we kept in touch for years, than, for some unexplained reason, silence. Dear little Catherine, I often think of her, wondering how the world has treated her, I like to think someday we will meet again and the struggle seems all worthwhile. I visited many of the churches with my friends, the church of my choice was, of course, the one of my first affiliation, I just happened to be one of the biggest in the city, I attended regularly but it lacked the warmth and fellowship that l had found in the little country church. The young people's evening services seemed to be the real lives wire of the church, everyone worked together to make it a real success.

My deepest interest outside the church was my school, I had visions of the day when I would sit with my classmates as a happy graduate, and I felt it was worth all of the cost and effort. We had all of the sport activities including triangular debate which prepared students for a speaking career, we had our own debate songs and wore our school colors, blue and white, the triangular debate was three school debating at the same evening, all of the affirmative teams stayed home to debate with the visiting negative teams from other schools in the state, we had as much excitement as any ball team. I wanted so much to finish school, I included God in all of my plans and promised if he would help me finish high school, I would devote the first year after graduation to anything he wanted me to do, I had a special college course on my mind but that would have to wait for an opportunity.

At the end of my school year, my mistress, Eugenia, was going back home to visit her parents and suggested I go visit my family at the same time, I had not been home for over three yeas, and she was paying my way, of course her decision to go home came up suddenly, I knew of no other family at this time who might want help in the home my age Eugenia, made no effort to find one for me, I did not have much of a choice on such short notice, it seems when we must make quick decisions we usually use our own snap judgment which doesn't solve our problems, just delays them, God is never in a hurry but is always there, if we just take time to tell him our trouble , he is never late. Sadly and reluctantly I agreed to go, I cried most of he night, she left for her home town and I went to my people from there; it was nice to see my father and family again but really I was not happy, my heart was back in Zanesville and my school

I did find pleasure in meeting old acquaintances and friends again; I met again the "boy next door", the boyfriend of earlier days before I went away, we walked again to churches we once visited and to the "box supers" or services at other churches Sundays or weeknights. I whiled away the days while waiting for that all important letter with a ticket and notice to meet Eugenia at her mother's to go back to Zanesville with them as had been planned. On Friday before school was to start, the letter came, alas, no train fare and no notice to meet her, instead, the chilling truth, my premonition was true--she explained they had decided not to keep help in their home for the coming winter, a bitter disappointment, but I would not give up. I wrote to a lady in Zanesville with whom I had stayed once for two weeks during school when Eugenia had gone to her parents. I asked the lady, Mrs. Anderson, if I could stay in her home for a while until I could find a permanent home just so I could start to school with my class, she was sorry, but her husband's business was being transferred to another state and they would not be in Zanesville. I wrote to another lady with whom I had stayed for two weeks while Eugenia was away during my school period. She too was sorry but her only extra room had been rented to a teacher, if she cold fined a place for me she would let me know, I never heard from her. By now half of September was gone and it looked impossible for me to get back to school, a painful disappointment. It seems all of the sad things to come my way were in the fall - beautiful colors but sad reminders.

Well, what to do now? No job, the country folk helped each other, so I joined in helping with the canning or whatever I could. I appreciated even more the friendships of old; the one I found the most happiness with was the boyfriend of our teens. He was a fine young man from an old fashioned family of high ideals and strong faith, during our earlier friendship, we were not very serious and thought we were too young to be really serious; our friendship was interrupted when I left the community. Since I hoped to finish school and have a career, I would be gone indefinitely and he would probably choose another, I never thought it would happen to us, although somehow I always hoped it would, he was the kind of young man I would have chosen for life. I never forgot him and occasionally we kept in touch, now that were together again or friendship grew stronger. We pledged our love to each other and decided to make it a lifetime pledge. We were married a year later, September 12 1923, the one big, happy event to come my way in a fall season.

Years later, his mother was ill; she called me to her bedside and said, "I have a confession to make. I should have made it a long time ago when Clarence told me you two were getting married; I objected, you were a poor girl; Annie, the other girl, would someday inherit a big farm. I hoped he would marry her. He said "Mom, I love Cleva and feel I can live a better Christian life with her." I said, "Marry her then. It was selfish of me for wanting him to choose the other girl, forgive me?" I said "sure, and I hope I have not disappointed either of you." " No, she said, you have both kept your vows and I have no regrets".

When we were first married, we lived a few months with his parents and then we went to ourselves, I hoped our first baby would be a boy and favor his dad, it all came true, everybody called him "Sonny", appropriately enough, he had a sunny disposition and, incidentally, was born on Sunday, he still bears his father's characteristics. We had six lovely children, four boys and two girls. There were the endless questions and answers and witty sayings. One day when Sonny, then about five, had been running hard and had a pain in his side, he asked," mom, could I have independence?" I said, "Yes, you have a bad case of independence, but you will get over it with out an operation." There were boxing bouts with an old alarm clock for a timing bell, operated by brother, Bud. Marie and Bud came down stairs dressed in some old lace curtains, Bud announced =, "I am Joseph, she is Mary". There were fights occasionally, but they always ended up without serious causalities. It made for a busy day but full of entertainment. I wish daddy could have lived to see them grow up, he would be so proud of them now, it would have been such a pleasure to have them and our precious grandchildren come to visit "grand mom and grand pop".

With all our love and happiness, we also had our share of trials, tears, and tests. When our third child Buddy was four months old, I was stricken with an illness and sent to the hospital, my case was diagnosed as Polio. The doctors told my family I would never walk again, after many tests the illness turned out to be a spinal infection and not Polio, it left me with partial paralysis in my left leg and right arm. I had been in the hospital about three weeks when my baby, now five months old, took whooping cough. His case was so serious that he was sent to the hospital for children just two blocks from me. His grandmother, who had been caring for him, came to visit me on a Sunday; she told me that they had taken the baby to the hospital on Friday night. He was very ill and would require blood transfusion and would be a very sick child, my floor doctor promised to keep me informed, but he managed to avoid me, at night I lay awake, crying and praying that God would permit us to return home together. After seven and a half weeks I was released but was still unable to walk for months, when I was able to walk and do some of my house work, I could not stoop to pick up things or sweep under the furniture, Sonny did this for me and carried in the wood, he even washed dishes, and seemed to get pleasure from all of this, my baby spent almost five months in "Harrist Lane" I had not seen him since he was four months old, he not only had whooping cough, he developed pneumonia and was in isolation so much that none of the family were permitted to see him, they could only inquire of his health, when they brought him home, we were all strangers to him, poor little fellow just looked at us wide-eyed and with wonder.

261

I was now able to care for my home and family in a limited way and with our love and as Buddy improved rapidly, and soon life was back to normal except for my handicap. The children were now in school except Anita, the five year old, who loved to be with Daddy and went almost everywhere with him, in the early summer of 1939, misfortune struck again, Daddy developed and illness that would later send him to the hospital but he stayed with his farm work helping to get the fall work done, when the work became less demanding, he told his boss he was going to the hospital for an operation, he went to the clinic on a Friday for examination. The doctor told us Daddy had an ulcer and a tumor, I don't know what Daddy's reaction was, but when the doctor said ulcer and tumor, the word "Cancer" flashed across my mind as clearly as if it had been written on the wall. The doctor didn't mention the word and neither did I until five weeks later when Daddy was released for the hospital, I asked the doctor quietly, "is it cancer?" after a moments thought, he said "Yes, but we don't want him to know it". On October 18 we took him to the hospital, on Thursday, October 22, he went through his major surgery, he was in the operating room two hours and forty-five minutes, our pastor, N.G.Mink, went to the hospital early to cheer and encourage Daddy. He was annoyed at Daddy's calmness and said Clarence was an encouragement to him, they were in the waiting room when we arrived, after a talk and prayers, the nurses came and took him to his room, he was placed in a wheel chair, given a needle and was taken to the operating room. His sister and I went with him to the door, we could not go further, but God went with him all the way, that door sometimes separates life and death but not God or love.

To get me away the family suggested we go for a cup of coffee, we went about two blocks away, we came back to the waiting room where we continued to wait and pray. Often the pastor wrote notes, I thought he was making notes for his Sunday sermon; it was a poem of faith and supplication entitled, "We Wait". A year later he wrote me a new copy and another poem, "We Still Wait".

After what seemed like ages, the elevator brought Daddy back to his room, a few minutes more of waiting and the nurse let us go into his room, he was so pale and cold. He looked like he had come from a torture chamber, I guess in a way it was. There was no odor of ether, I looked inquiringly at the doctor, he understood and explained it wasn't necessary and they deemed it a very successful operation, they had given him a spinal nerve block, he was like wood from his waist down, he was wide awake when they started the operation and was asked if he wanted to watch, of course he said "no". When his pain became severe, they put him to sleep temporarily, he awoke and asked if they were about through, they said "not quite" and they put him to sleep again. The block must have lost some of its effect, he told me about it later, and said that when they cut the large intestine, he thought he would die of pain.

We stayed with him until his folks had to go home, I got permission from the floor nurse and doctor and one of his surgeons to stay at the hospital for the night, I stayed a few moments past visiting hours with him, the night nurse came and said I would have to leave, as I left the room I met our pastor, he explained the situation and the nurse I could stay in the waiting room.

Later a good friend came it to see how Clarence was, she was on her way to prayer meeting and would stop buy for me and I should spent the night with her, she had been thorough the same experience and understood, we gave the nurse a phone number where she cold reach me in case he got worse, she took me to her home, and me a donuts and coffee, that was the best cup of coffee I ever drank, it was in a way, her "cup of water given in His name".

I went back to the hospital the next morning, the nurse was giving him oxygen to help his breathing, the nurse who had run me out the night before came to me and asked, " now don't you feel better after a good night's rest?' I answered, "no, I was worried about my husband, have you ever been married?" "No", "then you could not understand" later I took her a Christmas cake decorated with an angel announcing the birth of Christ. She was a Jew.

Daddy was a very sick man for the first few weeks, I visited him every afternoon and evenings for weeks, the fifth week they let him come home, what a homecoming! The children all gathered around him, even the old shepherd dog "Girlie" cuddled up to him, put her head on his knee and looked up at him as if to say "welcome home". Days and weeks went by and he was able to get out to help the boys with the small chores, feeding the stock, cutting and carrying wood, the children took their responsibilities seriously and without complaint, his family saw to it that the children had a way to church every Sunday, our sister-in-law, Arlo, was always so good to take us anywhere we had to go, sometimes Daddy didn't feel like going and a friend came in and stayed with him.

In January Daddy had to go back to the clinic for a check up, the doctors found that he was not healing inwardly, so they kept him for another week, they told me this operation was a minor thing, he would not have to be put to sleep and it was unnecessary form me to be there, when I visited him the next day, he told me what they had done and he was unconscious for threee hours, I know it must have been more serious than the doctors had told me, his room mate told me he was a very sick man and that he had never heard anyone pray as hard as Dadddy had, the doctors did not tell me the whole truth, "They had found nothing wrong". That and what I found out later almost destroyed my faith in hospitals and doctors, I still have reservations. They never closed Daddy's incision and it never healed, he was much concerned about this and voiced his fear that it might be Cancer. I was glad I was looking the other ways so he could not see my face, I tried to encourage him with an answer, truthfully as I could, I always looked through the evening news to find anything that might describe his case as Cancer or it's symptoms, I took out the whole page, he never missed it. I had never told anyone that Daddy had Cancer; I felt that some one in his family should know, so I told his youngest sister, she was not married and would not feel obligated to tell any one now, his mother was ill and we didn't not want to tell her. On the fourth of March a bleeding occurred and his doctor sent him back to the hospital, his nephew, Willard, took us. Daddy stopped at a store to get something, I told Willard that I had a strong feeling they would want to keep Daddy for another operation or send him home as helpless case. Willard tried to assure me that it was not that bad. While Daddy was in the clinic, I had a talk with the chief surgeon, I asked him for the true facts about Daddy's case, he said I was entitled to know the truth and he would tell me, At Daddy's last operation they had found a definite re-growth, and there was nothing more they could do. Asked if they could not remove the re-growth, that is what they did in the last operation and they could do no more, they considered him as living on borrowed time now, my heart seemed to stop. I felt frozen inside; I thanked him for the truth, which I think I fought to disbelieve all the time. The doctor sent me in to talk to the social worker, she advised me to act and look as if he wa going to live for years, I had just been told he was living on borrowed time; I had never pretended before; our lives were like open books to each other, here I am going home knowing his days are numbered and yet I should cheerful and smile while he is sent home with hope and looking forward to being able to resume his duties on the farm, my heart wanted to cry - but I dare not. He was so pleased when they told him it would not be necessary for him to come to the clinic again. His family doctor could take care of him; I thought going through the anxiety of his operation was bad; this was going to be my "Gethsemane". I could understand a little more deeply how Jesus must have felt, except, that my friends did not forsake me or go to sleep. I knew this trial would take more strength and grace than I alone had, I knew God would be my "Rock of Ages" through this stormy sea. Through all the days that followed, Daddy never murmured or complained, he was a good husband and father, making sacrifices for his family and so helpful around the house; he helped with all the household duties when he wasn't busy with outside chores.

In all the 17 years of married life, we never found anything to quarrel about, some cannot believe that, some were bold enough to say" I don't believe it". It didn't bother me if they believed it or not and I had a lot less to grieve about when he was gone. We were not the only couple who never quarreled. I heard a famous comedian once say that he and his wife never found any thing to quarrel about; they celebrated their 24th anniversary shortly before he made the statement. I believed him.

When we were no longer able to take the children to church, some of the family took them, the last time we was at church together was March 24. Our pastor preached a very encouraging sermon; it was the last sermon Daddy ever heard.

On March 15 Daddy would celebrate his 41st birthday. I had always baked him cake, just the year before, I had baked him one with the inscription, "Till Death Do Us Part" on it, little did I know that it would be just one later. His sister made the cake for him this year and would bring it down Sunday since they were coming for dinner after church and could not be with us on Monday. She had told Daddy's parents on Friday the nature of his illness so they were somewhat prepared for what would follow.

Daddy had a very bad pain on Saturday night but would not let me call the doctor out of bed that late at night; I stayed up until early in the morning, he called me and said he was all right and that I should come to bed. Early Sunday morning he said, "We must get up and get the children ready for church." After breakfast he helped dress the smaller ones, after they were off he dressed chickens we were having for dinner. He also peeled potatoes for me; I never did tell his parents that he had helped to prepare the last meal they would share together. Later in the afternoon Daddy became worse, we called the doctor, he gave him needles to ease his pain and said he would be back tomorrow, the doctor told me infection had set in and there was nothing anyone could do, he was sorry he could not do more. After church services Sunday evening, the pastor came and stayed until 4:00am, our sister-in-law stayed through the night.

Monday morning Daddy was no better, the doctor came back and gave him another needle, he seemed so sad that he could not do more than make him comfortable, he made so many attempts to leave, but kept turning back, I asked, "how is it with him Doc?" Sorrowfully, he said "I am afraid he is going, I can't even find his pulse, I'm afraid he is dying now" I suppose we had a defeated look on our faces, I said "doctor, since I have known this all along and I have never kept a secret from him before, I would like for him to know". He said, "Then go tell him". I had to confess I didn't know just how to tell him, I went to the kitchen to tell my sister-in-law the bad news. The doctor went to Daddy's bedside, he said to the doctor, "you didn't have good news for Cleva did you doc? He said, "No Clarence, I didn't". Daddy said "it's all right; I've thought it for some time. It's been hard on Cleva".

When I came back to the room, the doctor said, "Clarence knows it now". I knelt by Daddy's bed and said, "You are not afraid are you?" He said "no". I am ready and willing to go. If that is God's will, then it's mine. I wish I didn't have to leave you and the children so helpless." I said "Daddy, we won't be alone, God has taken care of us through the years, he will take care of us yet.

The doctor said he would call my pastor from his office, before he drove off, one of the children said he sat in his car and cried. He was not only a good doctor, he was a friend, the pastor came, and few friends came later, they talked, sang hymns together and prayed, all of which Daddy took a part. In the evening, more friends including his boss of ten years, he was not a Christian but he had a lot of faith and deep respect for Daddy. He stayed until Daddy's body was taken away; he told me later that Clarence's death hurt him as much as loosing one of his family.

Daddy talked to friends, thanking them for coming, he remained conscious to the end, I asked him if he would like to say a word to the older children, he said, "yes", Sonny came to his bedside, Daddy looked and said, "Son, I have to leave you, be a good boy and take care of your mother". Sonny said, "Yes, Dad, I will", and he surely did his part in taking Daddy's place.

I have never been in favor of giving dying Christians hypodermics which might render them unconscious in the last moments when they may wish to leave a last request or an important statement, I think my doctor shared my belief because he did not come back to give him the last needle, Knowing it was the last thing he could do, I think he wanted daddy to remain conscious, his pain became more severe and someone went for the doctor, he could not come, he had an emergency in his office, there was no medical aid we could give him, our pastor said, "Prayer always helps". He prayed and Daddy's pain ceased and he became calm. In a few minutes Daddy went to be with his God where pain and partings are no more, I knelt by his bedside, committed his soul and our keeping in God's care. I kissed my dear companion "Good night" for the last time. We had never gone to sleep at night without saying "Good night".

Through all the long days and nights that followed, we missed Daddy very much but I never questioned God's reasons for taking him away, some day he will make it clear to me, The children were so good, they helped me carry the burden willingly and without question, they seemed to understand fully, Thank God for my faithful children. Sonny kept his promise to his Dad, he quit school to take a job to help provide for us, he brought his pay home to me without reservations, when he was 18, he went into the Air Force, eventually to England, as gunner on a B-17 where he made 12 missions over enemy occupied territory, he wrote to me often, he came home safe and sound, thank God for his care, Sonny never broke a promise to me and still tried to help even though his pay was small, Thank you Sonny.

As my other children grow older, they went out on their own to be independent or work their way through school, the younger boys stayed home with me for a while, Ross was the man of the houses now. He helped me with the canning and we picked berries together, cut down trees, cut it into blocks and carried it to the house. It was hard work, but we did it together, the boys took care of stock to help pay for rent and the keep of our cow.

I have been sorry that I could not give them all they deserved, but I hope the love that existed between us and the basic fundamental training they got at home and church made it possible for them to face the responsibilities of their individual lives when they were on their own. I tried to teach them to be honest in all things, to tell the truth even when it hurt, and that "obedience is better than sacrifice". I recall one incident when Ross said something, and before I could comment, Ross said, "Don't say it Mom" it concerned sacrifice. I think he had absorbed the message. They are all married now and families of their own, the precious grandchildren and great grandchildren add pleasure to my life, sorrow sometimes, when I think how much Daddy would have loved them, too.

I am living alone now, by my own choice, with many happy memories to keep me company, even sad memories have their place, reminding me that God is still on the Throne, keeping watch over His own. As I said "Good night" to Daddy here, it will be "Good morning " up there, yes, someday we will all meet Daddy again "just inside the Eastern Gate, and together we can sing, "Jesus, Led Me All The Way".

These incidents of my life may seem dull and insignificant to others, but as I recall them, I find I have much to be thankful for, the revelations and proof that their is a God who loves, hears, and answers prayer and, "A very present help in the time of trouble". For what it has meant to me, the experience I gained-yes, all along the way, love and life has been good to me, I am looking to Heaven for the climax.

To all my good friends, neighbors, and families who stood by me in sunshine and sorrow, my most humble and grateful "THANKS". I hope this little reminiscence will explain to you my many moods, actions and reasons for my doing or not doing something's that seemed a little strange or mysterious. I hope you can profit by my mistakes and climb the mountains that I couldn't climb and do for your children that which I could not or failed to do for you, Remember, God is there when you need Him.

To you my children

I am glad to call you my children. My life has been blessed and enriched in having you as my own.

You are the best in the world, if only Dad could have lived to see you grow up, he, too, would have been proud of you.

Thank you for your love and care through the years, thank you for sanding by me and helping to bear my burdens during your father's sickness and death and the long years that have followed, you did your duty so faithfully and obediently.

I was sure when you had to go out on your own to fight your own battles of life, you had what it takes to be a winner and I'm sure you have done just that.

And even though you were far away and in different places, if I ever needed you, I would only have to call and you would be there, what more could a mother want?

Thank you for your love and devotion down through the years and May God bless you and your families as he has mine.

I have never been able to do for you what I would like to have done or give you much of this world's goods, I won't be leaving you much, but I believe I have given you something to strengthen your faith in God and, thereby, help you to build strong character and deep morals.

I think I have the best children in the world, the sweetest and dearest grandchildren and great grandchildren, and I know I have the best sons and daughter-in -laws than <u>any</u> mother-in-law. Thank you for your love and for being such good in-laws. My love has been quite and still - but deep.

My love to each one of you - now and forever.

Mom.

> Twilight and evening bell,
> And after that the dark,
> And may there be no sadness of farewell
> When I embark;
>
> For though from out our bourne of Time and Place
> The flood may bear me far
> I hope to see my Pilot face to face
> When I have crossed the bar.

Tennyson

ps: (please note: As difficult as her life was and the many disappointments she suffered, she never complained or had a bad thing to say about anyone. She was a wonderful woman)

CPSIA information can be obtained
at www.ICGtesting.com
Printed in the USA
FSOW02n0617210817
37747FS